PRAISE FOR *MELTING THE ICE CURTAIN*

In *Melting the Ice Curtain*, David Ramseur tells the fascinating story of U.S.-Russian relations at the border where our two nations have been linked for centuries. He focuses on a rare opening that began during the Reagan-Gorbachev years, when Alaska Natives, artists, and entrepreneurs moved faster than diplomats or politicians to bring the two peoples together. It's terrific story-telling about an era that has profound lessons for American policy today.

—*Corey Flintoff, National Public Radio Moscow correspondent, 2012-2016*

David Ramseur combines firsthand experience with thorough reporting to create an engaging account of a remarkable period of friendship between Russia's Far East and Alaska. Intimate details abound in this contemporary history of arctic neighbors with so much in common, including environment, blood relations, political entanglements, and intense curiosity about each other. Especially fascinating are the stories of dedicated citizen diplomats who helped reunite Native families separated by the Cold War, establish commercial and cultural ties, and crumble barriers between former enemies. This timely book reminds us that ordinary people of goodwill and determination can overcome suspicion and uncertainty to change the world, bit by bit, in even its most remote corners.

—*Sherry Simpson, author* Dominion of Bears *and* The Way Winter Comes

David Ramseur's book recalls a more hopeful time when Russia was striving for democratic reforms, and when U.S.–Russia relations were defined by cooperation and goodwill. It is also a valuable reminder that nothing is predetermined, and that we should never cease to work for a better tomorrow.

—*Vladimir Kara-Murza, Chairman, Boris Nemtsov Foundation for Freedom*

Those of us who have lived in Alaska know the hulking presence Russia plays less than three miles away at the closet point. Journalist and political aide David Ramseur tells a compelling story of a colorful era when Alaska and Russia helped end the Cold War across the Bering Strait. The lessons Ramseur draws from these productive decades of northern good will are instructive for today's uneasy relations between Washington and Moscow.

—*Peter Rouse, Chief of Staff to President Barack Obama*

For nearly three decades, David Ramseur has been one of Alaska's most persistent advocates for productive relations with Russia across the Bering Strait. Thanks to his tenacity in my Senate office, I eagerly stood up for human rights and against Russia's escalating dictatorship. Ramseur's fascinating account of this era is a must-read for anyone who cares about Russia or its former fur colony.

—*Alaska U.S. Senator Mark Begich, 2009-2015*

D0843878

This compelling, well-written account of a productive period in U.S.-Russia relations is timely and invaluable. David Ramseur's experience as a journalist makes him a keen and meticulous observer of a colorful but chaotic era. *Melting the Ice Curtain* dramatically shows how people of the Arctic have surmounted enormous obstacles to achieve high levels of cooperation, a model needed today.

—*Vic Fischer, author* To Russia With Love: An Alaskan's Journey

For Alaskans who want to better understand their state's history, and for Americans who need to better understand the complicated US-Russia relationship, this book is an invaluable read. With the insight of an insider, Ramseur traces the highs and lows of Alaska-Russia interactions with lively stories about people and places on both sides of the Bering Strait. He rightly concludes the Arctic is the most promising area for future U.S.-Russian cooperation and draws a roadmap for getting there.

—*Fran Ulmer, Chair, U.S. Arctic Research Commission, Alaska Lt. Governor, 1994-2002*

The U.S. and Russia need one another's help to tackle the problems that will matter beyond today's news cycle. Ramseur's book outlines a blueprint for cooperation in the Arctic region, which is vital not only for managing the region's precious resources, but for addressing looming threats to national and global security.

—*Matt Rojansky, Director, Kennan Institute at the Woodrow Wilson Center*

U.S.-Russia military relations have varied widely, from the enormously beneficial in World War II to the dangerously tense during the Cold War. We are now at another critical turning point in our history. While it is vitally important to remain firm in our values and defense of our national interests, we must also recognize that communication and collaboration are foundational to preventing conflict. Russia and the United States share deep native roots and cultural ties in the Arctic that can be embraced and leveraged. *Melting the Ice Curtain* tells a compelling story of the success of grassroots citizen diplomacy and details lessons for today's perilously poor relations between the world's superpowers. Ramseur is one of Alaska's experts on this topic and he offers valuable insights on how we may turn our challenges into opportunities. I was honored to have him address my command staff.

—*Air Force Lt. Gen. Russell J. Handy (ret.), Commander, Alaskan Command, 2013-2016*

For 40 years, Cold War politics banned Alaska and Russia indigenous peoples from practicing the sacred traditions they had pursued across the Bering Strait since time immemorial. With impeccable research, David Ramseur documents how these peoples pressured Moscow and Washington to reopen the border as they struggle to keep endangered cultures alive. *Ice Curtain* is must reading for anyone who cares about the ancient people of the Arctic.

—*Julie Kitka, President, Alaska Federation of Natives*

MELTING THE ICE CURTAIN

MELTING THE ICE CURTAIN

The Extraordinary Story of Citizen Diplomacy on the Russia-Alaska Frontier

David Ramseur

UNIVERSITY OF ALASKA PRESS

Published by
University of Alaska Press
P.O. Box 756240
Fairbanks, AK 99775-6240

Cover design by Martyn Schmoll
Cover images from iStockphoto
Back cover image by Steve Raymer/National Geographic Creative.
Interior design by Rachel Fudge

Library of Congress Cataloging-in-Publication Data

Names: Ramseur, David, author.
Title: Melting the Ice Curtain : the extraordinary story of citizen diplomacy on the
    Russia-Alaska frontier / David Ramseur.
    Description: [Fairbanks, Alaska] : University of Alaska Press, 2017. |
Includes bibliographical references and index.
    Identifiers: LCCN 2016056626 (print) | LCCN 2017010552 (ebook) |
    ISBN 9781602233348 (paperback : acid-free paper) | ISBN 9781602233355 (e-book)
Subjects: LCSH: Alaska—Relations—Soviet Union. | Soviet Union—Relations—
    Alaska. | Alaska—Boundaries—Soviet Union. | Soviet Union—Boundaries—
    Alaska. | Alaska—History—1959– | Diplomacy—History—20th century. | Political
    participation—History—20th century. | Friendship—Political aspects—History—
    20th century. | Soviet Union—Foreign relations—1985–1991. | United States—
    Foreign relations—1981–1989.
Classification: LCC F910.5 .R35 2017 (print) | LCC F910.5 (ebook) | DDC
    320.98047—dc23
LC record available at https://lccn.loc.gov/2016056626

SECOND PRINTING

To my parents, Joe and Susan Ramseur,
for instilling in me intellectual curiosity about the world.

1. *Build in Kamchatka, or in some other place in that region, one or two decked vessels.*

2. *Sail in those same vessels, north up the coast which, since its limit is unknown, appears to be a part of America.*

3. *Ascertain where it joins America and go to a settlement under European authority. If you encounter a European ship, learn from her the name of the coast off which you stand, and record it. Make a landing and so obtain more detailed information, prepare a chart, and return here.*

—RUSSIAN CZAR PETER THE GREAT, JANUARY 26, 1725.
INSTRUCTIONS TO VITUS BERING TO EXPLORE THE REGION
BETWEEN RUSSIA AND ALASKA. PETER DIED THREE DAYS LATER.

Contents

Author's Note

FOLLOWING THE 1917 Russian Revolution, the Union of Soviet Socialist Republics was established in 1922. The largest of the fifteen republics was Russia. On December 26, 1991, the Soviet Union dissolved after many of the republics took advantage of Gorbachev-era reforms to declare their independence. The Ice Curtain era, the focus of this book, began during the final years of the Soviet Union. Generally, the term Soviet Union, or USSR, is used in describing events occurring before the dissolution; the term Russia is used thereafter.

The easternmost region of Russia is the Russian Far East, composed of ten territories of varying powers. It spans from the northeasternmost point of Asia south to the Pacific maritime city of Vladivostok. Most of the events described in this book occurred in the Russian Far East. The extent to which Siberia, Russia's vast inland region, extends to the east is commonly misunderstood. Siberia sits west of the Far East republic of Sakha, stretching to the Ural Mountains, to what is generally considered European Russia.

This book uses the conventional English translation to refer to Russian places and names, such as Provideniya and Vladimir.

Temperatures are expressed in Fahrenheit and distances in miles.

The author at about one year old with his father's Marine Corps uniform near Camp Pendleton, California, where he was born.

Preface

I CAN STILL see the smiling man with the movie-star tan waving from the back-seat of a white convertible as the crowd thundered "Ken-a-DEE, Ken-a-DEE." I was two weeks short of my sixth birthday when my mother pulled me from first grade for my first campaign rally during Sen. John F. Kennedy's June 1960 visit to Albuquerque, New Mexico.

My mom, my three-year-old sister, and I arrived so early we could almost touch the candidate's hand from our second-row seats when his motorcade circled into the stadium.

Little did I know then that Kennedy's presidential campaign centered on getting tough with the Soviet Union by flexing America's nuclear muscle. After the rally, Kennedy soberly addressed the New Mexico State Democratic Convention, singling out Soviet leader Nikita Khrushchev for his threatening behavior.

"We meet here in a period of great peril for the world," the forty-three-year-old candidate said. "At no time since the Korean War have the voices been as angry or menacing."

While most Americans were rattled by the Cold War of the 1950s and 1960s, my family found itself on the front lines. We were in Albuquerque because my father, a Marine Corps gunnery sergeant, was assigned to the region's Sandia Base, learning to arm Honest John rockets with nuclear warheads for use against the Soviet Union in the event of war.

Six years earlier, my dad's orders had taken us to one of five national nuclear-weapons stockpiles in Nevada. At a Marine outpost there, he helped safeguard the warheads in reinforced-concrete igloos behind triple-layer security fences.

Up early one dark morning in the Nevada desert to feed me a bottle, my mom saw a bright flash across the horizon. The newspaper had warned against looking directly at that atomic-bomb test.

Later, in an elementary school near a California Marine base, air-raid sirens sent me and my classmates under our desks like dogs to a whistle to protect ourselves against incoming Soviet A-bombs. Three years after that New Mexico rally, when our fourth-grade teacher tearfully announced President Kennedy's assassination, my classmates and I childishly speculated on the playground that those Russian "commies" had something to do with it.

That early exposure to the Cold War stimulated my lifelong fascination with international affairs, especially those of the Soviet Union. The Vietnam War dominated my senior year in high school, as it did the lives of many draft-age American men. I was relieved when the draft ended the next year, and my college education proceeded with a political-science degree and graduate school in journalism. Itchy for more adventure than I found in my first newspaper job in South Carolina, I landed a reporting position at America's farthest-north daily, the *Fairbanks Daily News-Miner*.

The Cold War was alive and well in Alaska in the early 1980s. We wrote about Soviet Bear bombers threatening Alaska airspace, mysterious Soviet military equipment washing up on our Bering Sea beaches, and the occasional quirky adventurer attempting to walk or paddle the two and a half miles across the international date line separating Alaska and the Soviet Union before being snatched up by Soviet border guards.

Alaska went into high alert in fall 1983, when a Korean Air Lines passenger jet departed Anchorage for Seoul, drifted off course over the Soviet Far East, and was blown out of the sky by a Soviet missile, killing all 269 on board. That was the same year I moved to Washington, DC, as the capital correspondent for the *News-Miner* and the *Anchorage Times*. There, I reported on Alaska-Soviet interactions and took my first Russian-language classes.

After two years in Washington and homesick for Alaska, I returned to Anchorage, where I volunteered as press secretary for Steve Cowper's cash-strapped gubernatorial campaign. The "high plains drifter," as he was known, was making his second run in 1986 after losing the Democratic primary four years earlier by just 259 votes.

Appalled at reckless spending by a state government flush with petro dollars, Cowper campaigned on weaning Alaska from its oil reliance by capitalizing on its strategic proximity to global markets in Asia, Europe, and North America. The campaign couldn't afford to pay me, so my reward was occasional travel with the candidate. Politicking over steaming bowls of black walrus stew in western coastal villages and chunks of chewy whale blubber on the North Slope took us closer to the Soviet Union than we had ever been.

Cowper won that November and hired me as his press secretary, just as world oil prices collapsed, plunging the state into a deep recession. Trying to diversify the economy through international trade, Governor Cowper—with me in tow—led trade missions to Korea, Japan, Taiwan, and China. Alaska's closest western neighbor didn't make the list.

"Even though one of my ancestors was the ambassador to Russia in 1840, Russia never entered into any of the conversations I had," Cowper said. "The two countries had a mutual disdain for each other, and trade was not really something I associated with Russia."

Like me, Cowper had never visited the Soviet Union. Yet, halfway into his term, a fortuitous mix of local and global events changed that, changed our lives, and changed history. *Melting the Ice Curtain* tells that story.

It's a story of danger, where pilots on goodwill missions contemplate getting shot out of the sky crossing into Soviet airspace. It's a story of political intrigue, where staunchly capitalist politicians jockey for friendships in one of the world's most resolutely communist nations.

It's a story of compassion, where Alaskans reach deep into their pockets to better life for their Russian neighbors. It's a story of romance, where scores of Alaskans and Russians get together for love or economic convenience.

It's a story of bold diplomatic breakthroughs, where an Alaska peacenik befriends the Soviet Union's top image maker, who sees political advantage for his boss and his country. It's a story of opportunism, where Russians and Americans alike seek unbridled fortune in the turbulent Russian Far East.

Finally, it's a story of cultural preservation, where small clans of Alaska and Russian Natives separated by fifty-five miles of stormy seas struggle to preserve common languages and cultures in a technological world.

For many Americans, knowledge of Alaska's connections with its western neighbor is limited to comedian Tina Fey's "I can see Russia from my house" parody of former Alaska Governor Sarah Palin in the 2008 presidential campaign. For many Alaskans, Russia is a land of mystery and shared history that shaped their state but today puzzles and frustrates them.

Melting the Ice Curtain is especially timely for three reasons. First, whether we like it or not—and most Americans don't—Russia casts a long shadow across the world and is a force to be reckoned with. Americans snicker at the shirtless President Putin on horseback, yet are perplexed by his soaring job-approval ratings as he thumbs his nose at the United States. This work documents a chaotic but successful era of Alaska-Russia interactions, a model sorely needed today as US-Russian relations deteriorate to their most dangerous level since the Cold War.

Second, memories are rapidly fading on both sides of the Bering Strait about the origins and achievements during the heyday of Alaska-Russia relations. A chief catalyst for melting the Ice Curtain in the mid-1980s was reuniting Native peoples in Alaska and Russia who had long been separated by Cold War tensions. Now, many of those with firsthand knowledge of those relationships are gone. Of the nearly thirty Alaska Natives aboard the groundbreaking 1988 Friendship Flight from Nome to Provideniya, only a handful were still living in 2016. While adapting to twenty-first-century technology, Native peoples on both sides of the international date line struggle to keep alive millennia-old languages and traditions that link them to each other and to their rich cultural heritage.

Third, opportunities abound for fruitful cooperation between Alaska and the Russian Far East. From science to citizen diplomacy, the Ice Curtain era showed that local collaboration can improve overall relations between our countries. The area of most productive cooperation is managing a changing Arctic. Russia dominates the Far North, with nearly half of the Arctic within its borders as Russians comprise 40 percent of arctic residents. In the United States, Alaska is the only reason America is an arctic nation. That's a fact that only recently appears to have registered with federal decision makers as climate change dramatically alters the Arctic, especially passage through the Bering Strait shared by Alaska and Russia.

One hundred and fifty years ago, American and Russian diplomats consummated one of the world's biggest real-estate deals, the sale of Alaska to the United States for $7.2 million. Since then, the Alaska-Russia relationship has prospered and waned, contributed to global peace, and threatened the world with nuclear war. While some of Vladimir Putin's closest advisors have urged Alaska's return to the Motherland, President Putin himself laughed off the notion because Alaska is "too cold."

As the anniversary of the Alaska sale is commemorated in 2017, a reassessment of America's relationship with Russia is timely and crucial. The inspiration, courage, and persistence demonstrated by average citizens to melt the Alaska-Russia Ice Curtain is constructive to any effort to rebuild bridges across a widening gap in superpower relations.

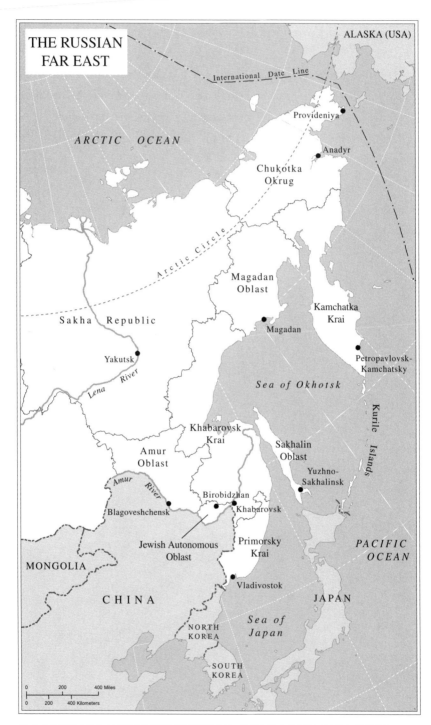

THE RUSSIAN
FAR EAST

ALASKA (USA)

International Date Line

Providéniya

Anadyr

ARCTIC OCEAN

Chukotka
Okrug

Arctic Circle

Magadan
Oblast

Kamchatka
Krai

Sakha Republic

Magadan

Yakutsk

Lena River

Sea of Okhotsk

Petropavlovsk-
Kamchatsky

Kurile Islands

Khabarovsk
Krai

Sakhalin
Oblast

Amur
Oblast

Yuzhno-
Sakhalinsk

Amur River

Birobidzhan

Blagoveshchensk

Khabarovsk

Jewish Autonomous
Oblast

Primorsky
Krai

PACIFIC
OCEAN

MONGOLIA

Vladivostok

CHINA

JAPAN

Sea of
Japan

NORTH
KOREA

SOUTH
KOREA

0   200   400 Miles

0   200   400 Kilometers

K. A. LABAY, 2016, MAPS OF THE RUSSIAN FAR EAST: U.S. GEOLOGICAL SURVEY

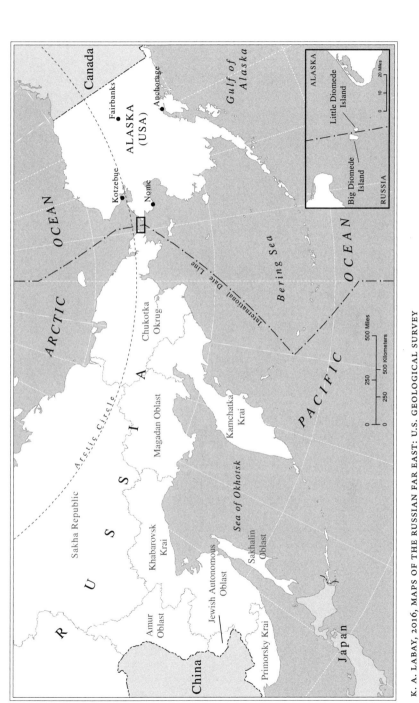

K. A. LABAY, 2016, MAPS OF THE RUSSIAN FAR EAST: U.S. GEOLOGICAL SURVEY

This map, published by the Royal Academy of Sciences in St. Petersburg, shows Russian discoveries on the northwest American coast as of 1730, including voyages by Vitus Bering.

Prologue

A N ESTIMATED THIRTY thousand years ago, bands of hunters followed their growling bellies from northeast Asia across a temporary land bridge into what now is Alaska. Outfitted in thick fur against the brutal cold, the Asiatic nomads lived in the Pleistocene Ice Age, which froze about 5 percent of the world's water. The reduced liquid lowered the earth's oceans about four hundred feet below current levels, exposing land beneath the shallow Bering Sea.

Across that new land bridge, scientists believe, Asian reindeer, mammoth, musk oxen, and bison migrated to a new continent. They were pursued by hunters adept at making and hurling sharpened projectiles with deadly accuracy.

Through a series of warming and cooling cycles over the next eighteen thousand years, enough of those frozen oceans thawed to reflood the Bering Land Bridge. Those stranded along the coasts of northeast Asia and northwest North America were forced to develop maritime technology—animal-skin boats—to continue their contact across fifty-five miles of sea. For centuries, the indigenous peoples of both continents lived in relative harmony, subsisting on marine mammals and vast herds of what Russians call reindeer and Alaskans call caribou.

That was the setting that Russian fur trappers encountered in the late sixteenth century, when they pushed into Siberia's major river basins in pursuit of the exquisite black fur of the sable, a species of marten. Encouraged by the czar, whose royal monopoly kept sable fur prices high, trappers pushed all the way to

Russia's Pacific coast. As they moved east, they regarded Siberian Natives much the same way other European colonialists of the era treated indigenous peoples— enslaving them and killing them with Western diseases.

As the 1600s transitioned into a more enlightened eighteenth century, a relatively progressive twenty-year-old Russian ruler ascended to the throne. Peter the Great was curious about the world at either ends of his huge empire. During one of his frequent visits to Europe, Czar Peter heard rumors of a North American landmass extending westward toward Russia's Kamchatka Peninsula. He dispatched two Russian navigators to determine whether the lands were connected. Based on a quick survey by ship and interviews with locals, the pair reported back that they were not.

On his deathbed in January 1725, dissatisfied with that report, Peter signed orders to a Danish mariner under contract to Russia to further explore and "ascertain where [Russia] joins America." It took Vitus Bering and his three dozen officers and shipbuilders more than two years to drag their tools and ship anchors across the four thousand miles from St. Petersburg to Kamchatka. There, they constructed a three-masted wooden ship, the *Saint Gabriel*, and in 1728 sailed northward along the Kamchatka coast and through the strait between Russia and Alaska, which today bears Bering's name.

Fog prevented Bering from viewing the North American coastline, but he ventured far enough north—above the Arctic Circle—to confirm that no land connection existed between the continents. Despite the historic adulation given to Bering's voyage, he failed to achieve Peter's chief objective: to identify new resources for Russia to exploit.

Bering got a second chance in 1738, when he and Russian explorer Alexii Chirikov were dispatched on the Second Kamchatka Expedition. In separate ships, the two explored regions of what today is Southcentral Alaska. To resupply freshwater reserves, Bering's ship spent a few hours at Kayak Island in southern Prince William Sound, about sixty miles from current-day Cordova. After the ships became separated in a storm and with his crew suffering from scurvy, Bering quickly set sail for Kamchatka through the Aleutian Islands.

Lacking the capability to calculate longitude, information that could have told the Russian explorers how close they were to home, Bering's ship, the *Saint Peter*, anchored in the Commander Islands, about one hundred miles off the Kamchatka coast. When the ship was destroyed in a storm, Bering and his crew were forced to winter on a desolate island. Nineteen died, including Bering, who succumbed on December 8, 1741.

The surviving crew arrived home the following summer, carrying fox and seal skins and fifteen hundred sea otter pelts, which were considered even more luxurious than the Siberian sable. Chinese merchants paid forty times more for sea otter than sable, setting the stage for a century of aggressive Russian exploitation of the newly discovered North American territory.

Within two years of Bering's death, successive expeditions of Russian fur trappers sailed to the Aleutian Islands to harvest sea otter fur. By the end of the eighteenth century, about one hundred such voyages had been made. They pushed increasingly farther east until reaching the Alaska mainland. The Russians soon determined that harvesting an ocean-based prey dictated a dramatically different operation than trapping the land-based sable.

In Siberian forests, the trappers largely knew their work and often pursued it on their own. But in the rough waters of Alaska's remote Aleutian Islands, they enslaved local Natives to hunt for them. The Russians held Native women and children hostage in their villages, forcing the men to harvest sea otter pelts for long periods. The enterprise required Russian managers over large swaths of territory and an expensive fleet of ships to collect and transport the pelts to Chinese markets. This system eventually led the Russian-American Company to expand from Siberia into Alaska.

A German doctor in the early employment of the company in Alaska, Georg Heinrich Baron von Langsdorff, described the brutal circumstances and eighteenth-century sentiments of the Russian masters over their Aleut Native subjects. "The Natives are so completely slaves of the Russian American Company that even their clothes and the bone tips of their spears belong to the Company. The oppression under which they live at home, the total want of care and the change in modes of living plus the Company's practice of sending away the best hunters from their home villages for months at a time" severely diminished the population.

Langsdorff found the Natives "generally kind-hearted, obliging, submissive and careful, but if roused to anger become rash and unthinking, even malevolent." The practice of washing their hair and clothes in human urine, kept in large buckets at the entrances to their underground abodes, "did not help sweeten their smell."

Those were the conditions Russian merchant Alexander Baranov faced when he was recruited to Russian America in 1790. Despite lacking a formal education, Baranov assembled a diverse commercial portfolio during his early career: glass factory manager, distillery founder, tax collector, and operator of a post on the Anadyr River that traded with local Chukchi Natives. Driven by wanderlust, the portly Baranov abandoned his wife for adventure and opportunity in Siberia and the Far East.

Russian-American Company manager Grigory Shelikhov pursued Baranov for years. He managed to finalize a contract for Baranov to succeed him in Alaska only after agreeing to pay off Baranov's debts. En route to Kodiak, Baranov demonstrated the resourcefulness that served him well during his time in Alaska. The ship carrying Baranov and a crew of forty-four ran aground off Unalaska in the Aleutian Islands. They were forced to winter over in dugouts fabricated on the rocky beach, subsisting on shellfish and seabirds when the weather was too rough to fish. Baranov used the time to plot company efficiencies and oversee the construction of three large *baidarkas*—Russian-style kayaks—for the crew and Aleut guides. In the spring, Baranov and his men paddled the remaining 750 miles to Kodiak.

During his twenty-nine years in Alaska, Baranov dramatically expanded the imprint of Russia's presence in America. At the cost of deadly battles with the Tlingit Natives, he moved his headquarters to what is now Sitka on Baranof Island. Established as New Archangel, Baranov located his house on a strategic hill, which his troops took from the local Natives. From this spot, he managed a far-flung operation that reached from Northern California to Hawaii to Kamchatka. Baranov acquired a mistress—likely the daughter of a high-ranking Aleut—and when his wife died in Russia in 1806, Baranov married her. They produced a son and two daughters.

As the Russian-American Company's operations matured at the turn of the century, modest conservation measures were imposed to stabilize the deteriorating sea otter stocks. To maintain their profits, Baranov expanded the company's reach across the colony and harvested walrus ivory, land animals, and even whales in the Bering Sea. The company later launched a successful ice trade with San Francisco and sold Alaska fish and timber in Hawaii and California.

International competition with the Russians in the Pacific Northwest intensified as the British, Spanish, and Americans sought to cash in on the fur trade and establish a foothold in the region. Meanwhile, in the Russian capital, the company's managers and their allies in government decided that a more enlightened administrator was needed for its colonial interests. In 1817, Baranov was relieved of his duties and died on the way back to Russia.

Over the next few decades, the Russians continued to extract enormous resource wealth from Russian America but faced encroachment from all directions. British explorers reached Alaska's northernmost Point Barrow. The Tlingit continued to harass company headquarters in Sitka. The California gold rush drew thousands near the Russian enclave in Northern California. And settlers found their way into the American West after crossing on the Oregon Trail. Russian leaders sensed an American destiny to occupy all of North America's western territory.

Even more troubling to Russia was a conflict on its western border, the Crimean War. Started in 1853 by the Russian invasion of current-day Romania, that action prompted a forceful reaction from a coalition comprising Britain, France, and the Ottoman Empire. As the war raged for three years, Russian leaders sensed their country's vulnerability in their far-away eastern colony and began an internal debate about selling Russian America. After Russia lost the Crimean War, a Russian naval audit found the value of the Russian-American Company in steep decline, requiring a government subsidy to pay dividends.

To cut his country's losses, Czar Alexander II directed his ambassadors to make simultaneous offers to sell Alaska to both Great Britain and the United States. The British, their hands already full managing wilderness provinces in Canada, declined.

In the United States, the Civil War prevented any serious consideration of the Alaska sale offer. After the war, over Christmas 1866, Czar Alexander convened his top financial and military advisors at St. Petersburg's Winter Palace to devise another sales proposal. Among those in attendance was Eduard de Stoeckl, Russian ambassador to the United States. Stoeckl was well versed in American culture and politics, having married an American woman and served as Russian consul general in Hawaii. After Alexander made the final decision to sell Alaska, Stoeckl was dispatched to Washington with instructions to accept not a kopek less than $5 million.

The US official whom Stoeckl targeted with his sales pitch was a gifted public speaker and anti-slavery advocate. Had he not been so overconfident of his abilities, William Seward might have been in his second term as president when Stoeckl arrived. Seward was born into a prosperous New York family, and his father was a slave-owning doctor. He entered politics in the 1820s, serving in the New York legislature and as governor, and gradually evolving into a pro-immigration abolitionist. In the decade before the Civil War, he was elected to the US Senate and was broadly regarded as the Republican Party's presidential nominee in 1860.

Seward was so confident of his nomination that he embarked on a grand tour of Europe to meet with kings and princes instead of focusing on the pedestrian task of campaigning for votes. A folksy Illinois lawyer named Abraham Lincoln mounted a come-from-behind campaign, shocking Seward and the political world by capturing his party's nomination and the presidency. Seward agreed to serve as Lincoln's secretary of state, becoming both the president's chief foreign policy advisor and one of his closest confidants.

When Stoeckl arrived in Washington in late 1866, Lincoln had been dead a year. Seward himself had been stabbed five times in the face and neck as part of the assassination conspiracy. He agreed to stay on as secretary of state to President Andrew Johnson, who grew increasingly unpopular over his management of the abolition of slavery. Over the winter, Seward and Stoeckl negotiated terms of the Alaska purchase and reached an agreement on March 30, 1867.

The United States would buy Alaska's land and its undeveloped resources for about two cents an acre. Assets of the Russian-American Company, including ships, outposts, eighty thousand fur pelts, and employee housing in Sitka, were sold to San Francisco merchants. They eventually formed the Alaska Commercial Company, which controlled other fur-harvesting operations in Alaska's Interior.

Convincing Congress to approve both the treaty and funding for the purchase was no easy sell. Opponents derided it as "Seward's Folly" or "Walrussia." The editor of the *New York Herald*, Horace Greeley, cynically advised European heads of state to unload their worthless land on Seward.

Congress had been distracted for a year trying to impeach the president. So getting the treaty approved required Seward's best diplomatic skills, reportedly greased with Stoeckl's bribes to congressmen. Seward commissioned studies to counter criticisms of Alaska as just a wasteland of ice and snow.

During debate on the treaty in July 1867, the Senate took a test procedural vote, and the treaty passed with one more vote than the required two-thirds. The formal approval followed on a vote of 37 to 2. The House approved funds for the purchase the following summer by a vote of 114 to 43.

In fall 1867, Americans streamed into Alaska's territorial capital in search of new opportunity. The State Department scrambled to consummate Alaska's official transfer before winter travel conditions jeopardized the schedule.

Around three p.m. on October 18, 1867, American and Russian officials gathered before a hundred-foot-tall flagpole at the governor's residence on Baranov Hill in Sitka. One hundred soldiers of the Siberian Line Battalion assembled, and a twenty-member US honor guard carried in the American flag. More than one hundred American spectators gathered as Tlingit watched from their canoes in Sitka Sound. As the presiding Russian captain ordered his nation's flag lowered, American and Russian ships began firing salutes.

"The last moments of Russian rule proceeded in much the same spirit of incompetence and misadventure as the previous eighty years of Russian administration," wrote one historian of the era.

About a third of the way down the flagpole, the Russian flag got stuck. According to a Finnish blacksmith who witnessed the ceremony, two Russian soldiers were ordered to cut it down but failed. A third soldier finally dislodged it, and the flag, bearing the double-eagle symbol of the czar, flittered down onto the fixed bayonets of the Siberians. The wife of the Russian company manager is said to have fainted at the sight. The US flag was hoisted up the flagpole by the fifteen-year-old son of the senior American officer, ending more than a century of Russian rule of Alaska.

Upon the election of President Ulysses Grant, Seward left office and spent his remaining years traveling. He crossed the country on the Transcontinental Railroad just weeks after its completion and sailed to Alaska, where he delivered a speech in Sitka and was received by Tlingit leaders.

In the immediate aftermath of America's acquisition of Alaska, contact with Russians across the Bering Strait slowed as developments set the stage for Alaska's treatment as a colony by a different master, the United States. A provision in the purchase agreement guaranteed Russians then living in Alaska the privilege of US citizenship, if they opted for it. Most did not, and instead returned to Russia or moved to California or the Pacific Northwest.

Alaska's new rulers were US military officers. Although Army General Jefferson C. Davis headed the Department of Alaska, it was the US Treasury's

Revenue Cutter Service—predecessor of the Coast Guard—that had the largest American government presence in Alaska, especially in the Arctic. Cutter Service men were dubbed "American Northwest Mounties" because they dispensed both law and humanitarian aid.

Meanwhile, Congress had little continuing interest in Alaska other than extending territorial laws governing commerce and navigation and prohibiting liquor. The boom many Americans expected never materialized. Sitka's population topped out at about nine hundred, including both military and civilian residents. Many early settlers blamed the federal government for failing to provide services, from mail delivery to land surveys so private land could be acquired and developed. Alaska Native people became wards of the US government.

Within a decade, American missionaries arrived to extend Christianity to Alaska Natives. Part of their mission was to eradicate all vestiges of the Russian culture, beginning with the Russian Orthodox religion. The Reverend Sheldon Jackson, a Presbyterian minister who made his first voyage to Alaska in 1877, predicted that "twenty-five years from now there will not be any Orthodox church members left in Alaska."

Just thirteen years after American administration began, the district of Alaska experienced the first of several waves of outsiders flooding in to exploit its rich natural resources. In 1880, a couple thousand adventurers descended on what would become Juneau in the first of Alaska's gold rushes. As the century rolled over, more gold was discovered in the Yukon, just east of Alaska's border with Canada, and shortly after that in Nome. The rapid growth of Alaska's population and the need to regulate industry led to the early development of territorial government.

For the seventy-five years between Russia's sale of its colony and World War II, interactions between Alaskans and Russians continued but were rarely productive. The increase in Caucasian fortune seekers deteriorated relations with both Russian and Alaska indigenous populations. Retired University of Alaska linguist Michael Krauss notes that while the Russian Far East was nominally under czarist rule at the turn of the century, the region's commerce was heavily influenced by the gold rush population around Nome, which "sold cheap goods, especially liquor, to Eskimo and Chukchi for good furs and ivory." The Russian word for such white traders—*khishchniki*—translates as "predators."

American whalers and traders plying the Bering Sea became regular suppliers of alcohol and disease to Natives on both coasts. Measles, influenza, gonorrhea, and syphilis took a huge toll, with the Northwest Alaska Native population falling from more than five thousand in 1860 to about one thousand in 1890.

Alaska and Russian Natives of the region continued to visit one another unimpeded. A collapse in the Northwest Alaska caribou population in the 1870s resulted in increased trade with Russian Natives as Alaskans sought to replace their local clothing source. Unregulated travel across the strait tightened in the mid-1920s as the Soviet revolution took hold in distant Chukotka. Under the new national collective policy, several Native villages were abandoned, moved, or consolidated as the Soviets forced the acculturation of different Native groups, such as a newly established "culture base" at Lavrentiya on the Bering Sea coast.

In 1938, the Soviet and US governments exchanged memoranda recognizing the historic visitation between the Native peoples of their countries and establishing a process for future interactions. The agreement allowed visits without passports or visas for up to three months, after checking in with local authorities. Visitors were allowed personal gifts in "non-commercial quantities" that could be traded for skins, furs, hides, and crafts. Banned from importation into the Soviet Union were firearms (including hunting rifles), narcotics, printed matter, liquor, and objects of religious worship.

The State Department confirmed the exchange rules in the flowery diplomatic language of the era: "The Secretary of State presents his compliments to His Excellency the Ambassador of the Union of Soviet Socialist Republics . . ." Alaska and Soviet Native peoples continued their interactions until global politics thousands of miles away interrupted their time-honored means of existence.

A U-2 spy plane similar to the type flown by Air Force Capt. Charles Maultsby from Alaska's Eielson Air Force Base in 1962. US AIR FORCE

1

A Call to Arms

I believe that in the future, whoever holds Alaska will hold the world. I think it is the most important strategic place in the world.

—US ARMY GEN. BILLY MITCHELL, 1935

FIVE DAYS AFTER President John F. Kennedy stunned America into fearing that nuclear war was closer than ever because of Soviet missiles in Cuba, a U-2 spy plane quietly lifted off from an obscure airfield outside Fairbanks, Alaska. It was dark and well below freezing at Eielson Air Force Base just after midnight on October 27, 1962. More than 4,100 miles away in Washington, DC, the atmosphere could not have been more heated.

At the height of Cold War tensions between the United States and the Soviet Union, American surveillance planes detected medium-range ballistic missiles in Cuba, just ninety miles off Florida's coast. The sixty-seven-foot-long missiles could turn the Eastern Seaboard into smoking rubble in just thirteen minutes.

On October 22, Kennedy reported the chilling discovery in a dramatic Oval Office address to the nation. He demanded that the country that Americans feared most—the Soviet Union—remove the missiles, and he imposed a quarantine on ships destined for the communist-led Caribbean island in hopes of preventing their launch.

For veteran Air Force Captain Charles Maultsby, his flight that night in far-away Alaska was routine. The Soviet Union had been conducting nuclear tests at Novaya Zemlya, an island off Siberia about one thousand miles south of the North Pole. As part of "Project Star Dust," Maultsby's mission was to fly his spy plane, nicknamed "Dragon Lady," to the pole and collect air samples on special filter paper to detect radioactivity. Most missions came back clean. Of forty-two already flown that month from Eielson, only six found radioactive material.

The elite flyer, a combination pilot and astronaut, preferred more action. Before this assignment, Maultsby had flown aerial acrobatics with the Air Force's famed Thunderbirds. After being shot down over North Korea during the Korean War, he had survived six hundred days as a prisoner of war.

As the nation steeled itself for war, the thin-mustached captain settled into the one-man cockpit for what he knew would be an eight-hour flight. He had prepared himself for the coming seventy-thousand-foot altitude by inhaling pure oxygen for several hours to rid his body of as much nitrogen as possible to guard against the bends. At just five foot seven and 150 pounds, Maultsby was a perfect fit in the cramped cockpit. To build an aircraft capable of flying fourteen miles high, U-2 designers eliminated weight wherever possible, starting with the fuselage. Most of the plane was wing surface, eighty feet from tip to tip.

As Maultsby's U-2 neared the North Pole, he knew his compass would become useless, the needle automatically pointing downward toward the earth's magnetic field. So he reverted to standard operating procedure: the celestial navigation method of fifteenth-century explorers, reading the stars. But in the late fall at that latitude, the sky was filled with dancing bright lights—the aurora borealis, or northern lights. Maultsby was prepared with a stack of celestial charts, but each time he tried to fix on a guiding star such as Vega or Polaris, the northern star, the shimmering aurora made it difficult to tell one from another.

After collecting samples over what he thought was the pole, Maultsby executed the standard maneuver for reversing course: turn left for 90 degrees and then reverse the turn for 270 degrees. He headed back for what he assumed was home base.

The regular practice for returning U-2 pilots was to rendezvous with a US air-rescue plane near Barter Island off Alaska's northern coast. The intercept aircraft, dubbed "Duck Butt," had promised to "leave a light on in the window."

Maultsby could see nothing but darkness from horizon to horizon. Concerned with the whereabouts of the U-2, the Duck Butt pilot radioed that he would fire flares every five minutes for Maultsby to follow. Nothing but black sky for the captain as radio transmissions from Alaska grew weaker. Finally, Maultsby picked up the faint signal of a local radio station: balalaika music and chatter in Russian. The captain was dangerously miles off course.

When Maultsby entered Soviet air space west of Wrangell Island off the Chukchi Sea, Soviet MiG fighters scrambled from two air bases in the Chukotka region, just across the Bering Strait from Alaska. Their orders: intercept and shoot down the intruder. Maultsby yelled, "Mayday, Mayday," over his emergency channel as he maneuvered his plane eastward.

By radar from nearly one thousand miles away at a Galena air station west of Fairbanks, interceptors tracked Maultsby's location. Because of the Cuban missile crisis, F-102 Delta Dagger intercept jets stationed there had been upgraded earlier in the week. When the squadron was elevated to DEFCON 3, their conventional weapons had been replaced with nuclear-tipped Falcon air-to-air missiles. Just one of the nuclear warheads could destroy everything within a half-mile radius. Using such weapons certainly would invite reciprocation from the Soviets. Two of the nuclear-equipped F-102s with distinctive red tails received immediate orders: intercept the Soviet MiGs and escort Maultsby home.

In the nation's capital, meanwhile, America's top leaders monitored the Cuban missile crisis around the clock. Shortly before two p.m. that Saturday, Defense Secretary Robert McNamara was conferring with the Joint Chiefs of Staff when he was passed a message: a U-2 spy plane was lost off Alaska. It had taken the Strategic Air Command (SAC) ninety minutes to report the missing plane to Washington. With Soviet and American armed forces on the highest alert across the globe, now this—McNamara was not happy.

THE PRESIDENT HAD just finished a swim in the White House pool to relax his back and was headed to the residence for a quick lunch when his defense secretary called with the troubling news. Conferring with his national-security aides, President Kennedy broke their tension over the missing U-2 when he laughed, "There's always some sonofabitch who doesn't get the word." McNamara canceled air-sampling missions worldwide, calling back another sampling plane already in the air.

As the Soviet MiGs screamed toward him, Maultsby maintained his altitude. Their supersonic engines made the fighters much quicker than the U-2, but they could only climb to about sixty thousand feet, leaving them ten thousand feet short of their target. Maultsby thought of fellow U-2 pilot Francis Gary Powers, who two years earlier was shot down over Siberia, harshly interrogated, and imprisoned for twenty-one months before being released in a prisoner exchange. The Powers incident had been a huge black eye for the United States and a domestic public-relations coup for Nikita Khrushchev. The implications of the downing of another American spy plane at the height of the Cuban missile crisis was unthinkable.

Already airborne for more than nine hours, Maultsby soon faced another complication: running out of fuel. With a light airframe and long wings, U-2s were capable of gliding on wind currents for up to two hundred miles without power. To save his remaining twelve minutes of fuel for an emergency, Maultsby reluctantly switched off the plane's single engine and battery power, isolating himself fourteen miles above the Soviet mainland without radio contact.

Still hundreds of miles inside the Soviet Union, Maultsby glided silently across the black sky. Below him, the MiGs tracked the U-2 for about three hundred miles before being forced to peel off in search of fuel. They were replaced by MiGs from Chukotka's capital city of Anadyr, which followed him across the Chukotka Peninsula. The SAC operations center 3,500 miles away in Nebraska tracked the cat-and-mouse intercepts. Finally, a glow of dawn on the horizon reassured Maultsby he was headed the right way, east to Alaska.

Maultsby continued to glide east as he slowly descended to twenty-five thousand feet. Suddenly, two fighter jets with red tails appeared off his wings. Maultsby switched his radio back on to hear an American voice: "Welcome home."

At the recommendation of the F-102 pilots, Maultsby backtracked about twenty miles to the closest landing spot, a snow-covered airstrip near Kotzebue on Alaska's northwest coast. Coming in too quickly for the short strip, Maultsby killed his engine, lowered his flaps, and deployed a parachute out the rear of the plane to slow his speed. The U-2 skidded along the icy runway and burrowed into deep snow.

Once the plane came to a stop, Maultsby remained transfixed in the cockpit, his legs numb, unable to climb out. What he later described as a "bearded giant" in a government-issue parka lifted the captain out by his armpits and set him down in the snow. The first order of business: he shuffled to a snowbank to relieve himself. Maultsby's ten-hour-and-twenty-five-minute flight was the longest ever recorded for a U-2.

The following day, after a thirteen-day standoff in which the world came closer than ever to nuclear annihilation, Soviet leader Khrushchev agreed to dismantle Soviet missiles in Cuba. In a message to President Kennedy, Khrushchev noted that the Alaska U-2 flight easily could have been mistaken "for a nuclear bomber, which might push us to a fateful step."

TWO DECADES BEFORE Captain Maultsby's harrowing flight over the Soviet Union, US-Soviet relations had plummeted to another low. The ink was barely dry on the pre–World War II diplomatic exchange allowing regulated visits by American and Soviet Natives across the Bering Strait when US paranoia grew over Soviet intentions in the region.

In 1940, Anthony Dimond, Alaska's territorial delegate to congress, alarmed his constituents when he announced that the Soviet Union was settling "thousands of Russians, supposedly colonists" on Soviet Big Diomede Island, just two and a half miles from Alaska's Little Diomede. The settlers were reported to be of the "younger generation" who were "carried away with the idea that they are to be the glorious conquerors of the world and they must sow the seeds of revolution."

Their first mission: "get their hands on Alaska which so idiotically was sold to capitalist America by the Czarist government." Within a few months, the crew of the US Coast Guard Cutter *Perseus* confirmed Soviet construction of an airplane hangar on Big Diomede. Alaska Natives also reported observing Soviet submarines berthed around Big Diomede's shoreline.

Americans saw the moves as part of broader Soviet muscle flexing in the region. "Simultaneously a string of nearly a dozen 'Soviet bases of culture,' which include army and navy contingents, have been established in this region, fortresses have been built, coast defense guns have been mounted, submarine bases are being built, airfields have been completed, and all foreigners are rigorously excluded from the whole area," reported the *New York Times*.

The newspaper's sources said the Soviets recently had deemed the Commander Islands (where Bering died two hundred years earlier) restricted to

Soviet military personnel, "although German naval officers continue to visit there with great frequency, which deepens the suspicion that a German submarine base is being prepared there."

Just a year later, Germany's invasion of the Soviet Union dramatically altered attitudes across the strait as suspicion gave way to international cooperation. Within weeks of the German aggression, President Roosevelt pledged all possible help to the Soviet people. He dispatched veteran Soviet observer and business-man Averell Harriman to Moscow to devise an American-British assistance pro-gram for the Soviets.

Soviet leader Joseph Stalin unconditionally rejected Harriman's idea to deliver US aircraft flown by American crews through Alaska to Siberia. He report-edly was nervous about provoking Japan. As the war raged, Stalin dispatched his key foreign-affairs advisor, Vyacheslav Molotov, to Washington to hammer out a deal for additional American aid. Arriving in such a hostile country for the first time, Molotov packed sausages, Russian black bread, and a pistol for survival.

The Soviets continued to resist the Alaska–Siberia route for warplanes, fear-ing the weather, unprepared Siberian cities, and an unwanted American presence in the Far East. However, with Soviet losses mounting, in June 1942 Stalin finally agreed to a Lend-Lease plan. Two months later, the first Soviet envoys arrived in Nome to implement the scheme.

The proposal called for flying aircraft from Great Falls, Montana, through the Canadian cities of Edmonton, Alberta, and Whitehorse, Yukon Territory, to Alaska airfields in Fairbanks and Galena. A major new airfield was constructed in Nome, the last stopping point before Siberia. US pilots flew the planes to Alaska then handed them off to Soviet pilots. The Soviet airmen were specially selected for their loyalty to the motherland and were housed in separate quarters from the Americans. Most of the Russian interpreters were uniformed Soviet women required to pass security clearances.

Cold weather, poor maintenance, aircraft overload, and liquor consumption by the Soviet pilots took a modest toll on the operation. Of the 7,983 planes deliv-ered to the Soviets between September 1942 and September 1945 on the Alaska route, only about 1.6 percent were lost to weather or pilot error.

Though deemed helpful to the Allied war victory, Lend-Lease was subject to conspiracy theories. Rumors abounded of uranium, gold bars, and American banknotes being smuggled to the Soviet Union in US aircraft. After the war, the Soviets minimized the program's importance to the war effort, arguing that American aid represented only 4 percent of overall Soviet production during the war.

Later, some Westerners received Soviet recognition for their contributions to the war effort but Lend-Lease participants did not. A generation after the war, Soviet leader Khrushchev charged that "American monopolists made billions of dollars on war deliveries" and "fattened themselves on the blood of the people lost during two world wars."

Six months after the war's end, in March 1946, former British Prime Minister Winston Churchill joined President Harry Truman in Truman's home state of Missouri to receive an honorary college degree. Churchill used the occasion to deliver what became known as the "Iron Curtain speech," which ominously altered the way the West viewed the Soviet Union. The speech was broadly considered to be the onset of the Cold War, which triggered a massive military buildup to block Soviet aggression around the world, including the Bering Strait region.

A few months after Churchill's speech, an incident soured relations between Alaska and the Soviet Far East. In July 1946, twenty-six Little Diomede Natives sailed their walrus-hide boats to Big Diomede for a friendly visit. Landing on the island's north shore, they were met by uniformed Soviet soldiers, including both Russian and Native troops. At gunpoint, the Alaskans were herded to tents on a rocky plateau and held for fifty-two days. They were interrogated about US military activities and fed saltwater soup once a day. One Alaskan died in captivity.

After their release, Alaska Natives were reluctant to venture across the date line, even to follow pods of whales or walrus. The Soviets soon exiled their country's Natives from Big Diomede to the Soviet mainland, further distancing them from their Alaska relatives. In their place, a border guard surveillance post was established on the island to monitor incursions across the strait.

Those incidents and increased Cold War tension elsewhere prompted an internal debate within the US government. On March 22, 1948, FBI director J. Edgar Hoover issued a memo concluding that US national-security concerns should outweigh the interests of local Alaska Natives. This cast a dark shadow on the ten-year-old agreement with the Soviets that had permitted relatively free exchange of Alaska and Soviet Natives. On May 29, 1948, the Soviet government concurred with Hoover, pronouncing the original 1938 agreement "invalid."

A Cold War Ice Curtain across the Bering Strait indefinitely sealed the border between the US and USSR, banning all contact.

Alaska's economy had benefited enormously from World War II, and the Cold War kept federal dollars flowing. Fearful of invasions by both Germany and Japan, the federal government spent millions of dollars in the territory to construct numerous military bases and build the Alaska Highway, the only surface link with the Lower 48. Thanks to the influx of wartime military personnel, Alaska's population jumped by double digits.

In 1940, the first year of the war, only about 75,000 Alaskans lived in the territory; that increased to nearly 140,000 in just ten years, with 18 percent of the population associated with the military. After the war, Alaska was spared an economic depression by a new military buildup for the Cold War.

Alaska's geographic location became a strategic asset against the feared "Red Menace." Developing weapons technologies made the continental United States vulnerable to air attack, so Alaska was a perfect location for early-warning radar systems and front-line troops. The territory was close enough to the USSR to monitor seismic anomalies from nuclear tests. Alaska contained ten of sixteen minerals crucial to Cold War industrial development. And Alaska was America's best place where troops could train for ground and air combat in cold-weather conditions similar to those in the Soviet Union. Compared to prewar expenditures of less than $1 million a year, military spending in the territory peaked at $513 million in 1953.

Cold War paranoia ran so deep in Alaska that the FBI embarked on a top-secret mission to recruit and train average Alaskans—fishermen, trappers, bush pilots, and other private citizens—to fight covertly against a feared Soviet invasion of its former fur colony. Dubbed by codenames such as "Washtub" and "Corpuscle," the operation had two phases, according to newly released classified documents. The first called for Alaska citizen-agents to be trained to hide in key locations during a Soviet takeover. They would find survival caches of food, cold-weather gear, and radios with guidance on how to send coded messages about Soviet troop movements.

The second phase, coordinated with the CIA, was an "evasion and escape" plan where civilian operatives could help rescue and evacuate downed US military air crews in danger of Soviet capture. Retainers of up to $3,000 were budgeted for civilian agents. The operation continued between 1951 and 1959. Documents show that FBI director Hoover soon got cold feet, handing Washtub off to the Air Force's Office of Special Investigations. The director feared that once shooting started, the FBI would be "left holding the bag."

With the limited success of Operation Washtub, Alaska's more effective eyes and ears trained on the Soviet Union were those of the Alaska Territorial Guard, also known as the Eskimo Scouts. Formed in 1942 in response to the Japanese invasion of Alaska's Aleutian Islands, many of the citizen-soldiers were Alaska Natives from coastal communities who served without compensation. After the war, the territorial guard was transferred into the "organized" Alaska Army National Guard, with armories constructed to recruit and train local Natives. Some Alaskans considered the guard a luxury that Alaska could not afford, arguing that it was unlikely that a territorial national guard would be able to forestall a Russian attack.

By the time communist aggression began in Korea in 1950, Alaska Army National Guard units had been established in about fifty communities between Ketchikan and Barrow with nearly 1,300 officers and enlisted soldiers. The growth of the Alaska Air National Guard had the added benefit of helping overcome prejudice against Alaska Natives with President Truman's 1948 military desegregation order.

By the 1950s, one of the primary roles of Alaska's military was tracking and intercepting Soviet aircraft flying along and across the international date line. A Distant Early Warning Line (DEW Line) radar system constructed along the northern and western coasts of Alaska and Canada helped monitor Soviet flights. The first documented interaction involving shots fired came in March 1953. Making what officials described as a weather-reconnaissance flight about one hundred miles east of a Soviet military base on the Kamchatka Peninsula, a US plane returned fire after being shot at by Soviet MiGs.

Not all US-Soviet aerial interactions were belligerent. The first Soviet aircraft reported on Alaska soil since World War II was an Antonov An-24 turboprop checking Bering Strait ice conditions in winter 1974. It was quickly intercepted by two Alaska-based F-4 fighter jets. Facing severe headwinds and fog, the An-24 had run low on fuel and landed at Gambell on St. Lawrence Island. An Air Force C-130 flew in fuel from Elmendorf Air Force Base near Anchorage to help the Soviet plane get home.

Nome's Jim Stimpfle doggedly pursued reuniting Alaska and Russia Native families separated by the Cold War Ice Curtain. PHOTO BY CLAIRE RICHARDSON

Extending Hands of Friendship

Never, perhaps, in the postwar decades was the situation in the world as explosive and hence, more difficult and unfavorable, as in the first half of the 1980s.
—MIKHAIL GORBACHEV, FEBRUARY 1986

A T FOUR A.M. one July morning in 1983, a ringing telephone jolted Leo Rasmussen awake at his home in the Bering Sea community of Nome. A forty-four-year-old volunteer fireman, city councilman, and mayor, Rasmussen was used to middle-of-the-night calls. But this one was different: the US State Department wanted him to go to the Soviet Union—and fast.

"As soon as I said 'yes,' my wife jabbed me in the ribs and said, 'What did you just say yes to?'" Rasmussen recalled with a chuckle.

His political mentor, Senator Ted Stevens of Alaska, had recommended Rasmussen for a special assignment. Some ten days earlier, seven members of Greenpeace, the environmental activist organization, sneaked ashore at the Soviet village of Lorino on the Bering Sea to investigate and film its mink and fox farm, a commercial fur-breeding operation.

For decades, the Soviets had set up collective farms in numerous northern Native communities as sources for village jobs and income. Greenpeace accused the Soviets of harvesting whales to feed caged mink and fox, in violation of International Whaling Commission regulations. Under the commission's agreements granting whale-harvesting quotas to indigenous peoples, whales could be taken only for human consumption. Soviet fur-farm managers countered that only waste whale meat was fed to the caged animals.

As a Soviet helicopter fired flares across the bow of Greenpeace's *Rainbow Warrior* and a merchant ship cut within fifteen feet of it, seven activists had scrambled onto the Soviet shore. One Canadian and five American crew members were arrested; a seventh American was plucked from the sea trying to make a high-speed getaway with film footage. All were threatened with up to three years in prison. They spent their initial days in captivity playing chess and working a Rubik's Cube.

About a week later, the State Department negotiated their release. To retrieve the prisoners, State needed an official US representative. That's when the opinionated Rasmussen received the call. Rasmussen, a staunch Republican in the heavily Democratic Nome, and Republican Senator Stevens were longtime political allies. Both were also early advocates of improving US-Soviet relations across the Bering Strait, and neither was fond of environmentalists. As a city councilman in 1971, Rasmussen had cosigned a letter with Nome's mayor to their counterparts in Provideniya, USSR, urging contact across the Bering Strait. Rasmussen and Stevens strongly disagreed with Greenpeace's actions and, like some Alaska Natives, feared the protest could jeopardize reunification efforts across the date line.

With Rasmussen on board with his special State Department designation, the *Rainbow Warrior* departed Nome and steamed overnight toward a rendezvous point in the Bering Sea. En route, Rasmussen recalled passing through large pods of gray whales of the type harvested by the Soviets. Suddenly, a Soviet merchant ship, the *Fedor Matisen*, appeared on the horizon, guns fixed at the Americans.

"I'm thinking to myself, here I am sitting on a ship that violated Russian territory and we've got the people who committed the crime on board," said Rasmussen, who contemplated a long Siberian prison sentence.

When the Soviets demanded his official papers, Rasmussen presented his passport and Alaska driver's license, both of which had expired. After an hour-long interrogation, the protestors finally were released into Rasmussen's custody. During the negotiations, Rasmussen and the Soviets' English interpreter struck up a conversation about dog mushing. Rasmussen was a longtime booster of the Iditarod Trail Dog Sled Race, which concludes in Nome each year.

"It was an odd friendship created under duress," said Rasmussen, who still remains in contact with the interpreter.

ABOUT THE TIME of the Greenpeace incursion into the Soviet Far East, Anchorage International Airport launched a marketing campaign billing itself as the "Air Crossroads of the World." The airport boasted that through international air connections, Anchorage was just nine and a half hours within 90 percent of the industrialized world.

One reason for the airport's claim was Korean Air Lines, whose regular flights through Anchorage helped make Korean Americans one of the city's largest minority communities.

In the early morning hours of September 1, 1983, KAL Flight 007 landed in Anchorage for a routine refueling stop after departing New York the night before. At four a.m., the Boeing 747 carrying 269 passengers and crew lifted off for the final seven-hour leg of its flight across the North Pacific to Seoul. Three hours before its scheduled arrival in the South Korean capital, flight attendants announced breakfast. It was never served.

Inexplicably, the airliner drifted off course to the north over the Soviet Kamchatka Peninsula. After tracking the plane into their airspace, Soviet military commanders scrambled two Sukhoi Su-15 fighters, the backbone of the Soviet interceptor fleet, from a base on Sakhalin Island. The Soviet pilots pulled alongside the jet to observe the two levels of windows common to the double-deck configuration of a civilian 747 and then fired warning shots with brightly lit tracers. The KAL crew maintained their course, appearing to be unaware of the nearby Soviet fighter jets.

Newly released transcripts of the KAL cockpit and Soviet military conversations indicate that the Soviet pilots were reluctant to take lethal action as they struggled to identify and alert the airliner. Finally, on direct orders from a general on the ground, a Soviet missile was fired into the passenger plane's tail, destroying hydraulic systems and severing cables. Flight 007 continued to fly another twelve minutes, according to a report to the International Civil Aviation Organization. The Korean pilots had time to announce an emergency descent and order the use of oxygen masks before the jet spiraled into the ocean, breaking apart on impact.

The downing of Flight 007 exacerbated American-Soviet distrust and heightened tensions across the globe. President Reagan called the KAL attack a "crime against humanity." His Soviet counterpart, Yuri Andropov, accused America of a "sophisticated provocation masterminded by the U.S. special services with the use of a South Korean plane." The disaster also gave birth to numerous conspiracy theories, including suggestions that the passengers survived and were held as Soviet prisoners. In the Bering Strait, the shoot-down shattered dreams for renewed ties between Soviets and Alaskans.

For many Alaska Natives, time for reunions across the strait was running out. Many of their contacts with distant relatives in the Soviet Union had taken place more than half a century earlier, before the US and Soviet governments imposed an Ice Curtain across the strait. For example, Willis Walunga's father came from Siberia in 1921. Willis, who in 2015 was ninety-one and living in Gambell, had visited relatives in the Soviet Union once—in a skin boat at age twelve.

Another Alaskan, Ora Gologergen, was a St. Lawrence Island playmate in the 1920s with another young Native girl, Uugsima Ukhsima. However, the two hadn't spoken since Ukhsima returned to her Soviet village many years before. By the mid-1980s, these few elderly Alaskan-Siberian Yupiit were overdue for a final reunion to introduce their children or grandchildren to long-lost relatives.

An eccentric Caucasian real-estate agent decided to do something about it. Raised in the affluent Washington, DC, suburb of McLean, Virginia, Jim Stimpfle attended ethnically diverse schools. After earning a history degree from nearby George Mason University in 1970, Stimpfle dreamed of becoming a diplomat and undergoing Foreign Service training at Georgetown University.

"The reality was my grades weren't high enough and the Vietnam War was going on," Stimpfle said. "I was a war protester and not in A-1 shape to go to Georgetown. I was more A-1 to go to Vietnam."

Many of Stimpfle's friends fled to Canada to avoid serving in a war they considered unjust. But his best friend, Steve Kramer, enlisted in the Army. Before shipping off to Vietnam, he named Stimpfle the beneficiary of a modest life-insurance policy. After completing most of two tours in Vietnam, Kramer was en route over the Pacific Ocean in a medical evacuation when he died from combat wounds.

Stimpfle used part of the insurance proceeds to buy a blue Ford pickup to get about as far away from Washington, DC, as possible—Fairbanks, Alaska. After more than a decade in that university town in the company of intellectuals and peaceniks, Stimpfle met a bilingual English-Iñupiaq teacher, Bernadette Alvanna, and followed her to Nome.

Stimpfle's new wife's family was from King Island, a remote Bering Sea outpost south of the Diomede Islands. Named by British explorer James Cook in 1778, the island was abandoned in the 1960s and most of its residents relocated to Nome. From his wife's elderly relatives, Stimpfle heard tales of visiting Russian relatives across the Bering Strait. The Nome real-estate market was slow, so with time on his hands Stimpfle stirred up local interest in renewing contact between long-separated Alaska and Russian Native peoples. He fired off letters to state and federal officials, most of which were ignored.

One August day in 1986, Stimpfle dropped by the Nome city dump, where he noticed a steady wind blowing west toward the Soviet Union. This gave him an idea. Instead of sending a message in a bottle tossed into the Bering Sea, he thought, how about attaching it to a balloon instead? After experimenting with store-bought balloons filled from his car exhaust, he sweet-talked the local National Weather Service out of two larger, more durable balloons. From his wife's elementary-school class, he got letters of friendship that a local Russian teacher helped translate into Cyrillic. Having heard the Native elders speak of trade across the strait, Stimpfle assembled a small collection of sugar, tea, sewing needles, and chewing tobacco.

On the day of the launch, he filled the balloon with helium, attached the letters and goodie bag, and weighted it with a few rocks so it wouldn't float off into the stratosphere. Tracking it through binoculars, Stimpfle watched the balloon rise and then slowly float down to the sea, where it bounced along the surface. Suddenly an Alaska seal hunter sped by in his boat, retrieved the balloon, and tossed it onboard. Stimpfle followed the hunter down the coast. It turned out to be a longtime friend, Tim Gologergen, who excitedly showed Stimpfle his gift basket from Russia.

After two failed balloon launches, Stimpfle refocused on assembling a local committee to write more letters—and figuring out how to get them across the strait.

One of the first such opportunities came in September 1987, when a US research vessel arrived in Nome to study the Chukchi Sea's ecosystem on a mission for the National Oceanic and Atmospheric Administration. The 292-foot *Surveyor* was loading scientists and equipment when Capt. Walter Forester received a surprising call from the State Department. It ordered him to proceed to Provideniya on a goodwill mission in response to an invitation from local city officials. No American vessel had visited the Soviet port city in sixty years.

Before the *Surveyor* departed for the 230-mile run across the Bering Strait, Stimpfle wrote a letter to Provideniya's mayor appealing for friendship. He knew nothing of Provideniya, not even the mayor's name. Other Nome citizens pushing for reunification collected bubble gum, coffee mugs with dog-mushing designs, T-shirts, and hats for the crew to present as gifts.

As the ship crossed the international date line, Soviet agents boarded the *Surveyor* to switch off sea-water intake valves so data such as water temperature and salinity could not be collected, recalled chief scientist Sathy Naidu of the School of Fisheries and Ocean Sciences at the University of Alaska Fairbanks. Twenty-two hours after it departed Nome, the *Surveyor* crew was met by grim-faced Soviet soldiers, who after a delay permitted the Americans to come ashore to visit carefully selected sites: the Lenin-Stalin Museum, a factory, and a medical facility. After a three-hour dinner washed down with considerable beer and vodka, crew members were deposited at a cooperative store and encouraged to buy Russian handicrafts and walrus ivory carvings. The following day, the *Surveyor* hosted an onboard open house. A Soviet Native dance group from the nearby village of New Chaplino performed for the crew.

Upon their return to Nome after a three-day visit, the Americans faced US Customs, which seized their recently purchased ivory carvings. Months later, Naidu received a Customs notice of a $1,000 fine for illegally importing ivory and failing to discourage other scientists from buying it. After considerable wrangling, the case was dropped.

The ship also returned with another treasure, a letter to Stimpfle from Provideniya mayor Oleg Kulinkin, who was enthusiastic about renewing ties across the strait. Stimpfle considered Kulinkin's response a breakthrough that finally lent legitimacy to his multiyear quest. Now no longer just an oddball real-estate agent, Stimpfle was invited to join the Nome Chamber of Commerce. With other advocates of renewed ties with the Soviet Union, Stimpfle formed a special Chamber group—the Committee for Cooperation, Commerce, and Peace, a play on the translated initials of the Union of Soviet Socialist Republics (CCCP).

IN ANCHORAGE, A separate effort to renew contacts between Alaskans and Soviets originated with a young man seeking to learn more of his mother, a distant relative of Russia's last czar. In 1946, Theodore Mala was born in Hollywood to parents whose best friends included some of Tinseltown's most glamorous stars. His father, Ray Wise Mala, was a handsome Alaska Native who became one of the most successful actors of the 1920s. Born in the gold rush town of Candle in Northwest Alaska, Ray Mala started as a cameraman and later played a starring role in the 1933 movie *Eskimo*, the first feature film shot on location in Alaska.

A dashing Hollywood playboy, Mala met a French-educated dancer whose parents escaped the Russian Red Army shortly after the Bolshevik Revolution. By virtue of her aunt's kinship to Russian Czar Nicholas II, the lithe Galina Liss also was known as Princess Kropotkin. In 1937, Mala and Liss eloped to Tijuana, Mexico. Nine years later, Liss gave birth to their son. Young Ted was six when his father died at age forty-five. His mother succumbed to pneumonia just ten months later.

Resisting the overtures of his Alaska Native family, Ted Mala's Russian grand-mother protectively raised the young boy, sending him to elite California board-ing schools with the children of other movie stars. Ronald Reagan's son Michael was among Ted's classmates. Intrigued by visits to the homes of Russians living in California where pictures of the czar hung over their fireplaces, Mala grew up curious about the country of his mother's birth. He graduated from DePaul, a Catholic university in Chicago, and majored in medicine at Autonomous University in Guadalajara, Mexico, before earning his master of public health degree from Harvard University.

Mala finally worked his way back to his father's birth state as Alaska's first male Iñupiaq doctor. In Alaska, he served in numerous positions, including staff member at the Center of Alcohol and Addiction Studies, associate professor of health sciences at the University of Alaska Anchorage, director of the Institute for Circumpolar Health Studies, and secretary general of the International Union for Circumpolar Health.

Around 1980, Mala attended an Alaska conference focused on environmen-tal impacts on public health to which a Soviet delegation had been sent. When the Soviets discovered Mala's ties to their homeland, they insisted he visit. In 1982, he made the first of what would become dozens of trips across the Soviet Union, proposing health exchanges with his Soviet counterparts. He focused on Novosibirsk, site of the country's Siberian research centers, and studied nutrition among the remote Natives of Chukotka.

Never a stickler for protocol, Mala wrote directly to Soviet General Secretary Mikhail Gorbachev, detailing his ideas for an Alaska–Soviet Far East health exchange. Gorbachev responded by setting up a Moscow meeting between the

Soviet health minister and Mala and his UAA delegation. In 1983, Mala and then-UAA chancellor David Outcalt returned from the Soviet Union with a draft agreement with the Siberian branch of the Soviet Academy of Medical Science.

The agreement called for information sharing about the health and social challenges of living in cold climates, especially among Native people. It focused on issues perplexing to scientists on both sides of the Bering Strait: Does diet affect living in the Far North? How can some thrive in harsh climates while others suffer frequent illness? What is the relationship between genetics and the susceptibility to alcoholism among Native peoples?

At their 1985 Geneva Summit, President Reagan and General Secretary Gorbachev also endorsed the idea of educational, scientific, and cultural exchanges, which had been largely frozen after the 1979 Soviet invasion of Afghanistan.

Mala was a gifted promoter of his Alaska-Soviet initiatives, signing a host of agreements, generating favorable media coverage, and occasionally running afoul of his bosses. For one of his early Alaska-Soviet exchange proposals, he secured the endorsement of Alaska's US senators when he organized a 1986 Washington, DC, ceremony for a health exchange with Soviet embassy officials. Senators Ted Stevens and Frank Murkowski signed as witnesses.

Mala won the backing of newly elected Alaska Gov. Steve Cowper, who attended a high-profile 1987 Siberian medical exchange signing ceremony to "help us lay the foundation of a new bridge for health, history and humanity." Mala also extracted funding from the Alaska Legislature for initiatives that had not been vetted through official university channels.

In 1989, Mala generated headlines by tempting UAA brass to fire him after accusing them of being "highly unethical" over management of the Institute for Circumpolar Health Studies, which he directed. The dispute even engulfed Cowper, who declined to take sides at a press conference kicking off his own extended trip across the Soviet Far East.

ANOTHER EARLY EFFORT to reunite Alaska and Soviet Native families was undertaken by a pair of international anthropologists who met far from the Bering Strait. New Zealander David Lewis was a veteran of several Antarctic expeditions when he encountered anthropologist Marianne "Mimi" George in 1981 in the South Pacific. They shared a passion for voyaging cultures, exploring how indigenous people ranging from Papua New Guinea to the Soviet Chukchi built and sailed vessels using ancient technology and navigation methods. They wintered over together in Antarctica two years later and documented the adventure in their book, *Icebound in Antarctica*.

The two first visited Chukotka together in 1988, when they transported eleven Alaska Natives from St. Lawrence Island to visit distant relatives in New Chaplino, near Provideniya. Their vessel, the *Cyrano*, was originally owned by American conservative thinker William F. Buckley and later donated for research use by Hawaiian Tropic suntan oil company. Lewis and George returned the following year to document the Soviet harvest of whales.

Early overtures, such as those spearheaded by Stimpfle, Mala, Lewis, the *Surveyor*, and others, chipped away at the Ice Curtain, helping lay the groundwork for renewed relations across the Bering Strait.

During a 1986 concert of Alaska Performing Artists for Peace in the Soviet Union, Juneau's Dixie Belcher is joined by Gennadi Gerasimov, who became President Gorbachev's principal spokesman, and former Alaska Gov. Jay Hammond. PHOTO BY BOYD NORTON

A Juneau Peacenik in the Kremlin

Our land and people are today divided by a political boundary. We are members of two great nations, both of which maintain powerful weapons pointed across the Bering Strait at each other. We share the same language, the same culture, and for some of us, the same parents.

—YUPIK ARTIST AND PERFORMER CHUNA MCINTYRE, 1986

PEACE ACTIVIST DIXIE Belcher believed music could change the world. Born and raised in Alaska's capital city, she returned to Juneau after college in Chicago to work for the state government. At age thirty-one, her life was dramatically disrupted when her husband was killed in a helicopter accident. She decided then to stay home to raise two daughters on her retirement income and Social Security, play piano and banjo, and travel.

As an average of five feet of rain soaked Juneau each year, Belcher frequently took cover in the local Catholic Church with a quirky mix of musicians attracted to Alaska's most liberal city. With Belcher as its musical director, the sixty-five-member St. Paul Singers toured the state, performing folk music concerts.

During a 1977 concert tour to Northwest Alaska, Belcher made a day trip to a remote, rarely visited spot, the tiny rock island of Little Diomede in the Bering Sea, just two and a half miles from Soviet Big Diomede. At the National Guard armory there, Belcher noticed a large sign: "If the Russians attack, surrender." As she watched Alaska Natives peer through binoculars across the foggy international date line at Soviets who could be long-lost relatives, Belcher decided the sign was one of the stupidest things she had ever seen. She vowed then to help warm the Cold War with music.

It took a while. Nearly a decade later, Belcher opened her rustic home surrounded by towering Sitka spruce to a peacenik from Palo Alto, California. Marty Behr of World Beyond War hoped to recruit new members with a unique appeal to send Alaskans to nearby Siberia to lobby for peace. Suddenly the image of that Little Diomede visit materialized in her mind as Belcher blurted out, "Let's take a group of Alaska performers across the Soviet Union and open the border!" A year later, in the fall of 1986, she did just that.

Converting that seemingly preposterous dream into reality played to Belcher's strengths: vision, persistence, and capitalizing on connections. And it accentuated her weaknesses: focus, organization, and money management. Over the span of her four-year activism with the Soviet Union, Belcher befriended two Alaska governors, one of America's top television network news anchors, and a top aide to Mikhail Gorbachev. She also incurred tens of thousands of dollars in debt, had to borrow money to eat, and persuaded former Alaska Gov. Jay Hammond to cosign a loan on her house so the bank wouldn't repossess it.

"Dixie, bless her generous, compassionate, gullible soul, is forever involved in extremis in some cause or another," Hammond wrote in a newspaper column. "As a result, chaos, confusion, apprehension and panic often swirl in her wake like pet puppies; nipping her heels, tearing her stockings and sometimes disgracing themselves on her carpet."

To deliver on her vision, Belcher opened two fronts: she recruited an eclectic group of performers willing to help pay their way singing and dancing across the world's largest country, and she milked connections at the highest levels of the US and Soviet governments.

To assemble the Alaska Performing Artists for Peace, she relied on some of her church singers and recruited other Juneau performers. She also attracted young Native performers, some of whom lived in remote northern villages. One of the most popular acts was the Savoonga Comedy Players. Mostly elderly Native women from one of Alaska's most remote villages on St. Lawrence Island, the players mixed slapstick with traditional Eskimo stories, spitting out their dentures to make funny faces. She also lined up five African American gospel singers from Anchorage.

Then Belcher focused on a major hurdle: securing Soviet permission to spread her seemingly provocative message. Her California peace-activist colleague helped land an appointment with Gennadi Gerasimov, then editor of the Kremlin-controlled *Moscow News*. Gerasimov became more influential than anyone in rekindling relations between Alaska and the Soviet Union. He welcomed Belcher and three Native performers to his newspaper office and was so intrigued by their dance demonstration that he published a prominent story about the proposed expedition in the internationally distributed *News*. Belcher invited Gerasimov to Alaska, hoping to impress him with the similarities between the Soviet Union and its former eighteenth-century fur colony.

Back home in Alaska, meanwhile, Belcher met stiff resistance to the proposed visit by a top Soviet communist. When she sought a required letter of invitation for Gerasimov from Alaska's US senators, Ted Stevens and Frank Murkowski, both declined. But a young staffer to Alaska's lone congressman, Don Young, slipped an invitation into a stack of correspondence awaiting signatures. Young unknowingly invited one of the Soviet Union's highest-profile communists to his state.

Alaska legislators summoned Belcher to the capitol to explain what they feared were her ties to the KGB, the Soviet spy and security agency. A powerful Native state senator, who represented the majority of Alaska's Northwest Native residents, threw Belcher's proposal back at her so hard it bruised her arm. Belcher said some Juneau residents even accused her of being a communist and called for her banishment from public schools.

IN MAY 1987, Gerasimov arrived for the first of four visits to Alaska. A New York correspondent for Soviet newspapers in the previous decade, he knew the US political process and headline-grabbing American slang better than most Americans. As General Secretary Gorbachev began moving his country toward more openness under *glasnost*, Gerasimov employed his wry humor to explain those policies to the world. He coined the term the "Sinatra Doctrine"—as in "I did it my way"—to characterize Gorbachev's reforms allowing Soviet satellites to go their own way. That helped Gerasimov become the first non-American named Communicator of the Year by the National Association of Government Communicators.

Gerasimov arrived in Juneau accustomed to the first-class style of a diplomat; Belcher escorted him across Alaska as a member of the proletariat. She drove him around Juneau in a car so beat up her daughters were embarrassed to be seen in it. As a guest of Jay and Bella Hammond's at their remote rustic homestead, he experienced his first Alaska outhouse.

Belcher had two goals for Gerasimov's visit: finding funds for her peace adventure and securing Soviet government approval for a tour by Alaska performers. Gerasimov and Belcher also traveled to Washington, DC, and New York to visit members of Congress and the national media. One meeting would pay key huge dividends later: a dinner with ABC news anchor Peter Jennings.

Back home, Belcher continued to beat the bushes for funding. She turned to the normally low-profile Alaska first lady Bella Hammond to lobby the Alaska Legislature for a grant.

"When she asked me to go to the legislature, I thought at first it was dreadful because I had never done anything like that before," the first lady recalled. "Some people in the legislature thought visiting Russia wasn't a good idea. But it worked out beautifully. They didn't argue and didn't have any problems funding a program like that."

Hammond extracted $63,000 from lawmakers.

Another attention-getting fund-raising event wasn't so lucrative. Belcher and other performing artists proposed a satellite "space bridge" linking Moscow and Juneau on New Year's Eve 1985. Folk and Native performers from both nations were slated to appear on live television. The Soviets planned to project the program onto a seven-story-tall screen erected for the International Year of Peace on Kalinsky Prospect, one of Moscow's main streets.

Alaska artists descended on Juneau from Sitka, St. Lawrence Island, and the remote village of Chevak. Technicians from Juneau's public television station and the state's Rural Alaska Television Network spent months resolving technical challenges. Just hours before the broadcast, officials of Gosteleradio, the Soviet State Committee for Television and Radio, called Juneau at three a.m. and without explanation pulled the plug. The Alaska performance proceeded as scheduled to hundreds in Juneau at noon on December 30, 1985. A local Tlingit dance troupe performed in hats modeled after those worn by Russian sailors who plied Southeast Alaska waters in the 1800s. Despite the Alaskans' frustration, public television mugs and T-shirts printed for the special occasion were shipped to the Soviet technicians who had struggled to relink Russia and Alaska.

Belcher's relationship with Gerasimov continued to pay off. She visited him again in Moscow in 1986, finally securing permission to lead her performers across the Soviet Union. As Belcher continued to seek underwriting until the day of departure, an ill-timed Cold War incident jeopardized the trip. That September, the United States arrested a Soviet United Nations employee for spying. Three days later, the Soviets retaliated with the Moscow arrest of prominent American journalist Nicholas Daniloff on espionage charges.

The *Juneau Empire* used the incident to editorialize against Gerasimov, who it said "recently visited Juneau parading around as the 'editor' of the *Moscow News*. What a joke! He is not an editor; he is a propagandist, bought and paid for by the Soviet government. To call him an editor is simply not telling the truth."

Short of cash as the departure date loomed, Belcher resorted to renting out rooms in her Juneau house. She racked up large credit-card bills flying performers to Anchorage for rehearsals. Inspired by Belcher's cause, a Ketchikan woman whose mother had died sent a portion of her modest inheritance. To cover remaining travel costs, Belcher was forced to take out a second mortgage on her home.

Just five days before departure for the Soviet Union, the ragtag performers gathered at Kings Lake, a camp retreat near Anchorage, to meld three hours of disjointed acts into an engaging program half that long.

"One of the terrifying things as a director was that I was taking a truly amateur group to a country that produces some of the best performers and performances in the world," Belcher said. "And when I really thought about it, I was petrified."

IN EARLY OCTOBER 1986, the sixty-seven performers and support crew packed their costumes and props and boarded a jet in Anchorage for the nearly twenty-four-hour trip to Leningrad. There, after a quick decompression, they prepared for their first performance in Russia's cultural capital. During the intermission, a group of Soviet students from the Leningrad Language Institute asked to meet the Alaska Native performers. As indigenous residents of Soviet Far East villages on the Bering Sea coast, the students excitedly asked about long-lost relatives. The visiting Alaska elders immediately recognized the name of a Soviet Native mentioned by the students, a distant cousin of Savoonga Comedy Player Kathy Noongwook. The Alaskans were elated to hear that Noongwook's cousin was alive and well in Provideniya, which they hoped to visit a few days later.

Alaskan Ora Gologergen enthralled the Soviet students with a tale of her own sole visit to their country forty-six years earlier. It took place after a tattered boat washed ashore one day near her St. Lawrence Island village. The Soviet Natives on board were in bad shape. The Alaskans nursed them back to health and, when the weather cleared, delivered them back to their home village.

"We spent four days in Siberia," Gologergen recalled. "The people were very thankful. They wanted to repay us for taking care of their lost fishermen."

Each Soviet Union performance of the Alaska Performing Artists for Peace was modeled after an Eskimo potlatch, a traditional gift-giving feast organized to celebrate births, deaths, weddings, and adoptions. Charismatic teacher and hunter John Pingayak of Chevak, a small Cup'ik village on Alaska's southwestern coast, was tapped as master of ceremonies. He introduced each performance to the beat of skin drums as kuspuk-clad dancers waved feathered dance fans. They were followed by the Gospel Singers, five African American women whose presence was a rarity in the Soviet Union, where encountering a black person was a novelty.

The elderly Savoonga ladies followed with comic relief, as they "field dressed" a cloth seal, extracting pantyhose, an old pair of pants, and a booze bottle, to the uproar of the Soviet audiences. The Juneau singers and cloggers wrapped up the show, inviting the audience to join in singing "Blowin' in the Wind," "We Are the World," and "We Shall Overcome."

Dubbed by the Soviet press "Alaska's gift to the Soviet Union," the Alaskans were received as rock stars. During one concert, 1,200 Soviets broke down a door trying to get in the concert hall. Each performance received multiple standing ovations.

"When the curtain fell, we collapsed from fatigue," acclaimed Yupik performer Chuna McIntyre told the *Moscow News*. "But the audiences were giving us marvelous ovations, so we jumped up and were prepared to dance over and over again. I can't imagine where we got the strength to dance so much."

Over nearly three weeks, the Alaskans traveled twice across the USSR's eleven time zones. They performed in concert halls and schools in Khabarovsk in the Far East; Irkutsk, Bratsk, and Novosibirsk in Siberia; and concluded in Moscow. Their major disappointment was the cancelation—last minute and never explained—of the planned visit to Providyeniya, across the Bering Strait from Nome, where they hoped to see Native relatives.

Before flying home, the group's leaders, including Dixie Belcher and Jay Hammond, joined Gerasimov at a Moscow press conference. The Alaskans presented him with an exquisite children's fur parka as a gift to Soviet First Lady Raisa Gorbachev.

In brief remarks, Governor Hammond said, "Martin Luther King, the well-known US personality, dreamed of a day when people would not be divided according to the color of their skin. Rephrasing it, I'd like to say that I hope people would not be divided according to their political views but by the end results of their activities."

Belcher and her exhausted troupe returned to Alaska to widespread media acclaim, changed lives, and $50,000 in debt. Headlines boasted "Soviet Audiences Enthusiastic" and "Russians Not So Different."

For gospel singer Shirley Staton, the visit was so inspiring she soon moved to Moscow and earned rubles singing in a jazz nightclub in the Cosmos Hotel.

"I had no idea of the impact of that experience at the time," Staton said nearly thirty years later. "It opened me up in a way that I did not expect. The experience whetted my thirst for wanting to connect with people internationally."

Yet part of Belcher's dream remained unfulfilled—reuniting Native families long separated by the Ice Curtain. When the Provideniya leg of the trip was inexplicably canceled by the Soviets, Belcher doubled down.

In early 1988 in Moscow and Washington, DC, aides to Ronald Reagan and Mikhail Gorbachev readied for the third and final summit between the leaders of the world's two superpowers. In Geneva nearly three years earlier, the two had endorsed a 50 percent reduction in offensive nuclear arms. A year later, at their second summit in Reykjavik, Iceland, they reached a tentative agreement on nuclear arms reduction. But the deal collapsed on the final day of the Moscow summit when Reagan rejected Gorbachev's insistence on limiting the US "Star Wars," or Strategic Defense Initiative. With Reagan leaving office in January 1989 and his legacy on the line, expectations were high going into the May summit.

As Gorbachev's principal spokesman, Gerasimov had embarked on a two-week US tour to spin the Russian view of nuclear disarmament in advance of the summit. Belcher persuaded him to add yet another visit to Juneau to his itinerary. In April 1988, Governor Cowper hosted a reception for Gerasimov at the elegant, white-columned governor's mansion. After the obligatory toasts, Cowper pulled Gerasimov aside to lobby for Soviet approval of a flight across the strait to reunite Native families and to open a Soviet consular office in Alaska.

Belcher had another idea up her sleeve. She was convinced that if Gerasimov visited the Bering Strait and witnessed firsthand the close proximity of the United

States and the Soviet Union, he would secure Kremlin approval to melt the Ice Curtain. The problem was that after flying a single-engine plane to Jay and Bella Hammond's Lake Clark homestead two years earlier, Gerasimov had vowed never to climb into a small plane again. A few days after his stay in the state capital, Belcher escorted the Soviet visitor to Nome to speak to the local Chamber of Commerce.

ABC NETWORK ANCHOR Peter Jennings, with whom Belcher and Gerasimov had dined two years earlier in New York, knew a great made-for-television story. So Jennings had arranged for a plane to transport Gerasimov and the media entourage from Nome to Little Diomede Island. With the prospect of favorable international media coverage, Gerasimov overcame his fear of flying and boarded a twin-engine plane for the forty-five-minute hop to an ice runway on the frozen Bering Strait. Gingerly making his way up slick steps to the village of Little Diomede, Gerasimov posed for the cameras in front of a giant sign that spelled out "peace" (*mir*) in Cyrillic.

"Everyone washed up and curled their hair to meet him," said Little Diomede resident Myrna Kunayak. "I'm glad he's here and I hope they open the international date line." Gerasimov declined to participate in the dancing performed in his honor. But he joined the call for more collaboration across the border.

"It's not an iron curtain, it's an ice curtain," he pronounced.

A month later, the eyes of the world focused on Gerasimov. As hundreds of reporters from across the globe descended on Moscow for the final Reagan-Gorbachev summit, Gerasimov appeared with Reagan's press secretary, Marlin Fitzwater, to explain their bosses' expectations. In the gilded briefing hall among that media mob was the Juneau peace activist named Dixie Belcher.

A Hollywood B-movie actor who launched his political career as a hard-line anti-communist, Ronald Reagan arrived for his first-ever visit to the Soviet Union on May 29, 1988. A light breeze rippled Soviet and American flags as Gorbachev welcomed the first American president to visit Moscow in fourteen years. The two superpower leaders were all smiles for the cameras in an ornate Kremlin ceremonial chamber, but tensions hung over the summit like a thunderstorm over the Russian steppe. Reagan criticized his hosts on human rights while the Soviets accused the Americans of arming rebels fighting the Soviet-installed government in Afghanistan.

After his visit to Little Diomede, Belcher found Gerasimov a changed man. He was reinvigorated seeing his homeland in person less than three miles away and hearing Alaska Natives speak of long-separated relatives. Belcher had scraped up just enough donations for a ticket to Moscow, where Gerasimov met her at the airport. "I had five dollars in my pocket—that was it—and he lent me money."

Upon her arrival at the summit, Belcher found a dejected Gerasimov. He had tried to sell the idea of opening relations between the Soviet Far East and Alaska to Gorbachev, Foreign Minister Eduard Shevardnadze, and other Kremlin leaders, but no one was interested. Belcher urged him to keep trying.

Later, during a break in the summit activities, Belcher encountered Gerasimov in a Kremlin hallway. He had shocking news. "We've got permission for Alaska Airlines to fly to the Far East," he told her. And that wasn't all. Gerasimov also had secured approval for Soviet and Alaska Natives to travel across the Bering Strait.

Belcher was so elated she asked Gerasimov about the possibility of a high-profile event to celebrate the opening of the border between the two countries. "Yes," he told her, "if you invite me."

Although President Reagan pronounced "the end of the Cold War" while walking through Red Square, the Moscow summit was broadly considered a failure. There was no further progress on arms control, and Reagan's repeated insistence on human-rights improvements met with a frosty response from Gorbachev. But even with the bureaucratic wording of the results, Alaskans were elated.

"Taking into account the unique environmental, demographic and other characteristics of the Arctic, the two leaders reaffirmed their support for expanded bilateral and regional contacts and cooperation in this area," reported an August 1988 State Department summary of the summit. "They noted plans and opportunities for increased scientific and environmental cooperation under a number of bilateral agreements as well as within an International Arctic Science Committee of states with interests in the region. They expressed their support for increased people-to-people contacts between the native peoples of Alaska and the Soviet north."

A forty-five-year-old banjo-playing peacenik from Juneau, who had been the object of derision when she began her effort to open doors, had secured Kremlin blessing for air service across the Bering Strait, exchanges of Native families long separated by the Ice Curtain, and openings for business development—and had set the stage for decades of cultural and educational exchanges that would follow.

Lynne Cox swims between Alaska Little Diomede and Soviet Big Diomede islands in August 1987 as doctors and the media monitor her progress. PHOTO BY CLAIRE RICHARDSON

4

Swimming Against the Current

You have embodied the essence of the American spirit.

—PRESIDENT RONALD REAGAN,

PRAISING ENDURANCE SWIMMER LYNNE COX, SEPTEMBER 11, 1987

A S A YOUNG girl growing up in New Hampshire, Lynne Cox was capti-vated by the x-rays her radiologist father allowed her to examine when they visited his hospital together. But Dr. Cox saw a darker side to radiation technology. As a World War II corpsman, he had witnessed the worst of war and feared the horrific results a Cold War collision could have on Lynne and her brother and sisters.

"He was the one who pointed out that the superpowers were so close together," Cox said, recalling her dad's fondness for perusing a *National Geographic* atlas with his children. "The relationship wasn't between Washington and Moscow. It was between these two islands in the middle of the Bering Strait. You could stand there and hold up binoculars and see people on the other side. That really humanized the border but also showed that in many ways we weren't that distant from each other."

Cox credits her dad with the outlandish idea of swimming across the inter-national date line between Alaska and the Soviet Union to draw attention to, and perhaps lessen, Cold War tensions. It was a goal she pursued for more than a decade, subjecting herself to increasingly challenging swims while pounding on doors at the highest levels of the Kremlin.

The sturdy youngster grew up in a comfortable middle-class family, attending to her studies and swimming in a local program. Even on chilly New England summer days when the other kids wanted out of the cold pool, Cox joyously kept warm swimming laps. At age twelve, Cox's parents saw such swim promise in their daughter that they uprooted the family to California so Cox could train with the US Olympic Team swim coach. He soon encouraged her to leave the comforts of a calm warm-water pool for a bigger challenge, the Pacific Ocean.

In her dramatic autobiography, *Swimming to Antarctica*, Cox documents her increasingly daring open-water swims between 1971 and 1985: Catalina Island, the English Channel, the Nile River, New Zealand's Cook Strait, South America's Strait of Magellan, and South Africa's Cape of Good Hope. She considered each one training for her ultimate goal—swimming the icy waters of the Bering Strait in a symbolic gesture for improved US-USSR relations.

"There's something poetic and beautiful about swimming from the present into the future," Cox said. "That was the hope, that we'd have a better future than present."

To realize her dream, Cox badgered each successive Soviet leader—Brezhnev, Chernenko, Andropov, Gorbachev—plus assorted diplomats and government officials in both nations. Her decade-long plea for Soviet permission to swim the Bering Strait went largely unanswered.

In spring 1986, Cox called at the Soviet consulate in San Francisco to register yet another request. As the consulate's heavy metal door slammed behind her, it reinforced her deep-seated fear of the Soviet Union, rekindling memories of the Cuban missile crisis and hiding under her elementary-school desk from a Soviet nuclear attack.

Finally, thanks to her persistence, Cox made a breakthrough with two influential contacts. The first was Ed Salazar, who worked on the Soviet desk at the State Department and became the first US diplomat to take Cox seriously. The other was Bob Walsh, who was organizing Seattle's Goodwill Games. Walsh was a colleague of television sports pioneer Ted Turner, who created the Cable News Network (CNN) in 1980. Salazar and Walsh both capitalized on their relationships in Washington and Moscow, slowly pushing through the US and Soviet bureaucracies Cox's long-awaited permission to swim the Bering Strait.

Salazar was a Foreign Service officer assigned to handle US-Soviet exchange ideas, many of them off the wall.

"When the secretary got a really wacky call, they sent it to me," said Salazar, now retired in London. "Lynne was one of those wacky calls—it was nuts."

After hearing her out, Salazar was persuaded Cox could pull it off. So he helped her build bipartisan support in Congress and pushed against the Reagan administration's inclination to nix citizen exchanges.

"The Reagan administration didn't want to expand this area of cooperation with the Soviet Union. They saw very little value in it," Salazar said. "But they also didn't think it would be productive to shut it all down. I think it's fair to say the Reagan administration allowed the exchanges to continue so they could be used as leverage against the Soviets to adopt changes in their foreign policy."

Like Dixie Belcher, Cox found raising money a persistent challenge to her international citizen diplomacy. She worked odd jobs to pay her bills and tried to win support through fund-raising letters to corporations. Kids she taught to swim handed over their allowance. A California swim team raised $230 with a swim-a-thon. Modest corporate contributions—$1,000 here, an airplane ticket there—slowly materialized.

A major barrier to approval for the swim was that no one believed the Soviets would permit her to enter their waters. To apply pressure on the Kremlin, Cox generated plenty of international media attention, with stories spanning the *Los Angeles Times*, CNN, and KNOM Radio in Nome. ABC News continued its interest in the melting the Ice Curtain by promising a "pre-story" that Cox could send to Gorbachev to persuade him to give the swimmer a green light.

In mid-June 1987, Cox gambled that the Soviets would finally relent. She relocated to Nome to finalize logistics and continue her cold-water training in earnest. Dave Karp, manager of the local Alaska Village Tours, volunteered to arrange housing and lent his office as the expedition's headquarters. As he was growing up in Nome, Karp said, he frequently heard about eccentrics trying to cross the strait. One wanted to float over in a bathtub; another proposed walking across the winter ice, camouflaged beneath a cardboard box painted white.

Cox's idea "seemed more legit" than the others. "While working out in the villages, I had become more and more aware that families had been divided at the border," Karp said. "This is kind of like the Berlin Wall, where there's no interaction but there should be."

For training swims, Cox walked each day to Nome's gravelly beach, the site of one of Alaska's biggest gold-rush bonanzas a century earlier. Regardless of weather—rain, fierce wind, sandstorms—she plunged into the fifty-degree Bering Sea and swam the coastline in nothing but a swim suit, cap, and goggles.

A major concern of doctors monitoring Cox's hoped-for Bering Strait crossing was her body temperature. In the mid-1980s, the winter ice usually retreated in the Bering Sea around the Diomede Islands by July, leaving water temperatures between thirty-eight and forty-two degrees. Exposure of the average person to those temperatures quickly produces hypothermia, a physical condition affecting the brain, heart, lungs, and other vital organs. Body heat is lost twenty-five times faster in cold water than in cold air.

In forty-degree water, hypothermia typically produces a loss of dexterity in about five minutes. Exhaustion or unconsciousness sets in within fifteen to thirty minutes, with death likely to occur within one to three hours. About six hundred Americans die of hypothermia each year.

Yet Cox was a different breed when it came to cold-water tolerance. A decade earlier, she was subjected to tests by the University of California Santa Barbara's Institute of Environmental Stress. It found that instead of floating on top of water like most women, Cox had a "neutral buoyancy," meaning she was an unusually efficient swimmer because she didn't need to expend energy staying afloat.

The other physiological oddity researchers discovered was that she generated more heat than she lost in cold-water swims. Most people swimming in fifty-degree water lose body heat rapidly, resulting in hypothermia.

To prepare for the Bering Sea swim, Cox swam a mile in thirty-eight-degree water in Southeast Alaska's Glacier Bay. It took her thirty minutes. With expected currents, the two-and-a-half-mile Diomede swim was expected to take about two and a half hours.

To monitor her internal temperature, doctors devised two options. The first was a "thermopill," a $1,000 large metal capsule containing a radio transmitter. Cox would have to choke down the horse-size pill before entering the water. To get a body temperature reading, she would have to roll over on her back while doctors extended a receiver on a broomstick near her stomach to receive a transmission.

The backup was a thin rectal probe, positioned in place with a liberal slab of K-Y Jelly and attached to a twenty-foot lead curled up outside her bathing suit. Her doctors and support crew agreed she would be pulled from the sea if her internal body temperature dropped to ninety-four degrees.

Another significant challenge for Cox's swim was support boats. Her team had contacted the US Coast Guard and local Natives seeking boats to accompany her. Just days before she hoped to hit the water, the Coast Guard gave a thumbs-down to Senator Murkowski's office with an inventive bureaucratic response: if the swim was too dangerous, the Coast Guard wouldn't allow it; if the swim wasn't dangerous, help wasn't needed. Little Diomede Natives had earlier quoted Cox the wildly inflated price of $5,000 for the use of two *umiat*, walrus-skin boats, to carry her doctors, support crew, and journalists.

In the days leading up to her proposed swim date, Little Diomede residents witnessed Soviets on Big Diomede moving in equipment and soldiers and deploying ships around the island. Still, despite frantic calls to the Soviet ambassador, no official permission had been received.

As would occur with many other citizen-diplomat initiatives during the Ice Curtain era, communications across the strait failed to keep pace with events. It turned out that Moscow had approved Cox's swim several days earlier, but word never reached the Alaskans. On Big Diomede, Soviets scanned the horizon for two days wondering when the American swimmer would splash ashore. Finally, Bob Walsh relayed Moscow's approval to Cox's gratefully teary team in Nome.

ON THE FOGGY morning of August 7, 1987, Cox lowered herself into the forty-two-degree Bering Sea just off the southern tip of Little Diomede Island. "Oh my God. It's like liquid ice," she recalled. "The frigid water punched the air out of my lungs. I popped up, gasping."

Cox forced her face into the water and swam hard. The Little Diomede boat crews had finally relented on their pricey demands and seven *umiat* formed a flotilla around Cox. As she churned ahead to stay warm, her doctors kept demanding she roll on her back to take temperature readings. Backstroking produced less warmth so as she reluctantly complied, the cold sea sucking heat from the increasingly irritated swimmer.

Through fog and heavy drizzle, Cox stroked ahead. Suddenly her crew and the journalists let out a loud cheer. They had spotted a Soviet ship; Cox crossed the date line into tomorrow. As Big Diomede's hills grew larger on the horizon, she fought stronger currents pushing her north as the water temperature dropped to thirty-eight degrees—just six degrees warmer than an ice cube. Cox's stroke rate slowed from seventy strokes a minute to fifty-six, concerning her doctors.

The Soviets had flown a welcoming delegation of dignitaries and national media to Big Diomede, including a doctor dispatched by Soviet first lady Raisa Gorbachev. KNOM radio reporter Claire Richardson recalls the Soviets prepared for Cox's arrival with cloth-covered tables on the beach and a white-jacketed waiter serving tea and cookies.

However, the Soviet welcoming party was on a snowy beach several hundred yards down shore from the landing area Cox was targeting. Cox heard a Soviet official yell at her to swim to them instead of swimming directly ahead on the shortest route to shore. With the current cutting her speed in half, she finally struggled to a rocky point covered with snow and ice. Too numb to climb ashore on her own, Cox was fished out of the sea by three Soviet soldiers.

"I can still feel the heat from their hands on my skin," she said. "To go from this abstract concept that we have a Cold War between the US and Soviet Union, and it's gone on for years, and one side might make a terrible mistake. Suddenly it comes down to humans on a beach and we have a picnic with a samovar and cookies and sing songs together."

Lynne Cox's defiance of the Bering Strait's brutal elements and its four-decade divide of the world's superpowers changed her life and altered history. In the immediate hours after the swim, the Alaska Native *umiak* captains—Pat Omiak, David Soolook, and Pete Ahkaulu—met for the first time in forty years with Siberian Natives flown in from Chukotka's Lavrentia region.

In the months after the swim, Cox was hailed as an international celebrity and goodwill ambassador. In Moscow's Red Square, Soviet citizens swarmed her. In the Vatican, she traded stories with Pope John Paul about swimming in Poland's cold lakes. In the Oval Office, President Reagan offered his congratulations.

In early December 1987, Reagan invited Gorbachev to Washington, DC, to sign a treaty—eight years in the making—eliminating nearly 2,700 American and

Soviet short- and medium-range conventional and nuclear missiles. At the White House dinner celebrating the historic disarmament achievement, Gorbachev stood to offer a toast.

"Last summer it took one brave American by the name of Lynne Cox just two hours to swim from one of our countries to the other," the Soviet leader said. "We saw on television how sincere and friendly the meeting was between our people and the Americans when she stepped onto the Soviet shore. She proved by her courage how close to each other our peoples live."

Within minutes of landing in Provideniya on the June 1988 Friendship Flight, Darlene Orr of Alaska met distant Soviet relatives. Here she visits with the Mumigtekaq family from the Siberian Yupik village of Sireniki. COURTESY OF DARLENE ORR

5

Historic Flight Approved

Now, with a suddenness that has created white-hot excitement on Nome's frozen, 20-degrees-below-zero streets, proposals for local flights across the border have been placed on the agenda for the Reagan-Gorbachev summit this week.
—WASHINGTON POST, DECEMBER 7, 1987

O N JUNE 8, 1988, the private phone interrupted the early-morning quiet in the governor's mansion in Juneau. The Soviet embassy in Washington, DC, was calling with a message for Gov. Steve Cowper. "Flight approved!"

The eagerly awaited Soviet approval of "Alaska Friendship One," the proposed Alaska Airlines' flight across the Bering Strait between Nome and Provid: eniya, had been years in the making. The effort by citizen-diplomats to reunite long-separated Native families across the strait picked up steam with high-profile events such as Dixie Belcher's 1986 musical tour across the Soviet Union and Lynne Cox's daring 1987 swim between the Diomede Islands. Now, a commercial airline flight became the first reunification effort with serious business interests behind it.

The timing was perfect for developers looking beyond Alaska's shores. As oil prices dropped in the mid-1980s, Alaska's oil-based economy hit the rocks. Cowper took the oath of office in December 1986 facing a nearly $900 million budget deficit. Between 1985 and 1987, Alaska's economy lost twenty-one thousand jobs, with another seven thousand about to go, according to the University of Alaska Anchorage's Institute of Economic and Social Research (ISER).

"We'll know the Alaska recession is over when we can open a newspaper and see no mention of layoffs or banks on the brink of failure; when we go to a store we haven't been to in six months and find it still in business; when we can drive around and see no notices for garage sales that say: Everything Must Go—Leaving State," wrote economist Scott Goldsmith.

To balance the state's books, the new governor offered up a host of politically radioactive proposals: resurrecting a state income tax, reducing payments to senior citizens, eliminating programs, cutting oil-industry tax breaks, and tapping the sacrosanct Permanent Fund savings account. Cowper also called for diversifying the economy to lessen its dependence on oil by looking abroad for new economic opportunities.

The prospect of making money by developing Soviet resources and selling consumer products to long-deprived Soviet citizens appealed to many Alaskans. After Jim Stimpfle spearheaded a special Nome Chamber of Commerce committee seeking to reunite Natives across the strait, the politically conservative Alaska State Chamber of Commerce smelled opportunity. George Krusz, who ran the chamber for a decade starting in 1981, said Alaska's resource industries—mining, oil and gas, timber, fisheries—were keenly interested in the prospect of developing Soviet resources. The more lax Soviet environmental constraints were icing on the cake.

Over a fall weekend in 1987, a handful of Alaskans gathered in Nome to plot strategy. They included Gunnar Knapp, a Russian-speaking economist from the University of Alaska; Ginna Brelsford from the governor's Office of International Trade; Nome Mayor John Handeland; and Jim Stimpfle. Shane Johnson represented the state chamber and Neil Colby represented the Nome chamber.

Another participant was Mead Treadwell, a friend of Knapp's from their days at Yale. Hailing from a patrician Connecticut family, Treadwell came to Alaska in 1974 as a campaign intern for former Gov. Walter Hickel, who had just returned to the state after being fired by President Richard Nixon as secretary of the interior. After attending Yale and the Harvard business school, Treadwell returned to Alaska to hitch his wagon to Hickel and dabble in Russia. The two made several trips to the Soviet Union, including a 1981 visit to Khabarovsk and Yakutsk in the Far East.

The weekend in Nome produced a framework, called the Siberian Gateway Project, designed to help open the Alaska-Soviet border. The fourteen-page document detailed plans to apply international pressure on the US and Soviet governments to reopen the Bering Strait with a new transportation link. The focus would be on "tourism, technological exchange, general trade, educational-sports and human rights."

The number-one reason for the state chamber's involvement: "This project would help all chamber members gain experience in establishing new international trade markets." The group envisioned a national committee of prominent citizens, ranging from the widow of pioneering aviator Charles Lindbergh to rock and roller Bruce Springsteen.

"The immediate goal of the Siberian Gateway Project is the inclusion of the Nome-Provideniya transportation links on the agenda for the Reagan-Gorbachev summit in June (1988) in Moscow," Knapp wrote in a report. The group also proposed an ambitious schedule of media events in Alaska, Washington, DC, and Moscow, slick promotional materials, and a flashy logo. Most of the ideas never materialized. But in Washington, Senator Murkowski advanced the chamber's message with a drumbeat of letters to the Reagan administration pressing for reopening of the Alaska-Soviet border.

"This issue—America's closest and most overlooked border with the Soviet Union—should be added to the list of U.S.-Soviet bilateral issues and discussed at any summit meeting between President Reagan and General Secretary Gorbachev," Murkowski wrote to Secretary of State George Shultz in October 1987.

A WEEK LATER, the senator jumped on a line in a speech Gorbachev had delivered in the western arctic city of Murmansk. The Soviet leader proposed a "conference of sub-Arctic states on the coordination of scientific research in the Arctic." Firing off another letter to Shultz, Murkowski urged the Reagan administration to seize Gorbachev's idea. Two years earlier, Congress had passed Murkowski's bill creating a United States Arctic Research Commission to coordinate American arctic policy. The senator told Shultz the commission "could serve as the focus of our effort."

In early December 1987, Murkowski issued a press release taking credit for the inclusion of Alaska-Soviet border issues on the agenda of the upcoming Moscow summit between Reagan and Gorbachev, set for the following May. At the request of the Nome Chamber of Commerce, Murkowski said, the two world leaders planned to discuss tourism flights between Nome and Provideniya.

"It's certainly keeping with the spirit of the season that we move forward to improve relations between our nations," Murkowski said. "Agreements on nuclear arms control, human-rights issues and on proposals like our Alaska-Siberia Gateway will go a long way toward promoting the security of peace for all mankind."

Meanwhile in Seattle, Alaska Airlines' charismatic chairman and CEO, Bruce Kennedy, also saw an opportunity. After attending high school in Palmer, Alaska, Kennedy earned his business degree from the University of Alaska Fairbanks and spent two years in the Army at nearby Fort Wainwright. In 1979, at age thirty-nine, he became Alaska Airlines' top executive. Kennedy believed regular service across the strait could work as a commercially successful expansion of his company's air routes, and he felt a moral obligation to reconnect Alaska and the Russian Far East to help reunite Native families.

At a 1987 San Diego planning meeting for Horizon, Alaska's sister carrier, Kennedy gathered company brass and pitched the idea of Russian service. It met a lukewarm response, with most executives dismissing such routes as more trouble than they would be worth. At about the same time, nearly three thousand miles to the north, Alaska Airlines hosted a community advisory meeting in Nome to hear from local leaders about the company's performance. Jim Stimpfle invited himself to the meeting to pitch flying to the Soviet Far East.

After the meeting, Stimpfle thought he had bombed. So he wandered across the street to the *Nome Nugget*, where *Wall Street Journal* reporter Ken Wells was looking for intriguing stories. Stimpfle regaled Wells with his grand scheme.

A couple of weeks later, on September 28, 1987, Wells produced a front-page story headlined "Gateway to Siberia? Nome, Alaska Feels It Has a Certain Ring." The story began: "NOME, Alaska—Imagine: A commercial jet thunders off a runway here and, as quick as a Wall Streeter can get to Grand Central Station, the passengers are in Provideniya, Siberia."

Stimpfle got a call from Jim Johnson, Alaska Airlines' public-relations chief, about the unwelcome publicity. But unknown to Stimpfle, Bruce Kennedy had prevailed with his company, securing a thumbs-up to pursue commercial air service to the Soviet Union.

To secure federal approval, Alaska Airlines immediately dispatched its Washington lawyers to connect with the US State Department, the Soviet embassy, and the state's congressional delegation. The airline also contacted New York officials of the Soviet airline Aeroflot about a possible maiden flight to Provideniya, to which an Aeroflot official responded: "Where the hell is Provideniya and why would anybody want to go there?"

THE GREEN-LIGHT CALL to Cowper for the Friendship Flight set off a frantic scramble from Juneau to Washington, DC, Provideniya to Moscow. It generated perplexing questions to which no one had immediate answers. Could an Alaska Airlines jet land in a remote Soviet outpost not visited by any US aviation official in at least forty years and take off again? Was the runway paved and long enough to accommodate a fully loaded 737? Were radio communications available and, if so, in what language? Who would get to pick the occupants for the limited seats destined to fly into history?

American aviation officials had no satellite images of the Provideniya airport. The few Soviet-produced maps in the hands of Americans were intentionally inaccurate to mask military facilities. So Alaska executives decided they needed to check out Provideniya in person before their jet tried to set down there.

On May 31, 1988, six Alaska Airlines officials chartered a twin-engine Piper from Nome's Bering Air for the one-hour hop to Provideniya. On board were Bruce Kennedy, Jim Johnson, flight-control vice president Bill Boser, and University of Washington consultant and interpreter Elisa Miller. The two Alaska pilots scheduled to fly the Friendship Flight, Steve Day and Terry Smith, occupied observer seats behind Bering Air pilot and company owner Jim Rowe.

Moscow aviation authorities reportedly had approved the Provideniya recon flight, but the paperwork got lost somewhere in the Soviet or American bureaucracies.

"We were in Nome about ready to depart when the FAA called and said if I wandered into Russian air space, I would be violating the law," Rowe said. "And then the insurance company called and said neither the airplane nor anyone on it would be covered."

Rowe summoned all the passengers into Bering Air's employee lounge, delivered the bad news, and asked Kennedy what he wanted to do. Everyone pondered their dilemma for a few minutes, exchanged glances, and gave a thumbs-up for departure. Rowe had been flying around the region for years, and landing in the Soviet Union was a long-held dream.

"I thought the likelihood of getting shot down was small," he said. "I had a wife and two kids at home and I had every intention of coming back alive."

Entering Soviet airspace under crystal-blue skies that May day, Rowe was unable to communicate with Provideniya's control tower. After circling the airport to give the Soviets a good look at his plane, he brought it to a bumpy stop on the gravel runway. The Americans—except Rowe—were welcomed by uniformed Soviet soldiers and Provideniya Mayor Kulinkin, who had been corresponding with the Alaskans for months over ways to reunite families and establish joint business ties.

Rowe was immediately summoned to the control tower to explain why he had failed to file a flight plan and landed without permission. "In typical Russian fashion, they all started waving their arms around and screaming at each other," Rowe said. "It finally got translated that they had sent all that information to Moscow but we never got it."

Mayor Kulinkin shepherded the delegation along the rutted ten-mile road into downtown Provideniya and treated them to a meat-laden Russian breakfast and city tour. A slight but muscular Georgian by birth, Kulinkin looked fresh off the set of a *Godfather* movie, given to slicked-back hair and black leather.

"Kulinkin was a lean-forward kind of guy with an electric personality," Stimpfle said. "He had so much lean-forward that a lot of shit happened."

The Alaska executives quickly determined the Soviet outpost to be inadequate for Alaska Airlines tourism packages, beset with what they diplomatically called "limited accommodations." They also decided that the town's six-thousand-foot compact gravel runway could handle a 737, but not fully loaded. Instead of the more than one hundred passengers they had envisioned for the Friendship Flight, the list had to be cut to eighty-two.

In the governor's office, planning for the flight fell to the Office of International Trade and to me. The trade shop was headed by Bob Poe, an impeccably coifed accountant more comfortable sipping fine sake with protocol-conscious Japanese than swilling cheap vodka with burly Russians. The bulk of logistics were assigned to Ginna Brelsford, an adventure athlete with a master's degree from the Fletcher School of Law and Diplomacy at Tufts University. The following spring, Brelsford caught the Russia bug so severely that she left her job to join a one-thousand-mile Soviet-Alaska ski and dogsled expedition across the Bering Strait.

Poe and Brelsford scrambled to Nome to negotiate seating. There they met up with Stimpfle, who already had helped area Native elders get US passports in anticipation of such a trip to the Soviet Union.

The opportunity to make history in a little-noticed corner of the world was the hottest ticket in Alaska. When a state legislator demanded a seat on the flight, Poe asked him, "Which Eskimo should I kick off to put you on?" The lawmaker backed off.

The passenger manifest was broken into categories: state, congressional, and federal officials; Natives and Nome city leaders; Alaska Airlines officials and their guests; and media. Protocol dictated that Cowper, the highest-ranking Alaska official, would lead the delegation.

Cowper's high-profile role exacerbated the political rivalry between the Democrat and members of Alaska's long-serving, all-Republican congressional delegation. Just two years earlier, all three federal lawmakers had endorsed Cowper's Republican rival for governor, Arliss Sturgulewski. After his election, Cowper and the state's senior politician, the hotheaded Senator Stevens, got into a shouting match at a congressional hearing over oil development in Alaska's Arctic National Wildlife Refuge.

The day before the flight, the Alaska Ear gossip column in the state's largest newspaper, the *Anchorage Daily News*, contained this blurb: "Did Sen. Frank Murkowski really come apart at the seams when he learned the Soviet embassy had notified Gov. Cowper instead of him that the Provideniya flight had been approved? Ear hears Frank worked behind the scenes on the deal and was incensed that his staff had to call the Democratic governor's office to get basic details. To add insult to injury, Cowper was named delegation leader."

Alaska's first lady was to accompany her husband on the flight. The Paris-born daughter of a wealthy Santa Barbara orchid grower, Michael Cowper was a stylish California lawyer who had married Cowper only a year before he plunged into his second campaign for governor.

Pregnant in the heat of the campaign, she delivered her son, Wade, just three days after Cowper's primary election victory. As the candidate's press secretary, I pushed the new parents to promote their family addition for all it was worth going into the general election. Michael was an easy sell. Still in her hospital bed, she dabbed on makeup, brushed her hair, and posed for the television cameras with her hours-old son and exhausted husband. The media ate it up.

From the congressional delegation, only Senator Murkowski signed up for the flight, along with his wife, Nancy. Murkowski was a member of the Senate Foreign Relations Committee, had visited Moscow a few months earlier, and was persistent in urging Reagan administration officials to open the "back door" to US-Soviet relations.

Cowper invited former Governor Hickel, a Republican, who had a long interest in Soviet affairs. As President Nixon's interior secretary, he established relationships with top Soviet leaders. After Hickel returned to Alaska, he was politically helpful to Cowper.

The Nome and Native delegations were given most of the seats. Stimpfle was the titular head of the delegation as chairman of the Nome chamber's Committee for Cooperation, Commerce, and Peace. Nearly thirty Alaska Natives from St. Lawrence Island, King Island, and Little Diomede Island were invited because of family ties or to perform in the celebrations in Provideniya.

About one-fourth of the seats were filled with a mix of national and Alaska journalists, who all wanted to transmit their stories within a few hours of the historic landing. That presented a major challenge for Alaska Airlines executives, who also wanted to get timely news coverage of the Friendship Flight to Alaska and across the world.

Making an international telephone call from the Soviet Union in the mid-1980s was convoluted and frustrating. The standard practice required dialing a Russian operator to place the call and then waiting around the phone, hoping for success. Sometimes the operator called back in a few hours. Sometimes it was days later; sometimes you never heard back. No one was willing to rely on Soviet technology to report some of the biggest international news in years involving Alaska.

A few months earlier, two executives of Alaska's top telecommunications company, Alascom, Inc., visited the Soviet Union as part of a US Information Agency program. Vice president for operations Lee Wareham and special projects administrator Harry Galekovich traveled from Moscow to Odessa to investigate ways to create a better international global communications network involving nations that sometimes did not cooperate with each other, including the United States and Soviet Union. Wareham pitched the idea of a telecom link between Alaska and the Soviet Far East to the vice chairman of the Soviet State Committee for TV and Radio.

Alascom had provided satellite links for Gennadi Gerasimov's visit to Little Diomede a few months earlier, which attracted international news coverage for the media-conscious Soviet official. With the Friendship Flight looming, Alascom managed in just one week to get a Soviet permit to uplink audio and video. The company scrambled to transport a ten-person crew to Provideniya to assemble and operate the equipment and document the event.

The plan called for putting together a twenty-five-foot-diameter earth station antenna to link to Alascom's satellite. The trailer-mounted antenna would be towed by a mobile electronics van. An eight-kilowatt diesel generator would power the operation.

The day before the Friendship Flight was to depart Nome, two planes loaded with Alascom's gear and crew left Anchorage for Nome and on to Provideniya. Alascom's Beechcraft King Air carried the passengers, and a civilian version of a Lockheed C-130 Hercules cargo plane hauled the equipment.

The King Air flight was a nail-biter, dropping through thick clouds just in time to spot the Soviet block-style apartment buildings that surround Provideniya. Moscow had provided a fifteen-minute window to fly through Soviet air space. But for the second time in two weeks, the flight crew could not raise the Provideniya control tower.

The weather was so bad that a delegation of English-speaking Soviet aviation officials trying to get to Provideniya had been stranded in Anadyr, an hour down the coast. Minutes from touchdown, when Alascom pilots finally connected with a Provideniya air-traffic controller, the Russian couldn't provide precise approach coordinates with his poor English. Both planes relied on their own instruments to land, once again irritating the Soviets.

On the ground, the crew spent nine hours assembling and orienting the dish to the Aurora satellite orbiting twenty-three thousand miles above the equator. Just fifteen hours before the Friendship Flight was scheduled to touch down, Alascom had in place video links to Alaska and the East Coast, including the Soviet embassy, and had installed a bank of direct-dial telephones for the media.

IN NOME, THE festive mood had been dampened a few days before by the disappearance of six walrus hunters and a teacher from the St. Lawrence Island villages of Savoonga and Gambell. After becoming separated from a hunting party in thick fog, they lashed their two boats together and drifted in heavy seas, occasionally pulling up on floating ice. Their disappearance prompted a massive search by Alaska air and Army guard units.

At Cowper's request, the Soviet maritime rescue service joined in and granted permission for Twin Otters from the Alaska Army National Guard to fly along the Soviet coast to search. These were the first US military planes to enter Soviet Far East air space—with Soviet permission—since World War II.

Cowper and I had arrived in Nome a few days before the flight to Provideniya. So we joined the search, flying coordinates for hours with the guard, peering out the tiny porthole windows over the white-capped Bering Sea. All the hunters were eventually rescued.

As the hour of departure neared, local residents and lucky ticket holders scurried to prepare for the historic flight. Alaska Airlines selected one of two 737-200 "combi" aircraft in its fleet equipped with "gravel kits" used in remote Alaska villages for the anticipated rough landing on Provideniya's unpaved strip. Painted in Cyrillic below the pilot's window were the words "City of Provideniya."

Nome recruited flag-bearing national guardsmen and local veterans to comprise an honor guard standing at attention along the tarmac leading to the plane. Jim Stimpfle was so thrilled that he was about to realize his two-year dream, he did a jig along the walkway. Most of the Alaska Native women wore colorful *kuspuks* and exquisitely sewn fur parkas. Many of their husbands opted for short-sleeved flowered Hawaiian shirts.

Each passenger received a souvenir folder adorned with a cover that featured smiling Native peoples, Vitus Bering, and an Alaska Airlines jet flying into history designed by Alaska artist Jon Van Zyle. It included messages from Cowper plus a Provideniya itinerary, a time line describing events leading up to the flight, and a concise history of the Soviet Native population from UAF Native language expert professor Michael Krauss.

As the crew managed to get the excited passengers buckled in for the scheduled 10:15 a.m. departure, Capt. Steve Day announced the two words every traveling Alaskan heard too often: "mechanical problem."

Author David Ramseur poses with a can of Spam before Provideniya's House of Culture during the Friendship Flight in June 1988 with Alaska UPI correspondent Jeff Berliner. RAMSEUR PERSONAL COLLECTION

6

Friendship Flight to Tomorrow

Now glasnost has come upon the land . . .
—*NATIONAL GEOGRAPHIC*, OCTOBER 1988

A s smokestacks bellowing black smoke from Provideniya's coal-fired power plant came into view below, Darlene Pungowiyi Orr felt uneasy. So did I. We were among eighty-two passengers on the first Alaska Airlines jet ever to land in this isolated Soviet outpost forty years after FBI director J. Edgar Hoover had closed the Bering Strait.

After a short mechanical delay that morning of June 13, 1988, Friendship Flight no. 1 departed Nome for the forty-five-minute flight into tomorrow. As soon as the plane reached the proper altitude, passengers jammed the aisle with excited chatter. Some traded autographs to mark the historic occasion. Politicians fine-tuned remarks they would deliver to the assembled Soviets. Reporters poured over inaccurate maps of the Chukotka Peninsula, struggling to understand the local geography.

Orr, a twenty-six-year-old Siberian Yupik, grew up in Alaska in the shadow of what Ronald Reagan just five years earlier had branded the "Evil Empire." From her St. Lawrence Island village, she could make out the Soviet mainland on the western horizon.

"I have drawings from when I was young of the mountains on the Russian side with snow on the hillsides, and you could see the sun on the hills over there," said Orr, whose great-grandfather was born in the pre-Soviet village of Old Chaplino on Russia's far eastern coast. "It was unattainable, yet you could see it."

Walking her village shoreline as a young girl, she would occasionally find strange little books in sealed plastic bags on the gravelly beach. They were Bibles translated into Cyrillic, dropped by American missionaries praying they would splash up onto Soviet beaches just thirty-six miles away. If the finder was lucky, the package might include a stick of gum.

"On the short-wave radio, we would occasionally hear Russian," Orr said. "For me growing up, that was the language of spies. I always envisioned frogmen coming out of the water."

Intrigued by the mystery of that radio chatter, Orr checked out a Russian language book from her Nome junior-high library, determined to teach herself the adopted tongue of her great-grandfather. In high school, she worked out a deal with her guidance counselor: she would teach him Siberian Yupik if he would give her Russian-language lessons. She later perfected her Russian at Dartmouth College and Russia's Yakutsk State University.

On that day, Orr prepared to set foot on Soviet soil for the first time. She came with two treasures: pictures of her family, hoping a distant Soviet relative might recognize someone, and three-cornered needles for sewing animal skins, a cherished gift for Soviet Native women.

For me, the Soviet Union still evoked the fear and intrigue of my childhood. Some of my earliest memories were of my Marine Corps father reporting to duty at various military bases in California, Nevada, and New Mexico in his starched olive-green uniform. I somehow connected his military assignments as keeping us safe from that obnoxious Nikita Khrushchev, who gave America the what-for on the *Huntley-Brinkley Report* my parents tuned in to on our black-and-white television.

I was jarred from those Cold War recollections when the plane bumped along Provideniya's gravel runway to wild applause. The curious Alaskans grinned through the airplane windows at the hundreds of children waving American flags who turned out to meet us. A freshly painted English sign adorned the crumbling airport terminal:

PEACE AND FRIENDSHIP
BETWEEN ALASKA AND CHUKOTKA!

Before a scrum of Soviet journalists, airport workers pushed a rickety set of stairs to the jet as we queued up inside. Governor Cowper and the first lady bounded off the plane and were greeted by young women clad in brightly colored Russian national costumes. They offered a ritual we came to look forward to in future visits to the Soviet Union, presenting a loaf of latticed bread and a small bowl of rock salt. This Russian tradition calls for distinguished visitors to break off a piece of bread—a symbol of wealth—and dip it in salt, protecting the consumer from evil. Cowper gladly poked the morsel in below his moustache and delivered the obligatory broad grin for the television cameras.

Soviet customs officials had planned a streamlined examination of the Americans' passports. But Michael Cowper had forgotten hers, offering the only ID she brought, an Alaska driver's license. The breach caused a stir among the uniformed Soviets but was finally waved off in the spirit of the day.

After a bumpy bus ride into town, another throng of sign-waving residents greeted the Americans in the central square beneath the ever-present statue of Vladimir Lenin. Scores of Russian Natives from nearby villages had been brought in to greet our Native delegation in what many hoped would be a common language. The day's media coverage focused on tearful reunions and documented several examples of long-lost connections reestablished.

Alaska Native Ora Gologergen, then seventy-two, found retired Soviet seamstress Uugsima Ukhsima, seventy-three. Ukhsima's chin and forehead were adorned with vertical tattooed lines common to Yupik women of that era, until Christian missionaries discouraged the practice on the Alaska side. Six decades earlier, the two women were playmates in the Alaska village of Gambell. After Ukhsima's family returned to the Soviet Union in the 1920s, they would not speak again until their Friendship Flight reunion.

Ora's brother-in-law, Tim Gologergen, carried to Provideniya a picture taken in 1947. It showed a Soviet official, identified as Tataaq, who had visited Gambell looking for two Russians who had defected. Gologergen was informed that Tataaq had died, but he found others whom he hadn't seen since last visiting Russia in 1942.

Gambell's Willis Walunga connected with a distant family member in Provideniya. "I met one relative and was able to talk to him in the Yupik language," the ninety-one-year-old Walunga recalled in 2015. "I was glad to talk to him—it had been forty years."

King Island hunter and carver Francis Alvanna remembered that when he was six, his father and uncle paddled across the strait in a skin boat, but he was too young to go along.

"When the plane landed we saw border guards, soldiers," Alvanna recalled of the Friendship Flight twenty-five years later. "It made me a little nervous at first, but when we walked to the meeting hall there were soldiers by the road and everyone was friendly. We spent many hours talking in Eskimo and Russian."

Most Americans had never met a Soviet, and vice versa. They all greeted each other as warm friends, exchanging packs of gum, chocolate bars, Frisbees, baseball cards, and baseball hats bearing Alascom and Alaska Airlines logos. Alaska's first lady dispensed Girl Scout cookies. An Anchorage television reporter brought rolls of toilet paper but was too embarrassed to hand them out.

The Soviets eagerly presented Lenin pins to the visitors. Bruce Kennedy of Alaska Airlines was pictured in *National Geographic* magazine, his sports coat lapels heavy with Russian pins, having become "an honorary member of every trade union and school in Siberia."

Provideniya was first established in the 1930s to supply coal to ships plying the Northern Sea Route. Much of the city looked as if it hadn't seen a fresh coat of paint since. But city leaders proudly showed off their community, welcoming visitors into freshly stocked Soviet stores.

Wall Street Journal reporter Carrie Dolan visited a workers' health resort, where, she wrote, "locals can take a dip in a coal-heated saltwater pool or take an 'electro-static shower.' The latter requires you to sit under an umbrella-like device that emits electricity and makes you feel as though you have bugs crawling in your hair."

After a long series of welcoming speeches and toasts over a banquet of cold cuts, French fries, black and red caviar on puff pastries, and locally brewed beer and vodka, the Americans were ushered to the *Dom Cultura*—House of Culture.

"Only Senator Frank Murkowski seemed able to out-talk and out-proclamation the Soviets," wrote *Anchorage Daily News* reporter David Postman. "Governor Cowper had the best line of the day when he talked about the purchase of Alaska from the czar: 'In Alaska, we understand that is why he was overthrown.' That got a big round of applause. Even bigger than when he presented a proclamation but said he wouldn't read it because it was too long."

The three-hour succession of speeches and Eskimo dancing concluded with a presentation of gifts. Cowper was given a walrus ivory tusk, more intricately carved by local Native craftsmen than most of the Alaskans had ever seen. The Americans handed over a copy machine, with a modest supply of paper and toner to keep it operating for a while. Stimpfle had complained of the enormous paperwork required to pull off the first visit to the Soviet Far East and thought a copier would help with future exchanges.

Both the Alaskans and Soviets were wowed by Alascom's technology that allowed instant telephone contact with the United States. During a break in the festivities, Governor Hickel wandered over to the company's mobile truck to place a direct-dial call to his wife, Ermalee, back in Anchorage.

"Mother? I'm in Provideniya," said a giggling Hickel. "Isn't that great?"

As the daylong visit neared an end, the Alaskans and Soviets gathered outside the House of Culture for a final round of speeches. After the politicians had their turns, one of the Soviet officials turned to a slight, elderly Yupik woman with a tattooed chin, a matriarch of the region.

"Naturally she spoke in Russian," recalled linguist Michael Krauss. "It never occurred to her to speak in her native language because Native people over there are so used to being the underdog." Krauss pushed his way through the crowd and whispered to her to switch to Siberian Yupik.

"She looked at me, confused and bewildered; she dared not speak Yupik in public," Krauss said. "But then her face and her whole being transformed into the most glorious state. And she launched into a completely different speech in Yupik. Suddenly this was the international language—Yupik. That was the only language that could be understood on both sides. A silence fell over the whole assembled throng. There was a transformed atmosphere."

For Darlene Orr, who spoke both Russian and Siberian Yupik, the day in Provideniya changed her life. After descending the stairs from the Alaska jet, she stood on ground that had mystified her for a quarter century from just over the eastern horizon.

"We would hear Russian on the short-wave radio and I would get goose bumps because you never heard good things about the Russians and we didn't quite understand the Cold War," Orr recalled nearly thirty years after the momentous day in Provideniya. "All we knew was that the border was closed and people could no longer go back and forth freely."

After landing that morning in 1988, Orr joined the other Alaska Natives slowly pushing their way through the hundreds of flag-waving Soviet children into Provideniya's tiny airport terminal. There, the first person she met introduced himself by his clan name—Qiwaghmii—the same clan of her St. Lawrence Island family.

"That was the most profound thing about the Friendship Flight," she said. "The very first person I met in all that chaos at the airport was this guy, the very same clan as me. To have that moment in time where I was actually there and actually connect with somebody from my own culture, is indescribable. I get emotional just thinking about it now."

Orr returned to the region thirteen times, researching the Siberian Yupik language and native plants. On one trip, she ignored Soviet warnings about visiting restricted areas, dressed herself as an average Russian, and took a long bus ride to the coast, where she spent the day harvesting seaweed and mushrooms. "It was worth any risk to me to visit the shoreline where my ancestors had walked," she said.

My own favorite piece of memorabilia from that day in Provideniya is a picture. It shows me holding a can of Spam in front of the House of Culture. For a couple of decades in Anchorage, a local musician dubbed Mr. Whitekeys operated a nightclub comedy show making fun of Alaska's quirkiness. Whitekeys' Fly by Night Club specialized in Spam appetizers and he encouraged the submission of photos of Spam in unusual places around the world. For years, my Provideniya picture was featured in the show.

In the photo, only two people are smiling: Lenin, from a billboard above the entrance, and me. Jeff Berliner, then a United Press International (UPI) reporter who brought the Spam, hid behind dark shades and his Rasputin-like beard. A uniformed Soviet policeman and a KGB official in black turtleneck and black leather jacket stood beside us, expressionless.

My visit was a dream fulfilled. As had many Americans on the Friendship Flight, I spent my childhood worried about a Soviet nuclear attack and took refuge under my desk in elementary school. The Friendship Flight demonstrated how much alike we all were despite divisions created by generations of Cold War propaganda. After that day, I couldn't get Russia out of my blood and made pilgrimages there a dozen more times, leaving my family for months to live and work in that frustrating but fascinating place.

To citizens of Provideniya, we Americans must have seemed equally mysterious. Provideniya is farther from Moscow—nearly four thousand miles across eleven time zones—than Alaska is from Washington, DC. The only previous contact the average Provideniya citizen had with Americans was the faint broadcast of a Nome radio station. We were welcomed with boundless generosity and formed lifelong friendships.

Leaders on both sides of the Bering Strait created high expectations that day in June: the promise of unbridled travel across a forbidden zone, regular contact between once-distant relatives, the promise of prosperity from new commerce and friendship. The Friendship Flight helped melt the four-decade-old Ice Curtain and offered citizen-diplomats an opportunity to realize those dreams.

State of Alaska international trade specialist Ginna Brelsford takes a break during Gov. Steve Cowper's 6,800-mile trade mission across the Soviet Far East in August 1989. PHOTO BY BRUCE MELZER

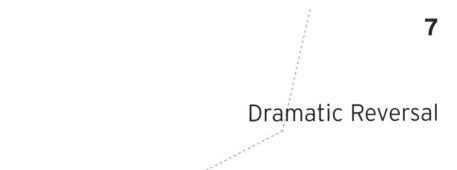

7

Dramatic Reversal

Business, cultural and educational exchanges between Alaska and the Soviet Far East and North continue to expand rapidly.

—ALASKA GOVERNOR STEVE COWPER
TO PRESIDENT GEORGE H. W. BUSH, NOVEMBER 27, 1989

AFTER THOSE TWELVE hours in the weathered outpost of Provideniya in June 1988, Alaskans and their Soviet neighbors couldn't get enough of each other. The Friendship Flight opened the floodgates to Cub Scouts, balloonists, rock and rollers, dog mushers, doctors, journalists, Chamber of Commerce boosters, World War II veterans, artists, scientists, educators, senior citizens, environmentalists, and even well-insulated members of the cold-water-swimming Soviet Walrus Club, all intent on face-to-face contact after forty years of Cold War separation.

This was a dramatic reversal of the paranoia that rippled through Alaska just five years earlier with the downing of Korean Air Flight 007. Despite initial outrage, that tragedy faded to regrettable history with the warm glow generated by the Friendship Flight. In the ten months after the Friendship Flight, Bering Air made one hundred flights between Nome and the Soviet Far East. To accommodate all the traffic across the strait, the US Immigration and Naturalization Service (INS) appointed its northernmost agent in Nome.

Attitudes at the highest levels of Alaska state government also shifted. As prospects for increased traffic grew in late 1987, the administration of Gov. Steve Cowper evolved from winging it to getting help from those who actually knew something about the Soviet Union. It turned to two Alaska experts in the Russian language and economy: Gunnar Knapp and Vic Fischer.

With a freshly minted doctorate in economics from Yale University, Knapp moved to Anchorage in 1981 to become an economics professor at the University of Alaska's think tank, the Institute of Social and Economic Research (ISER). As a Yale undergrad, Knapp spoke German, French, Swedish, and Latin and then learned Russian.

Knapp first visited the Soviet Union in 1977 as a member of the Yale Russian Chorus, when one of its concerts was aired on national television. In Anchorage, he connected with other Russian speakers to keep his language skills fresh and helped lead local teachers to Leningrad and Moscow.

Before most Alaskans had heard of the Soviet Far East, Knapp assembled ISER's first of numerous reports about the region for a 1987 academic conference. Largely a population study, it contrasted Alaska's development challenges with a Soviet region six times larger than Alaska with fifteen times more people. "Soviet massive use of forced labor for northern development projects under Stalin has no parallel in Alaska," Knapp noted.

At the governor's request, in April 1988 Knapp produced a more comprehensive report about Alaska–Soviet Far East trade prospects. This report served as the foundation for the administration's approach to the region, dubbed the Alaska–Soviet Far East Initiative. His coauthor was Elisa Miller, from the University of Washington's School of Business, who had worked as an Alaska Airlines consultant for the Friendship Flight.

Knapp said his charge was to bring order to the "grand ideas" of the citizen-diplomats. "I was the almost-sightless man in the valley of the blind because I knew something about the Soviet Union and Russian language," he said.

The report warned about the challenges of fostering commerce across the strait. "For the most part, the Soviet Far East is a competitor of Alaska's in international resource markets rather than a potential importer from Alaska," the report said. "It is more helpful to view the Soviet Far East as a region with many of the same problems as Alaska. There are many possible areas where economic cooperation and commerce can be mutually beneficial."

In the mid-1980s, the only Alaskan with deeper ties to Russian culture than Knapp was Vic Fischer. Born in Berlin, Fischer grew up in the Soviet Union as the son of parents intrigued by the communist experiment. Fischer's American father, Louis, wrote twenty-five books, including his influential autobiography, *Men and Politics,* which traced the causes of World War II and his years in the USSR. Fischer's Russian mother, Markoosha, wrote an autobiography that was a bestseller of 1944; in it, she recounted her hopes for and eventual disappointment with the Soviet Union. Fischer and his family left the USSR in 1939.

Armed with a master's degree in planning, Fischer fulfilled a lifelong dream when he moved to the Alaska territory in 1950. He joined the statehood movement and was elected one of fifty-five delegates to the Alaska Constitutional Convention, which drafted Alaska's constitution in 1955–1956, paving the way for statehood in 1959.

Fischer helped establish the university think tank that later hired Knapp, serving as its director in the late 1960s during the run-up to Alaska's oil boom. Fischer closely followed Soviet issues, even maintaining some friendships he had established there as a boy. As the Ice Curtain began to thaw, many Alaskans, including Knapp, relied on Fischer's knowledge of Soviet behavior and his Russian-language skills.

Fischer informally advised the state and university on issues related to the Friendship Flight. He had planned to go along as an interpreter. But his wife, Jane Angvik, landed a yearlong assignment representing Alaska at World Expo 88 in Brisbane, Australia. So Fischer and their daughter, Ruthie, had joined Angvik Down Under by the time the flight to Provideniya was finally approved.

Fischer returned to Alaska as the Ice Curtain was rapidly melting. He spent the next two decades leading the effort to better Alaska-Russia relations. Despite his liberal Democratic politics, Fischer capitalized on his nearly half-century relationship with Republican Sen. Ted Stevens to persuade one of the Senate's most prolific sponsors of budget earmarks—congressional directives to appropriate funds for specific projects—to funnel millions in federal dollars to the University of Alaska for Alaska-Russian activities.

Armed with Knapp's reports on the trade and cultural potential of Alaska-Soviet relations, the Cowper administration acted quickly to capitalize on those opportunities. In rapid succession, the governor dispatched two of his top aides to the Soviet Far East.

A month after the Friendship Flight, international-trade specialist Ginna Brelsford traveled nearly around the world through Moscow to Nakhodka, an industrial port city outside of Vladivostok, just across the border from North Korea. There she joined eighty-two trade officials from eleven countries for an international Conference on Security and Economic Cooperation in the Pacific Basin.

"The extraordinary political changes of Gorbachev's glasnost and perestroika have yet to filter through the sealed-off region of the Soviet Far East," Brelsford reported to the governor and other senior state officials in July 1988. "A measurable increase in border trade exists between China, Japan, and the Soviet Far East and with persistence, trade between Alaska and the Soviet Far East could also increase over the next year."

Building on the Alaska–Soviet Far East Initiative framework that the administration had roughed out with Knapp, Brelsford identified six areas for trade potential: tourism, construction, fisheries joint ventures, microeconomic projects such as marketing of reindeer products and Native crafts, telecommunications, and scientific and cultural exchanges.

She drew a road map for the private sector to capitalize on trade opportunities. This included proposed Alaska Airlines service to Vladivostok, Khabarovsk, and the Kamchatka Peninsula. She reported Kamchatka officials eager to establish sister-city relations with an Alaska community. Brelsford recommended that Alaska fisheries companies connect with the Russian fisheries conglomerate, Dalryba. And she urged Alaskans to seek new opportunities with a soon-to-be-created foreign-trade zone in Nakhodka.

While in the Soviet Far East, Brelsford also became one of the first recent Alaskans to visit Khabarovsk, the Far East's second-largest city across the Amur River from northeastern China. Her purpose there was prepping for Alaska's first Soviet trade mission. In fall 1987, Governor Cowper had traded letters of friendship with his counterpart in Khabarovsk, executive committee chairman Nikolai Daniluk. Cowper focused on Khabarovsk because of its key transportation links, a population larger than the more northern Far East cities, and the enthusiasm of its leaders.

About the size of California and the same latitude as Washington State, the region had a population of about 1.7 million. Khabarovsk is a major stop on the

Trans-Siberian Railway, with air links to Japan, Korea, and other parts of Russia. Having hosted the 1975 Washington State International Trade Fair Exhibition, Khabarovsk was already open to Western ties. And in contrast to the bleaker outposts in the north, the picturesque European-like city featured tree-lined avenues and better-than-average restaurants and hotels.

Cowper and Daniluk proposed establishing sister-province relations and exploring trade and cultural exchanges. To demonstrate his state's interests, Cowper was willing to personally lead Alaska's first Soviet trade mission to Khabarovsk. Shortly before the trip, however, Michael Cowper underwent a double mastectomy. Faced with the prospect of leaving the first lady recovering in the cavernous governor's mansion with their two-year-old son, Cowper decided not to make the trip.

The governor recruited a reluctant replacement to lead the mission—his chief of staff, Garrey Peska. An accountant, Peska had worked as a number-crunching legislative staffer in Juneau for fifteen years when Cowper picked him to head the state's Department of Administration, which runs the nuts and bolts of state government. Only six months into his term and consumed with Alaska's recession, brought on by low oil prices, Cowper recognized the need for more discipline and structure in his administration. He elevated Peska to become his right-hand man to crack a whip on the cabinet and calm a nervous state legislature.

Peska was dubious about the merits of engaging with the Soviets. "I couldn't understand why anybody was going over there with oil prices back home so low," he said. But like most Alaskans who interacted with the Russians, he was won over quickly.

With his receding hairline, scruffy goatee, and slight build, Peska bore a striking resemblance to the Soviet Union's founding father. Shortly after his arrival in Khabarovsk, the Soviets posed Peska beside a giant statue of Lenin's head and got a kick out of documenting the similarity with their Zenit cameras.

Five Alaska businessmen keenly interested in Soviet business opportunities joined the trip. They included Friendship Flight veterans Bruce Kennedy of Alaska Airlines and Lee Wareham of Alascom. Others were Ron Sheardown, president of Greatland Exploration, Ltd., a mining company; Sam Salkin, who ran the Alaska Commercial Company, the state's largest rural grocery-store chain; and Bill Phillips, an international lawyer and president of Alaska Joint Venture

Seafoods, who had close ties with Senator Stevens. Soviet specialist Elisa Miller went along to help coordinate arrangements, and Ginna Brelsford staffed it for the governor's office.

In addition to specific business proposals pitched by members of the delegation, Peska carried a stack of additional ideas offered by Alaska companies, ranging from oil-development services to reindeer-meat processing and sports exchanges.

IN THE MID-1980S, the Soviet Union had no "businessmen" in the Western sense; all economic resources and decisions were controlled by local, regional, or central government. The delegation spent most of its ten days in Khabarovsk meeting an assortment of government officials and those representing trade groups, such as the Association of Business Cooperation, freight shippers, and the seafood industry. They also traveled to Vladivostok, and a delegation of Magadan officials flew south to meet the Alaskans in Khabarovsk.

Despite goodwill demonstrated through countless vodka toasts, Peska was taken aback by the Soviets' ignorance of basic capitalism. For example, they seemed especially perplexed about how prices for products should be set in a country where the central government had dictated prices for seventy years.

The trip produced what was advertised as the first sister-state agreement between a US state and its Soviet counterpart, Alaska and the Khabarovsk Territory. Additional protocols were signed calling for various exchanges between Alaska and the Magadan region and the Primorskii Territory, which includes Vladivostok.

Among the more productive exchanges negotiated were between Soviet and Alaska universities and public schools, eventually resulting in hundreds of young people crossing the strait to experience each other's cultures. Both sides were effusive about the pioneering visit.

"The special significance of this agreement is that other states in the United States and in the Soviet Union can follow our example and establish ties with one another as well," said Khabarovsk chairman Daniluk. "We are so proud to have this happen in the name of both peoples."

Peska was so moved by his interaction with Soviets that he returned home and enrolled in Russian-language lessons. He transformed into a Soviet booster in the governor's office, made two additional trips to Russia, and eagerly welcomed future Soviet delegations to Alaska.

Soviet founder Vladimir Lenin looks out over the city of Magadan, which in the 1930s served as a transit point for political prisoners destined for the nearby gulags.
PHOTO BY PERRY EATON

8

Soviets Return the Favor

Let me hear your balalaikas ringing out,
Come and keep your comrade warm.
—"BACK IN THE U.S.S.R.," PAUL MCCARTNEY & JOHN LENNON, 1968

I N THE HEADY months following the June 1988 Friendship Flight, groups across every Soviet region, from reindeer herders in the far north to dealers of medicinal dried herbs in Vladivostok, were telexing joint-venture proposals to Alaska. And Alaskans were concocting their own ideas for goodwill, from mail-order brides to rock concerts. Managing high expectations and the new flood of traffic across the Bering Strait challenged both state officials and average Alaskans suddenly eager for civic and commercial ties with the Soviet Far East.

Just three months after the Friendship Flight, a fifteen-member Soviet delegation accepted Governor Cowper's invitation for a reciprocal visit to Alaska. It included Provideniya Mayor Kulinkin, who had grown close to those in Nome, and Vaycheslav Kobets, effectively governor of the Magadan region as chairman of its regional executive committee. A tall man with a bulbous nose and a quick aw-shucks smile, Kobets reminded the Alaskans of actor Jack Klugman from the *Odd Couple* television show. Cowper and Kobets hit it off in Provideniya and saw each other regularly over the next two years.

In an event dubbed the "Friendship Float," the Soviets landed in Nome in early September after a twenty-four-hour crossing of the Bering Strait on a research vessel, the *Dmitri Laptev*. John Handeland, then Nome's mayor, headed the welcoming party. The Soviet ship was too large for the city port so the Soviets transferred to a shallow-draft barge normally used for off-loading freight. Stretching down to the bobbing barge to welcome his Soviet counterpart, Handeland heard his pants split. "I had to wear my raincoat for the rest of the day," he laughed.

Scores of Nome residents eagerly signed up for the novelty of hosting a Soviet in their homes. Charles "Chick" Trainer, later appointed one of the first US Customs agents to handle all the sudden traffic across the date line, reported to retrieve his guest, a journalist for the Magadan *News*. As Trainer prepared to drive off with his Russian, an English-speaking Soviet intervened, insisting he needed to stick with the journalist to better facilitate communications. So Trainer put up both the reporter and the second unexpected guest, his KGB overseer, in the only space he had—children's bunk beds. Trainer said the Soviets' favorite activity during their brief stay was taking his rusty 1977 Plymouth for a spin around Nome's muddy roads.

Following a standing-room-only luncheon, the Soviets were treated to traditional Native games. Mayor Kulinkin took on a young former World Eskimo-Indian Olympics champion in the "ear pull," where a loop of twine is wrapped around one ear of two competitors facing each other sitting cross-legged. The event begins when the two competitors lean back against the tension until one surrenders in pain.

Handeland was tapped to host Kulinkin for the Soviet official's first-ever overnight stay in America. The Nome mayor recalls checking on his guest at three a.m. to find the Provideniya mayor sitting on the guest bed wide awake with excitement.

Cowper, Kobets, and Natives from both sides began initial talks that would lead to a sanctioned policy by their national governments to permit Bering Strait Natives to visit each other without the burdensome requirements of obtaining a visa.

Nome presented its visitors with the parting gift of a large television, a video cassette recorder, and blank tapes so the two communities could exchange videotapes. With the Soviet ship preparing to depart Nome, Kulinkin was spotted picking a handful of white beach stones from Nome's shoreline. As the *Dmitri Laptev* cast off, the mayor tossed the stones into the sea. The act fulfilled a custom that the Russians must return to America because they had left something behind.

The next big headline-grabbing interaction between Alaskans and their Soviet neighbors was not a business deal, international protocol, or exchange of schoolchildren. It was head-banging rock and roll.

Led by the man dubbed the "czar of rock," the Soviet Union's best-known rock band, the Stas Namin Group, blew the doors off concert halls in Anchorage and Juneau in late February 1989. Their Alaska performances were part of the biggest collection of Soviets to descend on Alaska since Lend-Lease pilots in World War II.

The rockers were the main attractions for Glasnost Folkfest, which capped a weeklong visit to Alaska by a ninety-member delegation returning the favor of the Friendship Flight seven months earlier. Even President George H. W. Bush got in on the act when Air Force One made an Anchorage refueling stop long enough to be entertained by Native dancers during the combination trade mission and cultural exchange.

Much of the Soviet visit was coordinated through a loose partnership between the Alaska State Chamber of Commerce and Dixie Belcher, who had pioneered early cross-border breakthroughs. Through her Cama'i nonprofit, Belcher produced the concerts while the chamber organized a trade show and business meetings as part of its Siberian Gateway Project.

Many Alaskans got their first peek at a real-live Soviet when a red, white, and blue chartered Aeroflot jet set down at Anchorage International Airport. Scores of students, business leaders, and politicians applauded their arrival. But the biggest cheers were reserved for the Reebok-wearing Russian rockers, who leaped up and down waving wildly from behind glass walls at the international terminal.

The Soviets spent the week in Anchorage, the Kenai Peninsula, and Juneau, staying in Alaskans' homes, visiting schools, shopping, and plotting future commercial opportunities with state and local politicians and businesses.

Governor Cowper greeted his comrade, Magadan Governor Kobets, with a hearty bear hug. "I'm proud to say that today Alaska is a leader in reestablishing the strong ties that once existed between the United States and the Soviet Union," Cowper said.

Kobets responded, "When we crossed the border between Alaska and the Soviet Union, we were followed by the sun and it has followed us all the way to Anchorage."

Within hours of their arrival, the spirit of goodwill clashed headfirst into bureaucratic reality. The chamber had planned a trade show at Anchorage's convention center where Soviets could show off local products to curious Alaskans. But the Soviets landed with an unannounced three tons of handicrafts, including wooden spoons, aprons and oven mitts, paintings, bed linens, tableware, leather and fur hats, mink pelts, clothing, and forty thousand picture postcard books.

In the 1980s, the Soviet Union and many eastern European nations did not rate favored-nation trade status with the United States. That meant their exports were subject to significantly higher tariff rates than more trade-friendly nations. For example, a US Customs officer explained to the perplexed Alaskans, products from a favored nation were taxed in the United States at 5 percent of their value while similar products from the Soviet bloc were subject to a 90 percent tax. That translated into a $100,000 upfront cash payment the Soviets would have to pay just to get their goods released from the airport.

A chamber official said that he had told the Soviets of the customs requirements weeks earlier in a phone call and had requested a list of merchandise in advance so an Anchorage broker could negotiate with Customs. No list ever arrived.

When the Soviets landed, they brought 115 boxes of unpriced goods and a partial inventory scratched out in Russian. "It's a regular Nordstrom of the North," one volunteer said.

After Governor Cowper's office and Alaska's senators intervened with US Customs and the US Fish and Wildlife Service, the state chamber agreed to post a bond to release the goods. In just the first day, curious Alaskans embarked on a nearly $100,000 shopping spree, raising enough to cover the bond.

Alaska business leaders, hoping to spur a new industry trading consumer products with the Soviets, wrote off the glitch as a learning experience and vowed to seek favored trade status for the Soviet Union. It took three years, but at a 1992 summit in Washington, DC, President Bush and President Yeltsin signed a package of commercial agreements giving Russia most-favored nation trade status for the first time in forty years.

Dixie Belcher envisioned Glasnost Folkfest as the US version of her Performing Artists for Peace tour across the Soviet Union almost three years earlier. She hoped her concerts—two in Anchorage and one in Juneau—would raise the profile of Native families separated by the Ice Curtain and "increase international understanding through music and dance." She initially had requested thirty-six Soviet performers, but the guest list nearly tripled by the time the Soviets landed.

As with her earlier Soviet tour, Belcher was plagued with fund-raising challenges. To handle logistics on the Soviet side, Belcher's nonprofit worked with a Soviet organization, the Foundation for Social Innovation. It was founded by Gennady Alferenko, a smooth-talking, well-connected Russian entrepreneur who helped organize several Alaska-Soviet exchanges before burning bridges with his American partners a few years later.

Belcher again enlisted many of the performers she had led across the Soviet Union. The first "folk" concert featured two Soviet groups: the Pokrovsky Singers, who performed traditional Russian folk songs, and the White Sail Dancers, a Chukotka Eskimo dance group with relatives in Alaska. The Alaska performers included Native dancers from Chevak and St. Lawrence Island, Yupik dancer and singer Chuna McIntyre, the Martin Luther King Anchorage Community Choir, Anchorage Children's Choir, and Belcher's Alaska Performing Artists for Peace.

The top-billed rock and rollers were reserved for the second night's concert, dubbed "Superpower Rock 'N' Roll." The Stas Namin Group had struggled for twenty years to make ends meet playing traditional rock in small clubs and university coffee houses. Twenty-five times the Soviet Minister of Culture had rejected the band's request to tour outside the country. But under Gorbachev's *glasnost*, the band became the biggest-selling rockers in the Soviet Union, filling twenty-five-thousand-seat venues and selling forty million albums.

Stas Namin, the band's founder and front man, was the rebellious black sheep in a well-connected Soviet family. His father was a Soviet hero—a fighter pilot—and his mother a classical musician who played with many of the Soviet Union's great performers. Namin, whose given name was Anastas Mikoyan, was named for his grandfather Anastas Mikoyan, who had been a close aide to Soviet leader Joseph Stalin. The elder Mikoyan was one of the few high-ranking Kremlin officials of that era to survive numerous deadly house cleanings.

American musicians such as Frank Zappa, Quincy Jones, Jon Bon Jovi, and Peter Gabriel all traveled to Moscow to do business with Namin. "At age forty-seven, with his Rod Stewart hairdo, leathered face, and Mick Jagger body, Namin is the Soviet Union's premier advocate of rock and roll," said the *Anchorage Daily News*.

The other Soviet band was Rondo, which had formed just two years earlier but was catching fire quickly after winning the country's main rock festival competition. The American performer was Eddie Money, a former New York City police officer whose first album went double platinum with the smash single "Baby Hold On."

The concerts helped melt forty years of nervous suspicion and replanted roots of friendship. Sovietmania dominated Alaska headlines for weeks and was profiled in the *New York Times* and *Washington Post*. When they visited local junior high schools, the Soviet musicians were mobbed like the Beatles. Namin's rendition of "Back in the U.S.S.R." left Alaska audiences in tears. Soviet leaders were pictured hugging Alaska children. Soviet and Alaska women shopped together, arm in arm. Alaska businessmen admitted to long lists of barriers to Alaska-Soviet trade but said they didn't care and would persist anyway.

"It was a love fest. It was a happening. It was the sixties all over again—but this time with a Russian accent," wrote one local music critic. Even Anchorage's two warring newspapers were inspired to do something rarely seen: publish laudatory editorials on the same day praising the concerts for reducing tensions.

In addition to the new friendships, the weeklong visit set the stage for many other joint activities. The Magadan governor brought officials from his ministries of trade, agriculture, industry, medicine, aviation, communication, culture, and education for talks with Cowper on implementing the Alaska-Magadan sister-city agreement signed four months earlier. One idea of particular interest to the Magadan governor was recruiting an Anchorage meat processor, Doug Drum, to teach the Soviets how to produce reindeer sausage Alaska-style.

A handful of Soviet journalists met with their Alaska counterparts to discuss professional practices and plan future journalism exchanges. Arctic explorers, including Alaska-trade specialist Ginna Brelsford, solidified final plans for a cross-country ski and dogsled trek across the frozen Bering Strait to begin just two weeks later.

AS ALASKANS CONTINUED to bask in the glow of Sovietmania, Belcher struggled to balance her books. She had counted on the concerts to raise enough to put her Cama'i nonprofit on firm financial footing. Instead, it lost more than $10,000. Just two weeks before the concerts, ticket sales were slow so Belcher was persuaded to cut the cost of the $20 tickets in half. The chamber assured her it would solicit local restaurants to donate meals for the Soviet musicians, but the arrangement never materialized. Her stage manager had to work full-time scraping up food from nonprofits and churches for the hungry Soviets.

Belcher agreed to give the chamber concession rights in exchange for its $25,000 donation to Cama'i, but that prevented her from cashing in on souvenir sales. The chamber netted an estimated $15,000 for those sales. As she did when financing her concert trip across the Soviet Union in 1987, Belcher again faced the prospect of losing her Juneau home.

Still, she claimed no regrets. "I think that week was fabulously successful in every way except financially. I think it was wonderful," she said.

However, the Soviets departed Alaska with thousands of dollars in unsold trinkets still sitting in Anchorage. The chamber mulled over options until a handful of local businessmen stepped up. One was Perry Eaton, an early and frequent visitor to the Russian Far East with ties to Magadan Governor Kobets. Eaton ran the Community Enterprise Development Corporation, which owned the Alaska Commercial Company. Another was Mead Treadwell, a confidant of former Alaska Governor Hickel who had worked with the state chamber on Soviet issues. The two took the lead in selling the remaining Soviet handicrafts to help pay for their trip.

Still aglow from their week of cultural sharing and hungry for more, Soviets and Alaskans bid a tearful farewell. While the new overtures generated international media coverage, however, the reaction from average Americans was sometimes less than enthusiastic.

When the *Dallas Morning News* carried a 1988 story about Alaska-Soviet exchanges, C. G. Bulin of Troup, Texas, sent a letter to Governor Cowper. He asked, "Have we reached the place in our Great Nation when we now display pictures of Lenin in our schools rather than our own Great Statesman [*sic*] such as George Washington, Abraham Lincoln, Patrick Henry, Nathan Hale or Franklin D. Roosevelt and any number of others?"

Cowper responded that the picture in Bulin's newspaper mistakenly identified a Nome school adorned with Lenin when in fact the school was in Provideniya.

"Rest assured," Cowper wrote him, "Alaska classrooms feature pictures of our own American founding fathers."

Alaska Natives keep breathing holes open in the Arctic Ocean ice north of Barrow to help stranded California gray whales in fall 1988. A Soviet icebreaker came to the whales' rescue and may have freed them, although no one spotted them in open ocean to confirm their release.
PHOTO BY JEFF SCHULTZ/SCHULTZPHOTO.COM

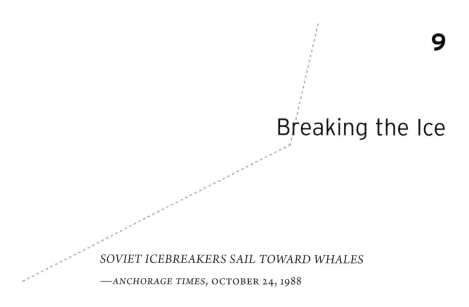

9

Breaking the Ice

SOVIET ICEBREAKERS SAIL TOWARD WHALES

—*ANCHORAGE TIMES*, OCTOBER 24, 1988

A S 1988 CAME to a close—ending a year of dramatic breakthroughs in relations across the Bering Strait—a freakish fate of nature focused the world's attention on Alaska and endeared the Soviet Union to schoolchildren and their parents across the globe.

Arctic Alaska was experiencing one of its coldest falls on record. Native whalers from Alaska's northernmost coastal community of Barrow were anxious to take their remaining whaling quota before the Arctic Ocean froze over. They were following the rules of the eighty-eight-nation International Whaling Commission, which two years earlier had imposed a ban on commercial whaling. But the commission allowed subsistence whaling by indigenous peoples, including some Alaska Natives. That fall, Barrow whalers had just three more chances to land a bowhead whale to help feed their community for the winter.

Scouting for his father's crew, Barrow whaler Roy Ahmaogak made his way to the slushy ocean edge and climbed an ice ridge for a panoramic view. Spotting no sign of bowheads, Ahmaogak started back across the ice pack toward town when he came across a small pool of open water. There, taking turns surfacing to catch a breath, were three giant California gray whales. Because of the cold—a record thirteen below zero that early October—the whales were trapped. They were too far from the open ocean to swim to freedom, and their breathing hole was slowly freezing over, threatening to drown them.

Normally by this time gray whales are long gone from a summer of feeding in Alaska's coastal waters. In the fall, they head back to warmer Baja California to give birth. Alaska Iñupiat hunters typically did not target grays, which had been hunted to near extinction by commercial whalers. It wasn't unheard of for grays to become trapped in the ice. Carcasses occasionally washed up on the arctic shore in spring, a fragrant meal for polar bears. Fortunately for these three whales, word of their dilemma spread quickly.

In less than a week, their plight received national headlines, whipped up by media-savvy Anchorage Greenpeace activist Cindy Lowry and biologists for the National Marine Fisheries Service. Initially, many of those intrigued by the stranded whales shrugged off their predicament. Some of the Barrow whaling captains thought the most humane act was to put them out of their misery.

However, news of the distressed whales spread so widely across the world that President Reagan called the head of the Alaska Army National Guard to pledge federal assistance and moral support for a successful rescue. At the request of Senator Stevens, the Pentagon was enlisted to help, too.

As press secretary to Alaska's governor, I fielded numerous media inquiries about the whales. Governor Cowper declined to join the media circus, suggesting a more cost-effective solution could be had at the tip of an explosive harpoon.

In attempts to free the whales, would-be rescuers considered or tried an assortment of techniques: soothing whale songs, dynamite, a Japanese "screw tractor," breaking the ice with an eight-thousand-pound concrete block suspended from a helicopter. Nothing worked.

Meanwhile, the whales gained an even wider international following as schoolchildren drew their pictures and called them by name: "Bone" (for the bone protruding from its nose), "Bonnet" (for the barnacle pattern around its blowhole), and "Crossbeak" (whose jaws didn't quite line up).

The Barrow whalers used chainsaws to cut a series of blowholes toward the open ocean. They hoped the whales would swim from one to the next and finally to freedom. But before the whales could be encouraged to move, the new holes kept freezing over. Two uninvited Minnesotans came to the rescue with their invention for Midwest ice fishing. Their electric bubblers circulated enough water to keep the blowholes open, even at below-freezing temperatures.

Two weeks after the whales were first spotted, a line of about fifty breathing holes had been cut into the ice two miles toward the open ocean. Two of the whales had been encouraged to move about a mile closer to open water. The third, Bone, had disappeared below the ice, never to be seen again. But the remaining whales refused to go farther, apparently stalled by a massive ice ridge that created subsurface obstructions. That's when the Soviets came to the rescue.

Two Soviet ships, the 443-foot icebreaker *Admiral Makarov* and an icebreaking cargo ship called the *Vladimir Arsenev* were en route back to their home port of Vladivostok after six months at sea. The Soviet Union boasted the world's largest icebreaking fleet, using dozens of thick-bowed vessels to service the 40 percent of the Arctic that is Soviet territory. By contrast, the United States had—and still has—only two aging icebreakers, dating back to the mid-1970s. When the whales were initially spotted, one of the US icebreakers, the *Polar Star,* was crossing the Northwest Passage eastward and declined to turn around.

Well aware of a potential public-relations bonanza, the Soviets on October 25 redirected their two ships to Barrow. The Soviet arrival on the scene is joyously portrayed in the 2012 movie *Big Miracle*, starring Drew Barrymore and John Krasinski. The Soviet involvement in the whale rescue helped repair their image as whale-killing villains, created when Greenpeace activists raided a fur farm in the Bering Sea village of Lorino five years earlier.

Scientists determined that the obstacle blocking the whales' escape was a thirty-five-foot-high solid wall of ice, formed by the pressure of ice floes squeezing against each other. Undaunted, the Soviet icebreaker went to work.

Over three days, the *Makarov* revved up its 41,400-horsepower diesel engines to ram the ridge repeatedly before the eyes of the world. The media-savvy Soviets invited American reporters on their ships for grand tours and even flew the US Stars and Stripes along with the Soviet hammer and sickle flag. The North Slope Borough reciprocated, flying Soviet journalists on its helicopter. The media deemed the multinational effort "Operation Rescue."

By the end of the third day of ramming, the Soviets had breached the ice ridge, opening a half-mile-wide gap for the whales to swim through. It appeared that the photogenic whales would be saved. At first light on October 28, helicopters took to the sky to pinpoint the whales' whereabouts. None could be spotted.

Scientists had considered attaching radios to the whales but rejected it out of fear of overstressing them.

"To the cheers of an unlikely team of Eskimos, scientists, environmentalists, oil workers, and Soviet sailors, two California gray whales trapped in the arctic ice for three weeks were last seen swimming behind a Russian icebreaker headed for the freedom of the open sea," UPI reported.

Although no one actually witnessed the whales' escape, the rescue was proclaimed a success by the federal biologists overseeing the effort. In Los Angeles, volunteers on Southern California whale-watching boats were provided pictures of the Barrow captives believed to be headed their way. But the whales were never identified.

While the whale rescue cost an estimated $1 million, it scored the Soviets an international public-relations coup. "I was impressed with the Soviets," said Alaska ice expert Bob Lewellen. "If it wasn't for the Russians, I'd say it was very unlikely they would have gotten free."

The Soviet effort even earned them a salute from that old Cold War warrior, President Reagan.

"The human persistence and determination by so many individuals on behalf of these whales shows mankind's concern for the environment," he said. "It has been an inspiring endeavor. We thank and congratulate the crews of the two Soviet ice-breakers who finally broke through to the whales."

Adventure Diplomacy Across the Strait

The purpose: to forget the cold and hot wars and to live friendly and peacefully on our planet.

—FAMED SOVIET ARCTIC EXPLORER DMITRY SHPARO, APRIL 5, 2016

I T WAS THE longest twenty minutes of Anatoly Tkachenko's young life. The baby-faced Soviet university student risked prison and punishment of his well-connected family when he stole, forged, and duped his way from Moscow across eleven time zones to a tiny American rock island in the Bering Strait. And then he committed the unthinkable.

On April 23, 1989, Tkachenko was among eighty-four Soviets who set down in bright orange Aeroflot helicopters on a windblown ice landing strip near the international date line. They were there to witness twelve rugged Soviet and American adventurers ski and dogsled across the halfway point of their three-month trek from the Soviet Far East to Alaska. The Bering Bridge Expedition was designed to generate international media attention to chip away at the Ice Curtain that had separated Alaska and the Soviet Union for four decades.

Two years earlier, a visionary Minnesota polar explorer, Paul Schurke, had conceived of the expedition. Schurke and his wife, Susan, operated Wintergreen Dogsled Lodge, providing winter dogsled expeditions in the northern Minnesota River Country. In 1986, Schurke co-led the seven-member international team to

Members of the Bering Bridge Expedition ski and dogsled into Provideniya during their March 1989 adventure, accompanied by village children. COURTESY OF SASHA BELYAEV

become the first to reach the North Pole without resupply, skiing from Ellesmere Island, Canada. Their family company produced the clothing and other equipment for the historic Steger International Polar Expedition.

In the aftermath of that high-profile expedition, Schurke hit the speaking circuit. Although that Canadian trip was thousands of miles from the Bering Strait, Schurke got an earful from Canadian First Peoples about the Ice Curtain preventing contact between indigenous people.

At a Montreal conference that spring, Schurke encountered another guest speaker, Soviet Dmitry Shparo. One of his nation's most celebrated arctic explorers, Shparo had once skied four hundred miles in two months across the Arctic Ocean in total winter darkness and had completed his own expedition over the North Pole from the Soviet Union to Canada. The two arctic explorers shared their frustration over the plight of divided Bering Strait Natives and agreed to embark on "adventure diplomacy" to do something about it. Schurke and Shparo traveled to Moscow to flesh out the idea for six explorers from each country to join forces.

Their plan called for a 1,200-mile expedition beginning in Anadyr, capital of Chukotka, the Soviet Union's northeasternmost province. The team would ski and mush dogs through fourteen largely indigenous villages to the coast closest to Alaska. Then they would traverse thirty miles of the ice-choked Bering Strait to Big Diomede Island, site of a KGB border guard post.

Just two and a half miles east of Big Diomede was Alaska's Little Diomede Island on the other side of the international date line. It was there the expedition would celebrate crossing from the Soviet Union into the United States. Then the explorers would make their way twenty-two miles across the US portion of the Bering Strait to the Alaska mainland. They planned to visit twelve Alaska communities before ending up in Kotzebue more than two hundred miles later.

In addition to co-leaders Schurke and Shparo, the team included experienced adventurers. Ginna Brelsford jumped at the chance to go. Taking leave from her job as lead Soviet trade specialist for Governor Cowper, she served as the expedition's diplomat, negotiating with Soviet and local officials along the way and helping plan the date line ceremony from the trail. The other Alaskans included three Natives from the Bering region: Little Diomede national guardsman Robert Soolook, Gambell college student Darlene Apangalook, and Kotzebue salmon fisherman Ernie Norton. The US team was filled out by Minnesota carpenter Lonnie Dupre.

The Soviet team included two veterans of Shparo's earlier expeditions: Alexander Tenyakshev, a communications professor, and research engineer Sasha Belyaev. Two other Soviet members were Eskimo hunters and reindeer herders from the region: Nicolai "Kolya" Attinya and Vadim Krivolap. The team doctor and driver of one of the dog teams was pediatrician Zoya Ivanova, also a leader of her Chukotka village dance team.

An expedition this ambitious normally took years to plan and secure government approvals. But Shparo was so well connected that Soviet authorities gave the tentative green light in just six months.

"Dmitry has a tremendous force of personality that's bigger than life," Schurke said. "He had access to all levels of the Soviet government, including the Kremlin, which led to Gorbachev's personal interest in the project."

Shparo believed the expedition got quick Kremlin approval because "it perfectly corresponded to the doctrine of a great man, Gorbachev, whose purpose was to emancipate the citizens of the Soviet Union."

After the initial planning meeting with Shparo in Moscow, Schurke scrambled back to Minnesota to line up American sponsors and work with his wife to produce the equipment and bright blue anorak parkas, pants, and other winter gear for the expedition. One of the chief sponsors was Alaska Airlines, which made available the same jet and flight crew that flew the Friendship Flight between Nome and Provideniya ten months earlier.

With the cargo hold packed with skis, howling sled dogs, and gear for three months on the trail, the Boeing 737 bearing Alaska's trademark smiling Eskimo departed Anchorage on March 1. A few hours later, it descended through the clouds for Anadyr. Pilot Terry Smith announced the weather: minus ten with a windchill of thirty-five below.

In addition to fostering friendship, the expedition agreed to take part in several scientific studies. One, by a University of Minnesota researcher who had done similar work for NASA's Mars team, examined how people exposed to extreme conditions for prolonged periods handled stress.

A second study, by the US Army's Cold Regions Research lab, looked at whether the human body built up resistance to cold after long exposure to it. To test that theory, a Massachusetts researcher joined the team along the trail. He plunged their hands into an ice-water bath and then examined them under an infrared monitor to see how the circulatory system was working. After weeks on a cold trail, team members didn't look forward to the test. But one finding was especially telling: Zoya Ivanova's hands melted the ice, proving her to be tougher than anyone for arctic travel.

With fighting sled dogs, ideological clashes, a fiery romance between two expedition members, and brutal trail conditions of hurricane-like winds and sub-zero temperatures, the trek tested the leadership skills of the American and Soviet co-leaders. The expedition's daily routine required skiing along the Soviet coast as dogs pulled sleds laden with food and gear. Some stretches between villages required five days of breaking fresh trail over coastal mountains and camping in tents. Some days, ferocious winds blew the skiers over like rag dolls; on others, rain and sleet slowed progress to a crawl and inflamed tempers.

As they entered each Soviet community, the adventurers were hailed as celebrities. They were welcomed with traditional Native foods such as seal, walrus, and duck, honored with hours-long Native dancing to the beat of sealskin drums, and delivered and listened to long friendship speeches. In most villages, the Alaskans were the first Americans the locals had ever met.

After six weeks on the trail, the expedition finally reached the jumping-off point to cross the strait, the Soviet village of Uelen. Known in Yupik as Ulyk, which translates to "the land's end," it is the easternmost community in Eurasia and the closest mainland Soviet village to the United States. En route to Uelen in driving snow and high winds, the expedition had been monitoring plans to celebrate the date line crossing, then scheduled for just three days later. But when Schurke finally reached an expedition contact in Nome, he was told that the same storm they were fighting had closed the strait for nearly a week. As a result, the Alaska governor's office had postponed the celebration for nine days, until April 23.

Expedition leaders devoted the next few days to figuring out how to get across the strait to Big Diomede Island, known to the locals as Ostrov Ratmanov. The storm had blown huge chunks of sea ice against the coastline, with shelf ice extending out another half mile. Beyond that was ice-choked open water. The only way forward was by boat.

Shparo consulted with local Natives, who warned him that the wooden boats used in Uelen for subsistence whaling were too heavy and unwieldy to maneuver in the ice floes. Better to use a lighter-weight walrus-skin boat known along the Soviet coast as a *baidar* or in Alaska as an *umiak*. The problem was *baidars* were no longer used in Uelen; the expedition last saw one in Sireniki, 170 miles to the south. Shparo capitalized on his goodwill with the Soviets, freed up a *baidar* from a Sireniki collective farm, and persuaded border guards to retrieve it by helicopter.

A few days later, the *baidar* arrived along with two Yupik hunters—the boat builder who was to captain the vessel and his crewman. The twenty-five-foot boat was supported by a wooden frame around which walrus hides were tightly wrapped and secured with rawhide ties. It was powered by a forty-horse Suzuki, with handmade wooden oars as backup.

The captain informed Shparo and Schurke that the boat could carry ten people maximum. But the expedition needed to transport twelve team members plus two guides, eighteen sled dogs, and hundreds of pounds of equipment. The leaders considered shuttling the expedition in two or more trips. But faced with the prospect of skittish dogs and a couple of days crisscrossing the rough seas thirty miles each way, they accepted the border guard offer to fly four team members, the dogs, and the gear to Big Diomede by helicopter.

Shortly after three p.m., with about six hours of daylight remaining, the team inched the loaded *baidar* over snowbanks and eased it into the dark sea. Brelsford and Schurke joined hands to offer a quiet prayer for a safe voyage. Putting along at ten miles an hour, the boat's progress was regularly jolted by submerged blocks of ice. A slow leak required team members to constantly bail seawater. Once they were in open water, a north wind rolled in waves higher than the expedition members' heads.

At one point, a curious walrus suddenly popped up next to the boat, threatening to overturn it. Chukchi hunter Vadim Krivolap managed to get off a shot with his rifle, scaring both the huge animal and the other passengers.

Twice the anxious sailors heard the chop-chop of a helicopter overhead. On the first pass, the Aeroflot helicopter dropped through the clouds to about one hundred feet over the sea but couldn't spot the boat. On the second pass, with photographers hanging out the doors, it got so close that prop wash threated to swamp the *baidar*.

About four hours later, the fog finally lifted enough for the crew to spot the rocky cliffs of Big Diomede. Unable to raise the Soviet border station by radio and blocked by shore ice, the crew was forced to land the boat about two miles away. To cover that distance took them hours of slogging over ice blocks and through slush-filled water, sometimes on all fours. Close to midnight, the weary team rounded a rocky corner to the welcome sight of the patrol station. The Soviet border guards had fired up every light they had as a beacon.

Those who had crossed the strait by boat happily reunited with their four teammates and the dogs who had flown in by helicopter. Schurke shared with the full expedition a telegram they had received shortly before casting off from Uelen. "I am greeting you with all my heart, you the members of the Soviet-American expedition with the name The Bering Bridge," said General Secretary Gorbachev. "The name is not just a symbol for me. This name represents my own true feelings. You are truly helping to build a bridge of friendship and cooperation between Chukotka and Alaska as well as between the Soviet Union and the United States. We are united by common challenges such as preserving northern culture, protecting the arctic ecosystem and, of course, the most important challenge, the strengthening of peaceful relations among all countries of the world. I wish you the best of luck, great success and may all your goals be accomplished."

IN NOME, 135 miles to the east, Governor Cowper was getting grouchy. Cowper was never enthralled with the show business side of politics. This time, though, we in the governor's office had dreamed up a real extravaganza. To celebrate the successful date-line crossing, we had proposed a signing ceremony in the middle of the frozen Bering Sea. On an orange line spray-painted on "the exact spot where today meets tomorrow." In April in a year with the harshest winter in four decades. Where scores of Soviets and Alaska dignitaries and journalists had to descend by helicopter at approximately the same time, tolerate some quick speeches, and escape before a blizzard or hungry polar bear ruined the party.

Cowper was distracted by developments in Juneau, where the legislature was snubbing his pleas for action to address one of the worst economic crises in state history. And here he was stranded in the Alaska Air National Guard hangar, grounded by thirty-knot winds, a windchill of thirty-four below, and poor visibility, which prevented the guard's helicopter from taking off.

For months, Ginna Brelsford and I had planned the date-line event to underscore progress in advancing relations between Alaska and the Magadan region. A few weeks earlier, in February, Cowper and Governor Kobets had expanded their friendship in Anchorage during the Glasnost Folkfest. Their staffs drafted another friendship protocol, this one focused on border crossings—easing visits by Natives of the region with visa-free travel and establishing a joint Alaska-Soviet commission to resolve border issues. What more photogenic place to sign it than on the actual border between the US and the USSR as weather-worn American and Soviet adventurers crossed from east to west on cross-country skis led by bounding sled dogs?

After the harrowing Bering Strait crossing, the exhausted members of the Bering Bridge Expedition collapsed in the relative comfort of the border guard station on Big Diomede. Six months later, I paid my own visit to the station with Governor Cowper and a handful of Alaska journalists. I found it the grimmest, most remote, and loneliest place I had been.

The outpost fell under the jurisdiction of the KGB. About seventy soldiers, young men who looked barely old enough to shave, were assigned there for two-year postings with a monthly salary of eight rubles, about $2. Their mission was to guard against a US invasion of the Motherland. But the only action they ever saw was the rare American adventurer who wandered across the strait illegally.

The only females on the island were the commander's wife and young daughter. The rusting playground equipment seemed out of place amid the military buildings.

"The Soviet border camp is perched on a rock overlooking the sea and reachable only by scaling what we're later told is one hundred steps," I recorded in my journal. "That's only after gingerly dancing along a path in the tundra made from metal airplane runway pieces nailed to boards submerged in the wet ground."

The enlisted soldiers slept elbow to elbow on rows of cots. Their bathroom was a six-hole outhouse suspended over a ravine; the stench was unbearable.

"They show up here as children—almost babies—and leave here as brave men," Commander Lt. Col. Vladimir Starukov told us during our brief visit on September 1, 1989.

For the weary expedition members, the lacy curtains, thick black bread, and hot tea were a welcome relief from the trail. The listening post's surveillance equipment blocked Schurke's efforts to connect with his base in Nome. But he learned through Little Diomede that high winds and poor visibility continued to keep Governor Cowper and his delegation grounded in Nome.

However, the Soviets planned to arrive on time and the ceremony was still on. So after a couple of days, the expedition loaded up for the short two-and-a-half-mile sprint to the date line.

Sun broke out as the team departed the Soviet island, but fierce gales hit them in the face as they rounded a cape on the way to Little Diomede. Visibility was reduced to near zero. Some of the Soviet guards had departed earlier on snow machines so the expedition blindly followed their tracks. About one hundred feet from the ceremony site, a portable satellite dish and Soviet and American flags snapping in the wind came into view.

On April 23, as Soviet border guardsmen and Alaska national guardsmen stood at attention, the expedition crossed into America across the orange line spray-painted in the snow and posed for pictures. A few minutes later, they had to reenact the crossing for late-arriving Soviet journalists before making a dash for the warmth of Little Diomede's school gym.

BACK IN NOME, National Guard helicopter pilots delivered bad news to Cowper and his entourage. They were grounded. The fuel-sucking Blackhawk helicopters slated to shuttle the governor to the date line had to gas up in Tin City, a radar outpost on Alaska's Bering Sea coast about one hundred miles northwest of Nome. But visibility was zero at Tin City.

Cowper had had enough of the frustrating wait in the Nome armory. So we quickly set up a speakerphone ceremony, with the Alaska governor in Nome and his Soviet counterpart on the phone in Little Diomede. Cowper and about fifty dignitaries, Native leaders, and journalists paraded across Nome and jammed in to the tiny offices of Alascom. The crowd gathered around a seven-inch screen to watch the date-line ceremony at Little Diomede, some hanging on to ladders amid the tangle of cables for a peek.

By speakerphone to Governor Kobets, Cowper signed a protocol that called for streamlined border crossings, the creation of a border commission to ease Native travel, radio communications links across the strait, and better trade and aviation ties. Kobets signed a Russian version, and both governors promised to send each other signed copies.

"Alaska is on the leading edge of improved relations with the Soviet Union and this is another important step forward," Cowper said. "I'm convinced it will lead to regular visits between Native people of both countries who have too long been separated by political barriers."

Back on the windswept icy Bering Sea landing zone at the foot of Little Diomede, Alaska Army National Guard Capt. Rex "Dusty" Finley was trying to stay warm. Suddenly his handheld radio crackled with a message: "A situation is developing and nothin' good's gonna come from it."

Soviet "journalists" Anatoly Tkachenko (left) and Alexander Genkin are interviewed by the Alaska National Guard after seeking political asylum during the Bering Bridge Expedition crossing ceremony on Little Diomede Island. COURTESY OF CAPT. REX "DUSTY" FINLEY

Deception on Diomede

Jesus, I mean, you guys do nothing but complain about how you can't stand it in this place here and you don't have the guts just to walk out?
—RANDLE MCMURPHY, *ONE FLEW OVER THE CUCKOO'S NEST*, 1975

C APT. DUSTY FINLEY had been dispatched from the Alaska Army National Guard headquarters in Anchorage to help oversee logistics for the Bering Bridge Expedition crossing. Western Alaska was his old stomping ground. He had served for a couple of years as an active Army Advisor with the First Scout Battalion of the 297th Infantry Regiment based in Nome with responsibilities for twenty-one villages. His assignment on April 23, 1989, was landing-zone control officer for the helicopters bringing dignitaries to the ceremony on the international date line. A West Pointer, Finley was the second highest-ranking Alaska guardsman on site.

Finley's superior was Col. William Wortman, an Anchorage-based guard training facilitator who also had been stationed in the Nome area. Wortman's father was an Army officer, and his family had once been assigned to the same Germany-based unit where a young serviceman named Elvis Presley was stationed.

A few days before traveling to Little Diomede to interact with the Soviets, Wortman noticed that the May issue of *Playboy* magazine had hit the stands.

Headlined "From Russia with Love," it featured Soviet screen star Natalya Negoda. Wortman urged his soldiers to buy up copies as Bering Strait trading stock with their Soviet counterparts.

As time neared for the border-crossing ceremony, Wortman traveled by snow machine nearly a mile toward Big Diomede, meeting his Soviet military counterparts at the temporary satellite earth station. Like many Alaskans caught up in the aura of growing US-Soviet friendship, the guardsmen dispatched to Little Diomede were committed to a smooth ceremony. Little did anyone anticipate an international political event that threatened to torpedo the goodwill so meticulously constructed across the strait over the previous three years.

After the wind-whipped crossing ceremony on the ice, the visiting Soviets made their way to the Little Diomede school, the largest building on the island. There they watched Native dancing and sipped hot coffee.

One of the twenty-two Soviet journalists trying to stay warm on Little Diomede was born into a privileged Moscow life. Anatoly Tkachenko's mother was a defense ministry engineer and his father a psychologist with the Ministry of Foreign Affairs. The elder Tkachenko's specialty was testing foreign diplomats for their ability to handle high-stress situations. A frequent discussion topic in the Tkachenko home in the 1980s was the merits of Western democracies versus the Soviet Union's communist government. Hooked on American television, Anatoly decided at an early age that he wanted to study journalism and travel to the West like his English-speaking father.

At seventeen, Anatoly took the admissions exam for an elite college where Soviet diplomats and foreign correspondents were trained. He scored well on English, geography, and history but his final paper failed. His professors determined that his composition, "The Responsibility of Journalists and Writers for the Truth in Their Works," lacked adequate references to Lenin and the Community Party.

Frustrated, Tkachenko left school to complete his two years' required national service as a KGB border guard on the Soviet-Finnish border. On his return, he passed the college's entrance exam on the second try and resumed studying journalism.

The restless Tkachenko was coming of age at a fortuitous time in the Soviet Union. After seventy years of Soviet central planning and top-down control, the relatively young Soviet leader, Mikhail Gorbachev, shook his country to its core with his duel reforms of *perestroika* (restructuring) and *glasnost* (openness). Suddenly, Gorbachev extended greater freedom to the media and religious groups and encouraged average Soviet citizens to express their opinions. He relaxed central control of the economy and even moved toward a reform most Soviets considered inconceivable: elected government.

That wasn't enough for Tkachenko, who grew increasingly disillusioned. At school, stories he prepared about American journalists working in Moscow and an interview with a US ambassador were spiked and he was reprimanded. He heard clicking noises on his parents' phone, raising suspicions that it was tapped.

A fellow student, Alexander Genkin, shared Tkachenko's frustration. Genkin was kicked out of school for his outspoken criticisms of Soviet policy in Afghanistan and Cuba. The dean told Genkin he could never be trusted to work outside the Soviet Union.

So the two privileged twentysomethings secretly plotted a risky effort to abandon their country. Failure could have meant years in a grim Soviet prison, or worse. Their first idea: stow away on a ship. Faking vacations, they traveled to two of the Soviet Union's largest ports—Murmansk on the Arctic Ocean and Leningrad on the Baltic Sea—to sneak aboard a ship headed to the West. But both times shipyard security was too tight, so they returned to Moscow, dejected.

One day in March 1989, Tkachenko was riding the subway across Moscow to his parents' flat when he spotted an announcement in a newspaper. A celebration was planned on American Little Diomede Island to celebrate a joint US-Soviet ski and dogsled trek across the Bering Strait. The Soviet expedition office was encouraging journalists to apply to cover it, no special visas required. Tkachenko convinced Genkin this was their chance.

The pair visited the expedition office in Moscow to inquire about the requirements: only an official application signed by an editor and 2,800 rubles (about $700) for expenses. Even this seemed insurmountable. Official documents were hard to come by in the security-conscious Soviet Union, and the prospects were nil that Tkachenko's dean would bless the idea. Plus, they each earned only around sixty rubles a month, the equivalent of $15. But the inventive Tkachenko went to work.

A few days later, he visited his college editor to pitch another story about frustrations with life in the Soviet Union—lousy dorms conditions that Nicaraguan students put up with while studying in Moscow. He drew out the conversation until his editor was called to another floor. Alone in the office, Tkachenko stole two sheets of official stationery from an open iron safe behind the editor's desk. After the college emptied out at the end of the day, Tkachenko typed two application letters in the dean's empty office. He forged signatures for the editor and school dean.

That wasn't good enough. The Soviet government was obsessed with seals and stamps to make documents official. So Tkachenko carried his letters to another university office where a fellow student worked as a receptionist. They struck up a conversation about the new American film, *One Flew over the Cuckoo's Nest*, which his friend had recently seen. They laughed about their classmates resembling the movie's mental patients and the dean the dictatorial Nurse Ratched. When the friend slipped out for a cigarette, Tkachenko rifled through her desk, found the school stamp, and added a fake authenticity to the letters. He was smiling when she returned from her break.

The next hurdle was cash. Between them Tkachenko and Genkin had saved only about three hundred rubles ($75). Amassing 2,800 rubles at their meager salaries would take years. So the next day they visited an enterprising engineer who sold American film and rock videos and electronic equipment out of his Moscow flat. The pair explained they were headed to America as tourists. They needed rubles and proposed to exchange them for dollars on the black market for a substantial markup. The Soviet entrepreneur liked the prospect of a significant return on his loan, so he counted out the requested 2,800 rubles.

Returning to the expedition office, Tkachenko and Genkin handed over their applications and the required fees. They were added to the official delegation of journalists. For the next ten days, as they readied for their adventure, they lived double lives in fear that their scheme would be found out. An innocent call from the expedition office to the university could get them expelled or perhaps sent to a Siberian prison. Both told their families and closest friends of their reporting assignment and downplayed their absences, saying they expected to be gone a couple of weeks at most.

As the days counted down, the two grew increasingly tense. One evening Tkachenko took his girlfriend, Natasha, to a café. He wanted to know if she'd ever consider leaving the Soviet Union to live with him in another country. Initially she resisted and pushed back. How can you leave your own country? Finally, she reluctantly agreed that perhaps someday—years in the future—she might join him if he moved abroad.

On his last morning in Moscow, Tkachenko had breakfast with his parents and teenage sister in the flat they had lived in for fourteen years. His mother tried to pin him down as to when he could visit his grandmother in the Ukraine countryside—June or July, she asked. July was probably best, he guessed, as he bid good-bye to his family.

Tkachenko and Genkin met up in the metro and made another high-stakes gamble that again paid off. Emerging from the subway with luggage in tow, they couldn't find a taxi for a ride to the rendezvous point near Red Square in central Moscow. Many Soviets who owned cars made extra cash by picking up pedestrians, happy to negotiate an off-the-books fare. Across from the subway station, Tkachenko spotted a black Volga of the type usually used by the KGB, its driver killing time behind the wheel. Tkachenko tapped the window and offered five rubles (about $1.25) for a lift.

Waiting for a bus to the airport, national journalists from *Pravda*, Novosti Press Agency, and *Gostelradio* (radio and television) were impressed when Tkachenko and Genkin pulled up. The two stepped from a KGB sedan whose KGB driver helped with their luggage and then bid them farewell. After that, the two considered themselves immune from suspicion.

The handful of journalists boarded a mostly empty Soviet jet for the 3,800-mile flight to the far eastern city of Magadan, the administrative center for a huge but sparsely populated arctic region. Magadan's claim to fame was as the major transit center for prisoners headed to remote gulags during the Stalin era.

Waiting in Magadan for the Bering Strait weather to improve, the journalists were entertained by local officials with barbecues and tours. To maintain their cover, Tkachenko and Genkin even interviewed Vyacheslav Kobets, chairman of the regional executive committee, the highest-ranking local official.

When the weather permitted, the delegation flew up the coast to Anadyr and then to the small indigenous village of Lavrentiya, across the Bering Strait from Alaska. Finally, on April 24, the fog lifted enough to make a run for Little Diomede. Now numbering eighty-four people, the government officials, journalists, and Soviet military escorts boarded four bright orange Aeroflot helicopters for the sixty-mile flight over the frozen Bering Sea. Before the last helicopter took off—the one carrying Tkachenko and Genkin—they wondered if it was the last time they'd ever touch Russian soil.

The Soviets arrived on Little Diomede's landing strip to witness the Bering Bridge Expedition cross the international date line, then hurried back to the school to get out of the blizzard. They killed time while the telephonic protocol-signing ceremony between Cowper and Kobets was arranged. Because of his strong English, Tkachenko was recruited to help translate media interviews. He was even summoned by the Soviet governor to serve as backup interpreter for the call with Cowper.

Finally, Tkachenko excused himself and sought out an Alaska guardsman standing alone. After a few minutes of friendly banter, Tkachenko looked Sgt. First Class John Michael Butzon in the eye and asked quietly, "What do you think about the possibility of us asking for political asylum here, for me and my friend Alex?" Butzon was stunned.

After a moment—what Tkachenko later said seemed like an hour—Butzon walked away to find a senior guardsman. "Wait here," he directed Tkachenko. Butzon left the school and quickly found Staff Sgt. Charles Jones. Jones got on the radio to his officers, Captain Finley and Colonel Wortman.

Wortman distracted his Soviet counterpart, border guard commander Col. Vladimir Starukov, while Finley called Nome for guidance. Conveniently stuck there together were Governor Cowper, Alaska Adjutant Gen. John Schaeffer, and Gary Johnson, deputy director of the Immigration and Naturalization Service. The three told Finley to honor the asylum request and, if necessary, lie to the Soviets to protect the two young defectors. Under US law, asylum seekers are entitled to the same civil liberties as American citizens, Johnson explained. After that call, Finley and Wortman directed the guardsmen to continue with their duties "so that it would appear as if nothing unusual was happening."

Sergeant Jones joined Sergeant Butzon in the gym. Under the guise of taking pictures outside, they casually walked Tkachenko and his comrade, Alexander Genkin, across a snowy trail to the village health clinic. There, the two young Soviets kept their heads down and were given sleeping bags and food.

"We didn't know if anybody was armed in the Russian delegation, we didn't know to what extent they would try to resecure their citizens so we didn't want to immediately show our hand," Finley said later.

As the Soviets prepared for a scheduled seven p.m. departure, Finley left his landing-zone post long enough to meet the defectors in person. In the clinic, he tape-recorded a sixteen-minute interview in which Tkachenko and Genkin reaffirmed their desire to defect.

"No methods, bribes, or coercion to stay here have been used on me," Tkachenko said. "I have made this decision of my own free will. I think that life in the United States is my only choice. My decision is final and irreversible."

WITH THE WEATHER closing in and darkness descending, the Soviets scrambled aboard their helicopters. The departure grew chaotic when a battery died on one of the choppers. Finley helped jump it.

It finally dawned on the Soviets that two members of their delegation were missing. At the demand of a Soviet interpreter, an Alaska guard scout was dispatched to the school to look for the missing pair. When he returned empty-handed, an angry Soviet charged up to the village to conduct his own search. The irate Soviets then demanded a house-to-house search. Finley declined, claiming the guard had no such authority. With fuel running low, the lone helicopter still on US soil lifted off at nearly eight p.m., buzzed Little Diomede for one last look, and disappeared into the dark sky.

Buoyed by the date-line ceremony yet still facing six more weeks on the trail in Alaska, the exhausted expedition members tried to rest on the gym floor. The exception was Soviet co-leader Shparo, who had been talking by radio to his base in Lavrentiya. He received puzzling news: two members of the Soviet delegation were missing.

It was nearly midnight when Shparo summoned Schurke and Brelsford. Schurke described him looking "more gaunt and weary than I'd ever seen him." Shparo had cashed in lots of chits for the expedition. Now he faced heat for the embarrassment of two high-profile defections from his own country.

Schurke and Brelsford discussed a late-night search of Little Diomede to find the missing Soviets. But they agreed to check first with Colonel Wortman, the ranking American official in the village. Awoken in the armory at two thirty a.m., Wortman played dumb and agreed to join the search in the morning.

Four hours later, Wortman came clean with the expedition leaders, telling them of the defection the previous day in the middle of the crossing ceremony. The INS soon issued a press release confirming the defections. The news was reported worldwide. "Soviets defect at border rite: timing was embarrassing," the *Anchorage Times's* headline blared.

Among Alaska citizen-diplomats urging better relations with the Soviet Union, reaction to the defections ranged from disappointment to outrage. One of the Ice Curtain–melting pioneers, Dr. Ted Mala, announced that he regretted the act and said it couldn't have come at a worse time.

General Schaeffer, the state's top military official and a Northwest Alaska Native, said, "The governor is trying to get along better with the Soviets and here comes a couple of people who are basically messing up the operation."

Nome Nugget reporter Sandra Medearis speculated about the reaction. "Unanswered is whether the defection will be a setback to warming and thawing relations between the cold and remote regions of Alaska and Chukotka, separated by the Iron Curtain since 1948," she wrote.

While public reaction to the asylum-seekers was cool, those stuck on Little Diomede with the defectors were steaming.

"It was such an ironic event to occur at this party over renewed Alaska-Soviet relationships. They really did rain on our parade in a big way," Schurke said. "I was deeply angry about it and took both those gentlemen to task in a big way, blew up at them in the little school complex in Little Diomede where we were all hanging out."

The continuing blizzard meant that the defectors, expedition members, and guardsmen were all trapped together for two more days on a tiny rock island in the frozen Bering Sea. The Soviet team members wondered aloud if the defectors had been bribed by the Americans to commit such a high-profile act as part of a pro-democracy demonstration or were being held against their will. Some news reports mistakenly depicted the defectors as Soviet members of the expedition. Soviet skier Sasha Belyaev feared he and his countrymen would be recalled to the Soviet Union, never to step foot in Alaska again. Other conspiracy buffs speculated that the defectors might be KGB agents trying to infiltrate US intelligence.

From Big Diomede, Soviet border guards demanded that their US counterparts grant them an audience with the defectors. The day after the defection, Wortman and Finley set up an interview by radio with the pair for Soviet border guards on Big Diomede. Tkachenko delivered "a well-rehearsed rap" about Soviet repression at home and abroad, and it became clear that the two weren't changing their minds.

Tempers began to cool as the expedition plotted how to cross the twenty-two miles to mainland Alaska while the guardsmen arranged transportation to get the defectors to Anchorage. Facing broken ice that prevented either a boat or a ski crossing, the expedition decided to load themselves, their gear, and their dogs on a Bering Air Beech aircraft for a hop to the village of Wales, on Alaska's northwest coast.

Before the flight, some of the expedition members made a final visit to Big Diomede to retrieve gear. On their return they could see in the distance what looked like an air show near Little Diomede, with three helicopters and two airplanes readying for takeoff. A contingent of uniformed guardsmen were escorting two men in plainclothes across the icy landing strip. A tall black fur hat gave away Tkachenko. The defectors were headed to freedom.

Once they were on the Alaska mainland, weather continued to dictate the expedition's schedule. Melting snow and open rivers forced them to cut the trip short. Instead of slogging all the way to Kotzebue, the team skied an additional eighty miles to Nome, and from there Alaska Airlines airlifted them to Kotzebue for a final celebration. The Soviets had approved two Aeroflot planes to carry seventy-six passengers from Chukotka villages to visit Kotzebue for six hours, the same amount of time Alaska Airlines was allotted in Anadyr three months earlier.

Political leaders, including Governor Cowper, sent congratulatory messages that were read to the hundreds jammed into the Kotzebue high school gym on May 10. Alaska Native leader Willie Hensley, who had visited the Soviet Far East ten months earlier on the Friendship Flight, read a telegram from Washington, DC:

> Crossing more than one thousand miles and the treacherous waters of the Bering Strait, your journey has been a remarkable demonstration of human strength and stamina. But more important, it has reminded us of the close ties which unite the Eskimo peoples on both sides of the Strait. You can be proud of your role in helping to strengthen those ties. In their official orders dated January 2, 1719, the Russian explorers Fedor Luzhin and Ivan Evreinov were told to answer the question "Are America and Asia joined?" Thanks to your efforts, this 270-year-old question can be answered "yes." May God bless you always.
>
> —President George H. W. Bush

After celebrating the end of the expedition, members jetted across the United States on a publicity tour from Anchorage to New York City with stops in Seattle, Minneapolis, and Duluth. The Soviets returned home as heroes. The Soviet government had hyped the expedition nationwide to underscore Gorbachev's new openness policies. It produced a commemorative postage stamp, banners, and two documentary films about the expedition. A bronze bust of Paul Schurke was cast for display in a Moscow art museum.

During a Soviet speaking tour, Schurke recalls visiting a Kiev aircraft plant where hundreds of assembly workers welcomed expedition members like rock stars. "As the airplane factory workers were fighting their way up to the stage to get signatures from our team members, I realized how effectively this Soviet PR machine played this thing up over there—and put a smiley face on their whole regime," Schurke said.

IN THE IMMEDIATE aftermath of the expedition, defectors Tkachenko and Genkin were processed into the United States by Anchorage INS officials, one of whom invited the pair to his home for a pizza dinner. Two months later, in a column for the *Anchorage Daily News*, Tkachenko described riding a bicycle through Anchorage neighborhoods where he was struck by the American flags waving from front porches.

"Speaking with the local people, you could hardly miss their feeling of pride for their country that gave them opportunities for advancing in anything they wish," he wrote.

Before the defectors left Alaska, several of the national guardsmen joined the pair for lunch to reminisce about their adventure together on Little Diomede. Captain Finley still treasures his *Anchorage Daily News* account of the incident, autographed by Tkachenko. At Colonel Wortman's recommendation, the guardsmen received commendations for their actions those four days on Little Diomede. The US Army interpreter assigned to the guard returned home with a treasure. He traded his *Playboy* for a Beatles album released only in the Soviet Union.

A year later, in summer 1990, Mikhail Gorbachev traveled to the United States for his second summit with President Bush, focused on the reunification of Germany. With the Soviet economy in decline and control over its Eastern

European satellites quickly eroding, Gorbachev secured an American economic-aid package and met US business leaders to encourage investment in the Soviet Union.

En route to California for a reunion with his old nemesis, Ronald Reagan, Gorbachev made a seven-hour stop in the American heartland in Minneapolis on June 3. Among those he sought out for a face-to-face meeting was Paul Schurke and his Soviet expedition co-leader, Dmitry Shparo, who flew in from Moscow. Schurke, who had learned elementary Russian on the expedition, was advised in advance that he'd have more time with the Soviet leader if he spoke in Russian. So he wrote out his remarks and Shparo helped him translate and practice them.

For the meeting with the Soviet leader, the duo was ushered into Minneapolis's Radisson Hotel ballroom, a large media scrum covering every word. After a gift exchange, Shparo spoke first and then turned to a nervous Schurke.

"When I launched into my Russian pitch, which I had rehearsed several times, I lost control of my monologue pretty quickly," Schurke recalled. "Then I had an odd and unpredictable response. Instead of just shutting down and reverting to English, I went into a nonsensical rant in completely unintelligible Russian. My gibberish got faster and louder when I noticed the president's face changed from a warm smile to a rather quizzical look.

"And then he did a beautiful thing. He very discreetly reached over ever so slightly and tugged the sleeve of my suit jacket and said to me in a voice low enough so the press corps didn't hear, 'If you can cross the Bering Strait in the wintertime during the Cold War, then you can speak to me in Russian. Now, Paul, slow down and start over.'"

Governor Cowper's 1989 Far East trade mission visits the Soviet border guard station on Big Diomede Island. The tiny outpost housed about seventy guardsmen, who watched and listened to Alaska from the far tip of the rocky cliff. PHOTO BY BRUCE MELZER

From Uelen to Vladivostok

Glasnost and geography are making the Bering Sea a well-traveled route rather than a barrier between the Soviet Far East and Alaska.

—ASSOCIATED PRESS, AUGUST 29, 1989

T HE LITTLE DIOMEDE defections sent shivers into advocates on both sides of the Bering Strait, who feared the high-profile incident might refreeze the Ice Curtain. But the momentum behind Alaska-Soviet citizen diplomacy was too strong, producing even more thawing in 1989 as the pace of activity accelerated.

The State of Alaska sought to bring order to the increasing flow of traffic between Alaska and the Soviet Far East by laying a foundation for permanent institutions to facilitate cross-border exchanges. Governor Cowper undertook the first extended tour of the Soviet Far East by a state chief executive, making good on a trip he had planned nearly a year earlier but delayed because of his wife's health.

In August 1989, the governor embarked on a twelve-day, 6,800-mile "trade and friendship mission." The ambitious trip included stops in some of the Soviet Union's most remote northeastern outposts and in each of the three principal Far East territories with budding relations with Alaska: Magadan and Chukotka, Khabarovsk, and the Primorskii region around Vladivostok.

In addition to Cowper and the first lady, administration officials included General Schaeffer and Ginna Brelsford, who had skied in the Bering Bridge

Expedition six months earlier. Cowper's interpreter was University of Alaska language instructor John Tichotsky, who had honed his knowledge of street Russian as a Bering Sea Soviet fish processor. Tichotsky had been at Cowper's side for most of his interactions with Soviet officials and evolved into an advisor on Soviet issues. A Tichotsky colleague and Alaska newcomer, Andrew Crow, helped the media with translation services.

The governor's office photographer and videographer, Marc Olson, went along to document the trip. I was there as Cowper's press secretary to work with the four Alaska journalists who joined us: AP bureau chief Dean Fosdick; KSKA public radio news director Bruce Melzer; Dan Grubb, assistant news director for Anchorage's ABC affiliate; and the station's videographer, Eric Sowl.

The Soviets treated the Alaskans as the first order of VIPs, making available Aeroflot helicopters and airplanes and accommodations usually reserved for high-ranking Communist Party members. We were welcomed to remote villages by flag-waving schoolchildren and sped through cities in motorcades of black limousines, American flags flapping from the fenders. While local Soviet stores were largely devoid of food, we were the overfed recipients of frequent multicourse meals of caviar, freshly baked black bread, Siberian dumplings, and endless toasts with local beer, vodka, and cognac.

The trip began in Provideniya, where ten months earlier on the Friendship Flight, Governor Cowper, first lady Michael Cowper, and I first stepped on Soviet soil. This time the Alaska National Guard deposited us in a US military Twin Otter, an indication of how open the Soviets had become so quickly to renewed relations with Alaska.

Provideniya was founded on the promise of the Northeast Passage or Northern Sea Route. Arctic visionaries had long dreamed of a shorter, more economic shipping route between Europe and the Pacific with vessels plying the arctic waters along the Soviet Union's northern coast. For decades, the route was passable only during a few summer months. But as global warming began melting increasing amounts of arctic ice in the 1990s, the route remained open longer.

Located close to the traditional southern limit of winter ice, Provideniya served as a coal and freshwater depot for northern shipping. The Soviet central government approved it as a settlement in 1946, just two years before the Soviet and US governments closed the Bering Strait to human interaction. By the mid-1980s, Provideniya's population had grown to nearly 5,400, with its port visited annually by about five hundred ships, including icebreakers and nuclear-powered freighters. Despite average winter temperatures well below freezing, officials kept the port open year-round.

In contrast to remote Alaska villages dependent on regular barge and air shipments of basic products, Provideniya was relatively self-sufficient. Residents lived in apartment buildings constructed of locally produced concrete. Central heat was generated from a coal-fired plant, which bellowed black smoke into the cold air. Beef, pork, dairy products, and vegetables were produced at local farms with patriotic names such as "Lighthouse of the North" and "Dawn of Communism."

Manufacturing employed about 220 local residents at a meat and milk company, leather factory, and print shop. Construction employed another three hundred, both in Provideniya and surrounding villages. Workers were attracted to the area for salaries up to three times higher than in the nation's heartland.

Provideniya caught the eye of Alaskans eager for renewed relations for two reasons: geography and the persistence of its mayor. The community boasted the largest port and airport closest to Alaska, so it could accommodate traffic from Alaskans. Its leader, Oleg Kulinkin, rivaled any American chamber of commerce booster with his enthusiasm. The youthful Georgian emigrated to the opposite end of his country, where he became chairman of Provideniya's Executive Committee of People's Deputies, effectively its mayor. He began pitching Nome on ideas for tourism and business as early as 1987.

"It's an attractive place for tourism. Just take a look at the region, at the tundra," Kulinkin bubbled to an American reporter in 1988. "You'll be convinced yourself. It's a beautiful place. How much nature. It's better to see one time than to hear about five hundred times."

Kulinkin's description may not have been the one that came to mind when we landed there in chilly fog and drizzle on August 31, 1989. But what the community lacked in polish its residents made up in hospitality. We were housed in the best local facilities and treated to steaming *pelmeni*—Siberian dumplings—washed down with locally brewed beer. To warm applause before hundreds of Provideniya residents, Governor Cowper was named an honorary citizen, a Miss America–type sash pinned across his chest.

Our Soviet hosts quickly loaded us into six military jeeps for what I remember as the bumpiest ride of my life across a barren, rocky landscape that looked more like Afghanistan. Our destination was Novoye, or New Chaplino, a Native village about twenty-five miles northeast of Provideniya. We had been scheduled to travel in Aeroflot helicopters, but low ceilings forced us into a ninety-minute crawl across a dirt trail. In the village's overheated community center, we endured hours of eating, friendship speeches, and Chukchi Native dancing to the beat of sealskin drums.

Left unsaid at the time was the plight of Chaplino residents, a tragic saga in the Soviet Union's treatment of its Native people. In 1958, in response to reports that its original coastal village site on an ocean spit was eroding, about 550 Chaplino residents and those from several other coastal villages were forced to uproot to a new location. Without consulting village elders, Soviet officials selected the current village site on the coast of Tkachen Bay. It turns out the bay is frozen at least eight months a year, so harvesting walrus, on which village residents depended, required a burdensome ten-mile one-way trip to open ocean. Within a decade, most of the elder hunters reportedly had died of "depression."

The next day, we made one of the more memorable visits of my dozen trips to the Soviet Union, to the border guard station on Big Diomede. After crossing sixty miles of ocean teeming with whales on a flight from the coastal village of Lavrentiya, our orange Aeroflot helicopter set down on this long-restricted, eleven-square-mile rocky outpost in the Bering Sea. Since the Cold War, average Soviet citizens—including Chukotka Natives—had been prohibited from the island.

FOR CENTURIES, THE indigenous peoples of this part of the world subsisted on whale, walrus, and seabirds in permanent villages on both Big Diomede and Little Diomede. Following the 1867 US purchase of Alaska, mapmakers placed Big Diomede in Asia and its smaller cousin in North America, with just 2.5 miles separating them. The 1880 US census counted forty residents on Little Diomede, which conservationist John Muir eight years later described as "the dreariest town I ever beheld."

A 1928 American Museum of Natural History expedition found residents of both islands "one of the most hardy and proud of all the Arctic peoples. Their everlasting struggle to survive has given them incredible stamina, just as their isolation has steeped them in ignorance and superstition."

As World War II US-Soviet tensions in the strait heightened, Little Diomede residents grew increasingly concerned about neighboring villagers on Soviet Big Diomede. According to minutes of a 1940 Little Diomede city council meeting, Alaska hunters encountered desperate conditions across the date line.

"The Big Diomeders said that they had hardly any meat, no kerosene, no gas, and no blubber," reported council secretary Roger Menadelook. The council agreed to assist the Soviet Natives, "knowing that if one of us is in a tough spot, the other would be ready to help, for after all, we are natives and are just handicapped by the present existing imaginary boundary lines set up by our big bosses, the whites."

After the 1948 imposition of an Ice Curtain, Big Diomede became the Soviet's first line of defense against incursions across the farthest northeast border with the United States. But that didn't prevent a series of odd adventurers from attempting to cross during the next forty years, most of them snatched up by Soviet border guards. Just two years before our visit, a San Franciscan named John Weymouth knocked around western Alaska villages before venturing to Big Diomede. Dubbed "The Wanderer" by the media, he was detained for two weeks and then sent home courtesy of an airplane ticket purchased by his mother.

In January 1987, another Californian, Castro Lazaro, became "the first American of the season" to cross the pack ice to Big Diomede. Out crabbing with Alaska Natives from Little Diomede, Lazaro suddenly dropped his gear and sprinted across the ice for Big Diomede. He made it about halfway up the island's shoreline cliffs when he got stuck. The Alaskans watched through binoculars as Soviet border guards and their dogs slowly made their way to Lazaro until darkness obscured the view. He was later returned.

Adventure-seeking Americans were not the only traffic to draw the attention of those living on remote islands in the Bering Strait. The Alaska Army National Guard maintained a thick file of sightings of Soviet aircraft, ships, military equipment, unusual dogs, and even UFOs. In February 1987, a Gambell woman was walking her daughter to school when a "very large, dome-shaped flying craft" with bright blue lights appeared on the western horizon. A sketch that accompanied a written report of the incident shows a jellyfishlike object hovering in the arctic sky.

Our reception on Big Diomede was less mysterious. Despite the intrigue surrounding this remote outpost, the approximately seventy border guardsmen warmly welcomed us. They showed off their quarters with neatly made bunks, a tiny museum dubbed the "room of international friendship," and a small mess hall with one wall painted green to resemble a garden. The young soldiers happily posed in their camo uniforms and laughed at our attempts at pleasantries in Russian.

Devices for monitoring Alaska were off-limits, although numerous antennas were in clear view, perched on a rocky outpost aimed across the date line. Rows of light automatic weapons and packs equipped with helmets and shovels were locked at the ready in a metal cage. In case they needed to identify them coming across the Bering Sea, posters of American, French, and British tanks and missiles lined the walls.

With the melting Ice Curtain, the post was getting more visitors than usual, including Soviet dignitaries and members of the Bering Bridge Expedition six months earlier. Yet there was no display to document social calls by the occasional adventure-seeking American. The outpost's commander, Lt. Col. Vladimir Starukov, told us his soldiers followed a standard procedure with such visitors. "We send them back," he said with a laugh.

Over the next two days, we focused on the modern lives of Soviet Natives during visits to the communities of Lavrentiya, Uelen, and Anadyr. For centuries, the majority of indigenous peoples of the northeast Russian mainland were Chukchi, who numbered about fourteen thousand in the 1980s. Mostly marine mammal hunters and nomadic reindeer herders, the Chukchi roamed over a massive area of the Chukotka Peninsula. Smaller groups of Natives included Yupik Eskimos who lived in the area around Providemiya and Aleuts who lived in the more southern Commander Islands off the Kamchatka coast.

The 1917 Bolshevik Revolution slowly changed the long-practiced subsistence way of life for many indigenous peoples. The new communist rulers ordered many villages abandoned and others consolidated, and forced the acculturation of Chukchi and Yupik people into the same villages.

Lavrentiya was one of these. Its name came from its location on Lavrentiya Bay, named by British explorer Capt. James Cook, who arrived in the bay on the feast day of St. Lawrence in 1778. The village was established by the Soviets in 1928 and became the site of a *Kul'tbaza*, or "cultural base," to ensure the ideological education of local Native peoples.

When we visited, the population was about three thousand. Our local host was an energetic Native leader, Yuri Tototto, who proudly showed off Native dancing and sports in the local school and traditional ivory carving. Tototto was a strong advocate of visa-free travel by his Native constituents and pitched us on his proposal for joint tourism opportunities with Kotzebue, a Northwest Alaska Native regional center.

We also made a quick helicopter stop in Uelen, the Soviet Union's eastern-most community of about seven hundred. Six months earlier it was the jumping-off point for the Bering Bridge Expedition before its harrowing boat trip across the Bering Sea to Alaska.

We Alaskans, impressed by Native ivory carving on our side of the border, were amazed at the intricate work we saw in Uelen. The village was famous for its masterpieces carved from walrus ivory, whale bone, and reindeer antler. The works of Chukotka artists from Uelen have won top awards in museums around the world. Although tempted to contribute to the local economy by buying some of the carvings, we knew US Customs would seize them on our return to Alaska.

On our way down the Soviet coast in an Aeroflot cargo plane, we over-nighted in the administrative center of the Chukotka region, Anadyr. Situated near a nineteenth-century trading post established by the brother of Russian-American Gov. Alexander Baranov, Anadyr was a key transit point for American Lend-Lease aircraft headed to the eastern front in World War II.

Deteriorating and weather-beaten during our visit, the city would undergo a dramatic revival a decade later when one of Russia's richest oligarchs was elected governor of the region. An oil and aluminum billionaire and confidant of Boris Yeltsin, Roman Abramovich was elected Chukotka's governor in 2000. He poured billions of his and his company's rubles into the region before stepping down eight years later to move to London.

After our week in remote northern communities, our next stop—Magadan—felt like a major metropolis. Established near the rich mineral potential of the Kolyma region, the city played a key role in the Soviet Union's dark past—a transit point for political prisoners destined for gulags during the Stalin era. In the 1930s and 1940s, prison laborers worked the area's gold, silver, tin, and tungsten mines.

After Stalin's death, high wages in the mining industry attracted workers to the region, pushing Magadan's population to more than half a million in the 1980s. Rather than hide from that shameful past, city leaders surprised us with a visit to the local gulag museum. It displayed gut-wrenching photographs of the prison camps and profiles of the many promising Soviet citizens who were worked to death in them.

Chairman Kobets jammed the four days with meetings to explore joint ventures in trade, tourism, fisheries, reindeer processing, mining, telecommunications, transportation, health, and education as well as citizen exchanges of artists, students, teachers, and sports teams. He and Cowper signed an agreement establishing an Alaska-Magadan Commission to carry out those activities. They again endorsed visa-free travel for Alaska and Soviet Natives and set the stage for future university partnerships. Kobets also promised to send two plane-loads of Soviet officials to a Northern Regions Conference the Alaska governor was hosting in September 1990.

Tipped off to Kobets's passion for fishing, Cowper presented the Soviet leader with an Alaska fishing pole, reel, and handful of artificial lures. Eager to try them out, Kobets loaded the Alaskans onto an Aeroflot helicopter and headed for a rustic fishing cabin outside Magadan. In a rapidly moving river, we hooked dozens of arctic grayling, keeping only a handful for our lunch of grilled fillets and fish-head soup.

On one cast, Kobets snagged his new Pixie lure on a submerged rock. The Alaska reaction would have been to cut the line and try again. Before we could get that advice translated, one of Kobets's aides stripped to his underwear, dove into the ice-cold river, and dislodged the lure. I warned Cowper not to expect the same service from his staff.

The Magadan visit solidified one of the most durable and productive relations between Alaska and any Soviet Far East community. Each day there Cowper was featured on the front pages of local newspapers. Alaska Airlines selected Magadan as one of its inaugural destination cities when it initiated regular service from Alaska in summer 1991. Magadan universities and the University of Alaska established long-standing relations that resulted in scores of Russian students attending UA Anchorage. Anchorage and Magadan were some of the first cities to adopt sister-city relations. Nearly a decade later, when the Russian economy collapsed, Anchorage residents donated tons of food and clothing to their needy neighbors on the Sea of Okhotsk.

Inspired by his grandfather's *National Geographic* magazines as a ten-year-old in North Carolina, Cowper had long been fixated on exploring the mysterious Amur River. Called the Black Dragon River by the Chinese, it serves as the eastern border between China and the Soviet Union. With headwaters in Mongolia, the Amur is the longest river in the Russian Far East, creating an 1,800-mile valley rich with giant fish and exotic wildlife, including the rare black sable and endangered Siberian tiger.

The governor got his wish during our three days in Khabarovsk, the Soviet Far East's second-largest city and capital of a region about the size of California. Ceded by the Chinese to Russia in 1858, Khabarovsk was an attractive city with wide avenues and massive, well-preserved czarist-era buildings.

Cowper's Soviet counterpart, Chairman Daniluk, rolled out the red carpet for the visiting Alaskans. Separating government officials from the reporters, our hosts lodged us in a Soviet guesthouse used previously by Gorbachev and other top foreign officials. Our VIP treatment made us increasingly uncomfortable as we saw scores of shawl-covered elderly women lined up along the streets for a rare sale of fatty meat or watermelon.

"Joint venture" was the one phrase every Soviet official knew in perfect English. We had meeting after meeting with government officials and local "businessmen" seeking joint ventures in areas from wood and fish processing to aviation and marine shipping to hairstyling and shoe repair. Khabarovsk proposed sending to Alaska its chamber orchestra, art exhibitions, students, and teachers to visit Alaska's Native boarding school and exchanging every sports team imaginable.

We disrupted the carefully choreographed schedule when Cowper insisted on taking a peak at the Chinese border from the Amur. The Soviets quickly produced three high-speed military patrol boats for a frighteningly fast run upriver. Along the birch-treed banks, we spotted several multiple-story wooden viewing platforms, remnants of Sino-Soviet border conflicts in the late 1960s in which several dozen Soviet soldiers were killed. Our only incident was nearly swamping a small skiff from which two Chinese fishermen were pulling in nets by hand.

Our final stop was Vladivostok, the Soviet Union's "window to the Pacific," site of the country's largest eastern port and home to its Pacific naval fleet. The area had long been closed to Westerners. We were among the first Americans in years permitted to wander the huge harbor and photograph the dozens of war ships rusting in the port. During our visit, regional leaders expressed hope to transform the area from a strategic military location to an international shipping center. They took us to the nearby port of Nakhodka, recently deemed a foreign-trade zone offering special incentives to encourage international trade. Meetings with Soviet officials focused on joint ventures in fisheries, marine shipping, and trade in herbal medicines—the latter of specific interest to this region because of its proximity to Korea.

The most memorable aspect of the Vladivostok visit came after another interminable multicourse state dinner on the last evening. The Soviets hoped to impress by housing the trade mission at a health resort outside Vladivostok, the same compound where President Gerald Ford and General Secretary Leonid Brezhnev had met for an arms-control summit in 1974.

"Although the Soviets had labored for ten days to spruce up the place and apply a fresh coat of paint to the main building, it still looked like an abandoned YMCA camp in the Catskills," Ford wrote in his memoir.

I remember sitting on a Pacific beach under bright stars with three traveling companions. Nearby, a Trans-Siberian train rumbled to its final stop after leaving Moscow a week and nearly six thousand miles before. Though weary of travel frustration, we each had been permanently affected by the adventure. We began the journey uneasy about the country we were raised to fear and irritated by the government handlers assigned to monitor us everywhere. We ended it with an enduring affinity for this long-forbidden neighbor, appreciative of a people with whom we had far more in common than different.

Two years later, those memories were fresh when I was recruited to help lead a Juneau delegation to its sister city of Vladivostok. A few days before our departure, Alaska wildlife managers had taken in an orphaned bear cub and suggested it be presented as a friendship gift. When we removed it from a dog kennel for presentation to a Vladivostok city official before the assembled local media, the feisty cub nearly bit the official's thumb off. Despite that, sister-city relations between the two regions prospered for years.

After our trade mission with Cowper ended, the governor and first lady left us to return to Alaska through nearby Japan. With the reporters, I retraced our route 2,500 miles up the Soviet Far East coast to Magadan and then to Provideniya. There, our National Guard plane was a welcome sight for the short hop to Nome and back to Anchorage.

THE MAJOR CHALLENGE in those heady days was managing expectations and demands. In Alaska, the Cowper administration heard from scores of well-meaning groups and individuals pitching every conceivable idea for an exchange with their Soviet counterparts, from dogsled races to timber harvesting. Some were driven by US industries, such as oil and gas and mining, seeking new, less regulated opportunities in the Soviet Far East. Other Alaskans were motivated by the intrigue of the forbidden Soviet Union.

We met the same enthusiasm from the Soviets during the trade mission. In virtually every community we visited, conference rooms were filled with heads of government departments, institutes, and associations armed with specific proposals for exchanges with Alaskans. *Perestroika* had opened the floodgates. Gorbachev's efforts to reorganize government meant that Moscow planners no longer dictated every production quota for distant Far East enterprises. He gave local authorities more autonomy within their regions and allowed them to deal directly with foreign entities. At the same time, more accountability was demanded of local enterprises as subsidies from Moscow were reduced.

The handful of Alaska state officials assigned to handle Soviet relations in those early days were quickly overwhelmed. The Soviet Far East is two-thirds the size of the United States with a population of 7.7 million people in the 1980s. Alaska was home to just half a million, a population that was declining monthly as low world oil prices continued to batter the state's economy.

Our response to managing this cross-border enthusiasm was to create an Alaska-Soviet Working Group responsible for contact with all three Soviet Far East regions. Some regions preferred their own bilateral agreement with Alaska instead of participating with other Soviet regions. In some cases, we relented. For example, Cowper signed a "Statement of Cultural, Economic and Medical Cooperation" with the interior Far East Yakutia Republic in August 1990.

Cowper also sought to establish an Alaska–Soviet Far East Commission by state statute as a more permanent entity for helping field the many requests for joint business and cultural ventures. His proposal called for a seven-member commission appointed by the governor to coordinate exchanges, collect information about current developments, and accept federal and charitable grants.

Another intriguing proposal to advance Alaska-Soviet relations came from state Rep. Kay Brown, a former journalist and among the more thoughtful Alaska lawmakers. Brown called for a citizen-diplomacy program under which Alaskans could become citizen-diplomats, financing trips to Russia with their Permanent Fund dividend—the annual payment to Alaska residents from the state's oil wealth. Each citizen-diplomat was required to complete a five-hour course and host a Soviet diplomat in exchange.

"One of the things I like about this idea is that it gives people hope—a feeling they can make a difference, a tangible contribution to world peace," Brown wrote. However, the idea never gained traction.

Less than a year after solidifying regional ties across the Soviet Far East, Cowper took his Alaska-Soviet initiative to the highest levels in Moscow. Because of Alaska's groundbreaking activities across the Bering Strait, Cowper was invited in May 1990 to address the largest gathering of business leaders from the two countries, the US-USSR Trade and Economic Council. We coupled the visit with a daylong stop at an oil terminal in northern Scotland. After the *Exxon Valdez* oil spill the previous spring, we wanted to see the terminal's state-of-the-art spill-prevention technology.

I wrote Cowper's keynote speech during our long flight to Moscow. When I plugged the bulky laptop into an outlet in our Soviet hotel, the computer fizzled and ate my masterpiece. I stayed up all night reconstructing it for his delivery the next day.

To the one thousand business leaders, Cowper boasted of Alaska's breakthrough relations with its Soviet neighbors. He recounted the dramatic reunions between Native families during the Friendship Flight and said that Alaska's relationship transcends business.

"We are pursuing a multiplicity of activities with our neighbors to the west, with a growing sense that we have a special mission for which we are uniquely qualified, both geographically and historically," the governor said.

Successfully dealing with the Soviets, he advised, rested on four principles: business ethics, personal relationships built on trust, "mutual benefits," and patience and flexibility. At the closing banquet, Cowper's dinner seatmate was Yevgeny Primakov, one of Gorbachev's top Kremlin economic advisors who later became prime minister under Boris Yeltsin. Cowper still cherishes his banquet photo with Primakov and Gorbachev.

During the visit, Alaska became one of just four states to sign a cooperation agreement with the Russian Federation. It called for numerous exchanges of people and information in science, education, tourism, manufacturing, and the arts, with annual meetings in Moscow and Alaska. We also called on Gorbachev's spokesman, Gennadi Gerasimov, whom Cowper had hosted in the governor's mansion a year earlier and who had been so helpful in pushing Alaska-Soviet initiatives through the Kremlin.

In Leningrad, we were scheduled for a stop at the People's Deputies, effectively the city council of the Soviet Union's second-largest city. We arrived to find the deputies in session. After Cowper was introduced from the gallery, he was invited to address the lawmakers. He still considers that brief speech, from the dais of a historic gilded chamber to the assembled communist parliamentarians, one of the highlights of his time as governor.

Another was a discussion of opportunities in the Far North with Soviet arctic explorer Artur Chilingarov, a Hero of the Soviet Union. Slight, with a bushy gray beard and boundless energy, Chilingarov received international derision nearly two decades later when he piloted a submersible fourteen thousand feet below the North Pole and planted his nation's flag, proclaiming "the Arctic is Russian."

Cowper used his Moscow trip to recruit participants for the 1990 Northern Regions Conference. More than 550 participants from ten countries, including sixty Soviet officials, gathered in Anchorage in September. The conference built on a concept first proposed in 1971 by leaders in Hokkaido, Japan, that regional rather than national governments were best equipped to address common problems.

The conference began with a governors' summit that included nine Soviet governors or deputies and others from Japan, Greenland, Sweden, Canada, Denmark, Finland, Norway, China, and the United States. Presentations and discussion topics ranged from arctic security to circumpolar health. Senator Stevens, Governor Hickel, and Soviet explorer Chilingarov were among the keynote speakers.

The conference helped lead to the creation of a permanent organization of regional international leaders, the Northern Forum. The conference was Cowper's last engagement with Soviets as governor. He had announced in spring 1989 that he would not seek reelection.

Alaska visa-free commissioner Vera Metcalf of Nome participated in a Beringia Days conference in Anadyr, Russia, in 2009 with marine scientist Martin Robards of the Wildlife Conservation Society. The US National Park Service sponsored the conferences in Alaska and Chukotka to advance the shared Beringia heritage across the Bering Strait. COURTESY OF NPS/BERINGIA PROGRAM

13

Visa-Free Reunification

Many Native people in the region have family members who reside across the
international border, who they have not been able to visit since 1948 . . .
—ALASKA GOVERNOR STEVE COWPER AND
MAGADAN CHAIRMAN VYACHESLAV KOBETS, APRIL 23, 1989

R EUNITING NATIVE FAMILIES separated by the Cold War was always a chief goal of renewed relations across the strait. The 1988 Friendship Flight emotionally illustrated that urgency as aging Alaska and Russian Natives struggled to rekindle memories of contacts more than half a century earlier. A long succession of Alaskans and Soviets pushed to make that dream a reality, including Governors Cowper and Kobets during their 1989 telephonic protocol signing between Little Diomede and Nome.

The two proposed that Native visits should be permitted across the strait for up to ninety days, with advance notice by telex or radio not less than ten days before the departure date. They also called for creation of a border commission of Alaska and Chukotka officials "dedicated to discuss[ing] border problems and incidents related to the border between the two regions."

The American and Soviet national governments gave voice to such reunifications when Gorbachev and Reagan endorsed "increased people-to-people contacts between the native peoples of Alaska and the Soviet north" at their May 1988 Moscow summit.

Half a year later, in January 1989, George H. W. Bush took the presidential oath. Reagan's former vice president adopted the tough-on-the-Soviets stance of his predecessor. Facing the new president were two key bilateral issues: Reagan's Star Wars space-based defense system and sea-launched cruise missiles. It quickly fell to the top two foreign-affairs appointees from the United States and the Soviet Union to tackle those details in advance of a likely Bush-Gorbachev summit the following year.

Bush quickly appointed fellow Texan James A. Baker III, Reagan's former chief of staff and treasury secretary, as his secretary of state. Gorbachev had surprised Kremlin watchers with his 1985 appointment of Georgian Eduard Shevardnadze as Soviet foreign minister. A dyed-in-the-wool Communist Party member, Shevardnadze evolved into one of Gorbachev's closest advisors and most outspoken *glasnost* proponents.

For their September 1989 ministerial meeting, Baker and Shevardnadze settled on an inspiring venue—a spacious lodge outside Jackson Hole, Wyoming, with unmatched views of the Grand Teton mountains. Although dubbed a "ranch," it had served primarily as a high-end vacation destination for wealthy East Coast families since the 1930s.

"The Baker-Shevardnadze meeting was marked by trout fishing, moose ogling, and good fellowship," reported the *New York Times*.

The meeting also produced the first agreement governing contact between Alaska and Soviet Far East Natives since J. Edgar Hoover froze the border in 1948. Signed on September 23, 1989, the five-page agreement defined which Native "relatives" qualified to participate, specified by geographic region.

In Alaska, those regions included the Nome, Seward Peninsula, and Kotzebue areas closest to the Soviet Union. The Soviets included the Chukotka region north and east of Anadyr, including the coastal communities closest to Alaska. Those permitted to travel without obtaining a visa included "blood relatives, fellow clan or tribe members, or native inhabitants who share a linguistic or cultural heritage with native inhabitants of the other territory."

The agreement endorsed the Cowper-Kobets border commission idea, specifying that three commissioners were to be appointed by each side to oversee the exchanges, with a chief commissioner in each country. To cross the strait, Native visitors were required to have a passport, secure a written invitation at least ten days before the proposed visit, and disclose details about where they planned to go. Visits could last up to ninety days. Travelers were prohibited from selling goods acquired in the country they visited.

Alaska Iñupiaq leader Charlie Johnson was selected Alaska's first chief commissioner. A gregarious man with a quick smile under his walruslike moustache, Johnson was born just outside Nome in White Mountain. A former chairman of the Alaska Federation of Natives, the state's largest Native organization, he had held numerous science-related posts during his career.

Johnson and his Soviet counterparts spent the following decade attempting to implement the visa-free agreement through unreliable telex and fax communications as the pace of Natives crossing the strait increased. In a 2000 memo to then–deputy secretary of state Strobe Talbott, who visited Alaska later that year, Johnson pronounced the visa-free program a success. He reported that visits to Alaska by Chukotka Natives had reached a peak of 250 in 1995 but then dropped to 172 four years later because of challenging economic conditions in the Russian Far East.

Based on those successes—and in response to pleas from Natives from other regions of both countries—Johnson and several Native groups lobbied to expand the program. Alaska Natives generally could afford to travel to Russia and were motivated to assist Russian villages that were in steep decline.

"The collapse of the Russian economy has made life difficult for Russian indigenous peoples," Johnson wrote.

The Aleutian Pribilof Islands Association portrayed especially grim conditions for the eight hundred Aleuts registered as living in Russia. Enslaved and transplanted from Alaska during the nineteenth-century fur trade, the Russian Aleuts were among the last speakers of the western Aleut dialect.

"Supply lines to the Commander Islands have been almost completely severed since the economic downturn in Russia," reported the association. "Russian Aleuts are presently without fuel, many basic provisions, and medicine."

Inside the US State Department in Washington, DC, discussions had been under way on how to streamline the program. But progress bogged down in bureaucratic jurisdictional issues, as detailed in an internal 1997 agency memo that raised numerous questions: What's the definition of a "native person"? How are members appointed to a border commission; how can they be replaced or terminated; and how is the commission funded? What are the ports of entry on the US side? Nome and Gambell, so close to the Soviet Union, seemed obvious but what about Unalaska and Barrow? Is it a conflict of interest for border commissioners to also serve as immigration or customs inspectors?

In 2000, the United States proposed expanding the range of territory covered by the original agreement. In Alaska, the Aleutian Islands and North Slope Borough were proposed for addition, plus Anchorage and Fairbanks for special meetings such as the annual Alaska Federation of Natives convention and Alaska Inter-Tribal Council. In Russia, new territories included more of the eastern part of the Anadyr region, the Kamchatka Peninsula, and the Commander Islands off Kamchatka's east coast. The seventeen-island Commander group remains a hallowed place for Russians and Alaskans alike as the place where Vitus Bering died in 1741.

Between 1993 and 2015, nearly 4,800 Soviet and Russian Natives visited Alaska under the US-Russia visa-free program, according to statistics gathered by the US Customs and Border Protection. A high of 1,008 visits were recorded in 2013.

As traffic across the strait by citizen-diplomats increased, the US and Soviet governments also embarked on an effort to recognize and preserve the region's common heritage. The idea was an international park spanning the Bering Strait and extending far into the landmasses of Alaska and Chukotka.

Conservative Alaska politicians and resource-development promoters who came to abhor the idea may be surprised to know it originated with Richard Nixon, one of America's most rabid anti-communists. In his 1950 US Senate race in California, the future president helped launch his political career by branding his opponent, Democrat Helen Douglas, "pink right down to her underwear." It worked in that Cold War "red scare" era, propelling Nixon to a 60 percent election victory. Facing down communists helped set the stage for Nixon's diplomatic breakthroughs with the Soviet Union and China during his presidency.

Nearly a quarter of a century after his Senate election, President Nixon traveled to Moscow to sign an environmental-protection agreement between the United States and the Soviet Union. The 1972 Agreement on Cooperation in the Field of Environmental Protection created a framework "aimed at solving the most important aspects of the problems of the environment and will be devoted to working out measures to prevent pollution, to study pollution and its effect on the environment, and to develop the basis for controlling the impact of human activities on nature." The agreement reached by Nixon and General

Secretary Leonid Brezhnev specifically called for protection of "arctic and subarctic ecological systems."

In 1986, US and Soviet conservation agencies finally acted to implement that agreement by setting up a working group to address "conservation and management of natural and cultural heritage." One of the goals was conservation of Beringia, defined as "that expanse of Siberia, Alaska, and Canada once connected by a bridge of land" spanning the Bering Strait.

Three years later, a joint American-Soviet team of planners and scientists spent ten days in Chukotka and eight in Northwest Alaska to explore the common heritage of Beringia. That heritage "covers the natural resources, the migration of man over the land bridge and archeological evidence of that crossing, the influences of more recent developments and the common traditions that endure—language, arts, traditions, and the subsistence use of resources."

The joint group produced a Beringian Heritage Reconnaissance Study and recommended the creation of an international Beringia Park. Presidents Bush and Gorbachev endorsed it at their June 1990 summit in Washington, DC.

Pushed by international conservation groups, preservation of the Beringia region started gaining support. More than one hundred countries, including the United States and the USSR, signed a 1988 resolution calling for designation of the region as a World Heritage Site. The National Audubon Society launched a Beringia Conservation Program that included initiatives ranging from a children's environmental-protection fund to nature-oriented tourism.

In the Alaska State House, Democrats introduced a 1989 resolution supporting creation of a Beringia International Biosphere Reserve. In the US Senate, moderate Sen. Claiborne Pell, a Democrat from Rhode Island, introduced federal legislation in 1991 to establish a Beringian Park. It noticeably lacked the support of Alaska's Republican congressional delegation.

The idea of such an international park quickly ran into a buzz saw of opposition, largely over fears of restrictions on resource development such as mining. Ironically, many of the Native village councils in the affected region, which so strongly advocated closer ties across the strait, opposed the idea. One was Kawerak, Inc., a Native nonprofit corporation established in 1973 to provide educational, health, cultural, and economic development services in the Nome region. According to retired Kawerak president Loretta Bullard, the National Park

Service (NPS) and its allies moved too quickly to try to establish a park without first consulting the affected locals.

At the urging of twenty-two Native groups from the Kawerak area, the AFN, the state's largest Native organization, adopted an anti-park resolution at its 1991 convention. In part, it said, "We have never seen a project where so little effort has been made to solicit Native participation and decision-making into the project . . . Alaska Native people are fed up with outside agencies and conservation groups who purport to have our best interests in mind, hoist their own agendas and regulations on our way of life."

Bob Gerhard, the park service official who ran the Beringia program for thirteen years, agreed the situation could have been better managed. "Everybody thought this was such a good idea that the park service came on a little strong and went to villages in Northwest Alaska and ran into opposition they didn't quite expect," Gerhard said. "Designation of an international park is largely symbolic; it's just a matter of two countries saying they're going to cooperate. But that didn't stop a lot of people [from] saying [that] we're giving up sovereignty, the United Nations is going to come in to take over, and black helicopters are going to come over the horizon."

Conservative members of Congress, including Rep. Don Young of Alaska, attempted to derail the park planning with a proposed 1997 law, the American Land Sovereignty Protection Act. It required explicit congressional approval before any US land was subject to "restricted use" under an international agreement. The Alaska House jumped on the bandwagon by overwhelmingly adopting a resolution in 1999 objecting to the designation of World Heritage Sites or Biosphere Reserves in Alaska "without the specific consent of the Alaska State Legislature."

As part of its Beringia effort, the park service also funded millions of dollars in scientific studies, many of which were awarded to NPS or non-Alaska research entities, which further offended some Native groups.

In the face of such opposition, the park service changed strategies. Instead of pushing for a park designation, it broadened its grant program to encourage cultural exchanges designed to achieve the same goals of the park—improved relations across the strait. The projects were overseen by a five-member Beringia Panel including Native representatives from Northwest Alaska. Between 1991 and 2015, more than $10 million worth of projects were funded, ranging from traditional knowledge of walrus to research into the Wolf Dance on a no-longer-inhabited Alaska island.

The park service also hosted a series of Beringia Days conferences where American and Russian researchers and Native representatives met to discuss the shared Beringia heritage. Numerous Russian organizations, including the far eastern branch of the Russian Academy of Sciences, and the Chukotka government supported the effort through funding and participation in projects and meetings.

The US and Russian governments reiterated their support for Beringia twice during the Obama administration. In May 2011, President Obama and Russian President Dmitri Medvedev declared their intentions to "deepen cooperation in the cross-boundary Bering Strait region." A year later in Vladivostok, Secretary of State Hillary Clinton and Russian Foreign Minister Sergey Lavrov agreed to pursue a "Transboundary Area of Beringian specially protected natural territory in consultation with local and tribal governments."

In Russia, support for Beringia appeared to be enthusiastic. In 1993, the Chukotka government established a regional park. Ten years later, the national government established a series of five federal parks in Chukotka, which, combined, constituted about half the size of the regional park.

The Beringia project continues to attract detractors in the United States. Republican US Sen. Rand Paul included it in his occasional "Waste Report," a list of government spending the Kentucky Republican considers wasteful. Paul targeted a $150,000, three-year NPS grant to explore what the grant application termed supernatural occurrences "such as little people, unexplained lights, sea monsters, invisible sea birds, animals with transformative powers, a variety of other non-human persons, landscape features with special powers, and other similar phenomena as defined by participants." The grant was awarded to Kawerak, Inc., which said it would collaborate with most of the region's tribes.

In 2014, Russia's incursion into Ukraine threatened the Beringia grant program as the US State Department opposed spending federal dollars within Russia. But joint projects continued, including one of the largest reunifications in memory when thirty-one Chukotka Natives traveled to St. Lawrence Island for two weeks of cultural celebrations in summer 2016.

Alaska Airlines advertised "Golden Samovar Service" with its charter service to the Soviet Union beginning in 1970. "Alaska's colorful Russian heritage comes alive on Alaska Airlines!," the company boasted. COURTESY OF
ALASKA AIRLINES

14

Golden Samovar Service

This year, 4,000 nonconformists will be sent to Siberia.

—ALASKA AIRLINES NEWSPAPER ADVERTISEMENT
PROMOTING ITS FLIGHTS TO RUSSIA, 1990

L OVELY STEWARDESSES IN elegantly long, black wool maxi-coats welcome you aboard," promised the brochure featuring a broadly grinning male customer reclining in an airplane seat surrounded by eager female flight attendants in fake bearskin hats. "Authentic Russian *balalaika* melodies set the mood as the hostesses in tailored Cossack tunics serve a special beverage from the Samovar— the 'Bolshoi Golden Troika' specially created by the House of Seagram."

That was Alaska Airlines' pitch in 1970, when the scrappy Seattle-based regional carrier surprised the airline industry by initiating air service to the mysterious Soviet Union. Although it barely broke even operating fewer than three dozen charter flights over three years, the adventure helped inspire a new generation of Alaska Air executives to connect Alaska with the Soviet Union two decades later.

The airline's first foray across the international date line was the initiative of a hard-charging, hard-drinking decorated combat pilot. Charles F. Willis Jr. enlisted in the Navy in 1940 and was stationed at a Hawaii airbase on that 1941 "day of infamy" when Japanese fighters headed for Pearl Harbor passed overhead. Willis dodged Japanese bullets running to his airplane and survived to fly 250 combat missions in the Pacific and thirty-five in Europe. Using saved-up military pay after the war, he founded an air-freight business and grew it to an international shipping company.

In 1957, Willis was selected president of Alaska Airlines as it was suffering from an "image of dull, uninspired service, its lowly status as an unimaginative nonentity in the postwar explosion of air travel and above all, its failure—despite its name—to be the dominant air carrier within Alaska itself," according to Robert Serling, author of *Character and Characters: The Spirit of Alaska Airlines*. Willis tried to turn the company around by promising to buy the still-being-tested Boeing 747 jumbo jet, adding stand-up bars in the rear of some planes, and pioneering flights to Alaska's neighbor to the west.

Willis acquired rights for the Soviet flights by massaging his connections in Washington, DC, and with his impressive vodka tolerance demonstrated during negotiations in the USSR. After finally giving in to Soviet demands to pay steep rates to service his planes, Willis, the president of one of America's smallest airlines, achieved a coup. The green light for Soviet service came on so suddenly that he had to lease a Pan-Am 707 because the USSR was beyond the range of Alaska's 727 fleet.

The company boasted of its newly dubbed Golden Samovar Service "Alaska's colorful Russian heritage comes alive on Alaska Airlines! A feast of history from the day when Russia ruled the great state is now yours to enjoy first class or coach on every jet flight." To live up to its promise, the airline located a supply of Russian samovars in New York City and had them gold-plated.

In the first year, fourteen charter flights were scheduled between Anchorage and Khabarovsk, the Soviet Far East's transportation hub. Flights were added in subsequent years over the North Pole to Leningrad. From those Soviet cities, passengers could connect on Aeroflot to even more exotic destinations such as central Asia and the Black Sea resort of Sochi. A round-trip flight and fifteen-day tour package cost $1,249.

To considerable fanfare, Alaska's inaugural Soviet flight departed Anchorage for Khabarovsk on June 10, 1970, almost seventeen years to the day before the airline's Friendship Flight departed Nome for Providcniya. On board were 130 passengers, including business and civic leaders and a Russian navigator and translator to traverse Soviet air space. Despite promises of service "fit for royalty," the VIPs ended up in coach because the first-class seats were filled with a relief crew for the return flight.

"It was 103 years ago that the United States bought Alaska, then Russian America, from the czars for two cents an acre," wrote *Seattle Times* reporter

Stanton Patty, who joined the flight. "But Alaska and Siberia might as well have been planets apart since then because of political collisions and other obstacles."

As would occur nearly two decades later during preliminary flights to the Soviet Far East, anxious confusion broke out in the cockpit as the jet crossed the date line. Suddenly two Soviet MiG fighter jets appeared off the wing. The Russian navigator translated to Capt. Bill "Dark Cloud" Lund that Moscow apparently had failed to notify Soviet air defense forces of the flight. When asked the consequences if the flight continued to Khabarovsk, the navigator formed his hand into a gun and uttered a threatening "rat-tat-tat." As Lund changed course for Tokyo to refuel and await clearance, Charlie Willis is said to have exploded into an alcohol-fueled rage, threatening to fire the entire crew unless it proceeded to Khabarovsk. Lund ignored his boss and, after several hours on a Japanese runway, resumed the flight to Khabarovsk.

The following summer, a host of Alaska dignitaries helped inaugurate Alaska's service to Leningrad, including Gov. Bill Egan, US Rep. Nick Begich and his wife, Pegge, and *Anchorage Times* publisher Bob Atwood and his wife, Evangeline.

Pegge Begich recalled the flight as a "great unique experience" with many passengers taking full advantage of the special samovar concoction. During several evenings in Soviet cities, she and other Americans wandered into the downtown square to mingle, sing, and dance with Soviet citizens—until KGB agents suddenly appeared to shoo the Russians away.

Nearly half a century later, one experience in her Leningrad hotel still remains vivid. During that era each floor of a Soviet tourist hotel was monitored by a *dezhurnaya* ("woman on duty"), who retained room keys and unlocked the guests' door for them. Begich broke Soviet custom with occasional tips to her "key ladies." One evening, two of the Soviet women followed Begich into her room, where they pointed to her hairbrush and asked to buy it. She refused their kopeks, handing over the brush as a gift instead.

"I had long, really thick hair at the time and the only thing I could think why they wanted it was maybe they thought it would make their hair thick," said Begich, who struggled to find a brush replacement in Leningrad's sparsely stocked shops.

After years of operating in the red and amid predictions that the company would be out of business by the end of 1972, the Alaska Airlines board fired Willis in May of that year.

Company public affairs chief Jim Johnson remembers waking at two a.m. in Seattle to call Intourist officials in Moscow to assure them that money had been deposited before the Soviets would clear the flights for takeoff. The charter service to the Soviet Union operated into 1973, when light passenger loads led Alaska's new management to end it. But it won the company worldwide acclaim.

"The Russian trips got the airline coverage on *60 Minutes*, a Lowell Thomas film, stories in every major newspaper and magazine in the nation and in many foreign countries," reported Archie Satterfield in his book, *The Alaska Airlines Story*.

FIFTEEN YEARS LATER, a confluence of circumstances created an environment favorable enough for Alaska Airlines and other carriers to make another run at flights to the Soviet Union. In Moscow in the late 1980s, Secretary Gorbachev tried to revive his nation's sluggish economy by pushing *perestroika* reforms on the Soviet Union's foreign economic sector. This allowed far-flung regional and local enterprises to engage directly in foreign trade instead of meeting centralized quotas set by the foreign trade ministry in the far-off capital. Under a new joint venture law effective in 1987, foreigners could invest in the Soviet Union through joint ventures. Shockingly, joint ventures were even permitted to be majority-owned and controlled by foreigners.

At the same time, Alaska Airlines' youthful chairman, Bruce Kennedy, was looking to take advantage of recent deregulation of his industry by expanding routes. After linking winter-weary Alaskans to warm-weather spots in Mexico, Arizona, and Southern California, Kennedy considered another exotic destination. Through his Alaska roots and religious humanitarianism, Kennedy wanted to help Alaska Natives reunite with Soviet relatives. He also saw potential business opportunity in what many Alaskans hoped was a rapidly changing Soviet Union.

"With the collapse of the Soviet Union and the opening of Russia, was it going to become the next great frontier? Would people go in and make giant amounts of dollars exploiting their almost unlimited resources? That was the sort of business justification for going there," recalled longtime Alaska Airlines lawyer Tom O'Grady, who helped clear the legal hurdles for the new Soviet venture.

Nearly eighteen months before the 1988 Friendship Flight, Alaska Airlines applied to the US Department of Transportation for approval to provide regular service between Nome and Provideniya. In its January 1987 application, the company boasted of its 1970s success as "the last U.S. carrier to have operated regular service to Siberia and is therefore particularly well-suited to provide the proposed service." A competitor, Markair, made a similar application but later withdrew it.

In May 1988, the US State Department formally proposed a new "annex," or addition, to the US-USSR Bilateral Civil Aviation Agreement approving the Nome-Provideniya route. But after the two visits to Provideniya—the Friendship Flight and the earlier surveillance visit—Alaska Airlines executives decided that the outpost was inadequate for regular service.

Shortly after the Friendship Flight, the company announced plans to abandon Provideniya flights, citing "slow high-level Soviet response to the airline's initiative." Alaska shifted its focus to the larger cities of Magadan and Khabarovsk.

Finally, in December 1990, Alaska Airlines announced three round-trips weekly between Anchorage and Magadan and Khabarovsk for the next summer. It coupled the direct flights with tour packages of up to eight days, with an optional Trans-Siberian Railway visit to Irkutsk on the shore of Lake Baikal, the world's deepest freshwater lake. Cost for a round-trip Anchorage–Magadan flight was $1,100; to Khabarovsk, $1,500.

The company marketed the Soviet service with an eyebrow-raising ad campaign featuring a picture of Soviet founding father Vladimir Lenin. The ad appealed: "Be one of the first westerners to experience Magadan, a port city literally built from the ground up by the prisoners of Joseph Stalin's notorious gulags."

Securing government approvals for the flights seemed easy compared to the initial logistical challenges of operating in the Soviet Far East. Radio tower communications were sometimes incompatible, terminals unfinished, runways inconsistently maintained, and fuel scarce.

Alaska Air dispatched a food-service official to explore meal options for the return flights to Alaska. In a Khabarovsk market shopping for chicken breasts or thighs suitable for an airplane meal, he found only whole chickens. Of several commercial kitchens he visited, only one had hot water. The airline decided to load meals in Anchorage for both legs of the flights.

To safely guide the new American airliners into Soviet airports, the University of Alaska Anchorage hosted Soviet air-traffic controllers for an intensive eight-week course. It was called "English for a Special Purpose" and was supported through a partnership of the National Air Transportation Association and the Soviet Ministry of Civil Aviation. The first class of twenty-five Soviet controllers graduated in summer 1991.

In the early days of operations, Alaska officials were especially fearful of notorious fuel shortages. But Mark Dudley, who opened and ran the airline's Magadan station for the first two years, said fuel arrived reliably to Magadan by barge. The Soviets then filtered it nine times to assure quality for aviation use. Dudley's biggest challenge was flying in tons of metal detectors and x-ray machines to comply with a new aviation-security system.

To participate in Alaska Airlines' inaugural flight to Magadan and Khabarovsk, 126 excited passengers assembled at Anchorage International Airport the afternoon of June 17, 1991. About half were Alaska and Lower 48 business and government officials who joined a trade mission organized by the Alaska State Chamber of Commerce. Others included a CBS News crew, several newspaper reporters, and a bicycle team that planned to pedal from Khabarovsk to China. A Russian-speaking Alaska mechanic joined Flight 29—and every subsequent flight to the Soviet Union—to be available to deal with maintenance problems.

Dozens of Alaska Airlines employees and onlookers gathered at the departure gate to hear newly named Alaska CEO Ray Vecci hail the Soviet service. Following speeches by politicians and state chamber chairman John Sims, a new commemorative painting was unveiled, *Russia-Alaska Reunion* by artist Barbara Lavallee. Shortly after Flight 29 departed Anchorage in a Boeing 727-200, the first-class dinner was rolled out featuring caviar canapés and filet of beef shashlik washed down with chilled Stolichnaya vodka.

The state chamber aggressively pursued prospects in the Soviet Far East, egged on by a handful of Alaska businessmen. Dave Heatwole, an Atlantic Richfield Company (ARCO Alaska) executive who served as state chamber chairman, called economic potential in the Soviet Far East "the opportunity of the decade." After partnering with Dixie Belcher to host scores of visiting Soviets to Anchorage's 1989 Glasnost Folkfest, the chamber's businessmen itched to set foot on Soviet soil.

More than a year before Alaska's inaugural service, in March 1990, about forty members of the state chamber chartered an Aeroflot Tu-154 trijet for a ten-day tour of the Far East. Industries represented included oil, mining, tourism, aviation, fisheries, and construction. Meetings and tours were held in Anadyr, Magadan, Khabarovsk, and Irkutsk. A scheduled visit to Vladivostok was canceled without explanation.

After many signed agreements calling for future joint ventures, the Alaska business officials returned home like modern-day Marco Polos. "The companies that come first will be very profitable and the ones that come later will be profitable, but less so," Heatwole predicted.

A year later, even more business officials jumped at the chance to prospect for opportunity in the Soviet Far East. Sixty chamber members shelled out $3,200 each for the June 1991 inaugural flight with Alaska Airlines. Their itinerary included Magadan, Khabarovsk, Vladivostok, and, for the first time, Sakhalin Island, site of one of the country's largest oil and gas developments. Activities included meetings with Soviet counterparts to explore joint ventures, a gulag tour, and a Russian tea party.

Participants were a who's who of the Alaska business community, including top officials of Native corporations, communications, real estate, energy, transportation, and tourism. The New York-based US-USSR Trade and Economic Council sent its national president along with a dozen of its members in oil and gas, timber, and medical products.

When Governor Cowper's term ended in December 1990, I went to work for State Rep. Tom Moyer of Fairbanks as staff director of his international trade and tourism committee. During the 1991 legislative session, we assembled several committee hearings focused on commercial opportunities in the Soviet Far East. When Alaska's maiden flight firmed up, Moyer jumped on it.

A major complaint we heard about Alaska-Soviet exchanges was the burden on Soviet citizens in obtaining visas for US travel. At the time, Soviets were required to visit an American consulate for an in-person interview before being granted a visa, and there were no consulates in the Soviet Far East.

I wrote protocols for Moyer and his Alaska Senate counterpart, Sen. Arliss Sturgulewski of Anchorage, to sign with Soviet officials in each city they visited as part of the chamber trade mission. The agreements called for establishment of an American consulate in the Far East and a Soviet consulate in Alaska "to more quickly and efficiently process the required approvals for Alaska-Soviet exchanges and visits and to further encourage the warming relations between our two countries."

A little more than a year later, in September 1992, the State Department reestablished its consulate in Vladivostok. Seventy years earlier, it had been the last American diplomatic mission to close after the Soviet Revolution.

AFTER THE INITIAL flurry of excitement, Alaska Airlines' Soviet Far East service steadily ramped up. In 1992 and 1993, with summer service only, flights between Anchorage and Magadan and Khabarovsk were about half full. Passenger loads reached a high of 85 percent in September 1994 on flights from Magadan to Anchorage and dropped to a low of 22 percent in January 1998. The convenient direct flights accelerated the exchange of citizen-diplomats across the strait.

Beginning in 1993, millions of dollars in federal earmarks began flowing to the University of Alaska, which established business training centers across the Russian Far East and brought Russians to Alaska and transported US business experts to Russia. Buoyed by federal travel funds, business travel, and adventure-seeking tourists, Alaska Airlines expanded its service to Vladivostok in 1993, to Petropavlovsk-Kamchatsky in 1994, and to Yuzhno-Sakhalinsk in 1997.

Operating in the Soviet Far East continued to challenge the company. One of the more legendary incidents occurred in June 1993 when an Alaska Air MD-80 flying from Khabarovsk iced up after landing in Magadan. Peculiar to that aircraft, the top section of the wing often became icy twenty minutes after landing, even at seventy degrees. With no deicing fluid available in the summer, the crew asked the Russians to warm the wing with a jet engine mounted on a flatbed truck usually used to clear winter runways. But the truck was broken down.

Capt. Zip Trower got a laugh from his puzzled ground crew when he suggested using vodka. But then it dawned on them it might work. After retrieving twenty-five bottles from the local liquor store, an Alaska mechanic emptied the bottles into a borrowed fire extinguisher. As he sprayed the vodka on the wing, the ice quickly melted away. The impressed Russians gathered to witness the chemical innovation. The airline later boasted of its employee ingenuity, but the company also reportedly was sanctioned by the Federal Aviation Administration.

Another problem required middle-of-the-night intervention by the US State Department. Bad weather in Magadan had forced an Alaska jet to land in Anadyr near the Chukotka coast. The Anadyr airport was shared by civilian and military aircraft, dating back to its construction in the 1950s to service long-range Soviet bombers.

According to Kit Cooper, the airline's international operations chief, Aeroflot controlled Anadyr's fuel supply and planned to keep the revenue from selling fuel to Alaska Airlines. But the local military demanded its share. The Alaska jet sat stranded on the runway for nearly twelve hours while Cooper aroused company and State Department officials in Washington, DC, to mediate the standoff.

"Every flight to Russia was like giving birth," Cooper said, quoting a colleague's favorite phrase.

Alaska Airlines generated lots of headlines with its Soviet service. But it was not the first US airline to take advantage of the melting Ice Curtain. In spring 1974, Jim Rowe was seeking a little postcollege adventure when he joined three friends and flew a Cessna 195 from northern Michigan to Nome. There they ran out of money. Intrigued by the Bering Sea coastal town, he settled down to race sled dogs, fly for a local air service, and raise a family. Five years later, Rowe incorporated Bering Air, delivering mail, passengers, and cargo to Nome- and Kotzebue-area villages.

After flying near the Soviet coast—he refused to say if he entered Soviet air space—Rowe first sought FAA permission to fly to the USSR in 1974. It took more than a decade to get approved. During those years, he worked with other Ice Curtain–melting advocates such as Jim Stimpfle to renew relations across the strait.

Ten days before the 1988 Friendship Flight, Rowe shuttled Bruce Kennedy and other Alaska Airlines brass to Provideniya to check the condition of the landing strip. Over the following year, he made twenty-two more flights to the Soviet town, transporting scientists, business and cultural exchanges, and medical evacuations. In July 1989, Bering Air won FAA certification to transport passengers to four additional Soviet communities. Rowe also helped ease border crossings by bringing Anchorage-based US Customs inspectors to Nome at his expense to clear Soviet and returning Alaska passengers into the state. Bering's early chartered passenger rates ran about $350 one-way to Provideniya; today one-way rates can top $1,000.

Despite flying to the Soviet Union and Russia 225 times himself, Rowe says he counts on one hand the number of problems there, mostly flat tires. Bering Air was among the first Western companies to open a Soviet bank account in Provideniya because the company was prohibited from taking dollars into the country or rubles out. Rowe said that by the mid-1990s, Bering had quietly amassed about $250,000 worth of rubles in the Provideniya bank.

One day he was tipped off by his Russian driver that bank inspectors were en route from Magadan to seize the account. Bering Air had a flight scheduled the next day so Rowe assigned himself to pilot the plane. He hustled to the bank and withdrew his accumulated rubles, which filled about twenty banker boxes. Rowe and his driver then sped around Provideniya in a Soviet jeep, giving away the ruble-stuffed boxes to the local orphanage, women's shelter, and school while the Magadan bank inspectors circled overhead. For what he called his "Harrison Ford incident," Rowe was later celebrated by Provideniya schoolchildren.

"As long as I'm around—and who knows how long that will be—I'll stick with it," Rowe said. "A sane person probably would have given up a long time ago."

Another carrier that tried to capitalize on the melting Ice Curtain was the world's largest, the Soviet airline Aeroflot. Established just six years after the Soviet revolution, the government-owned carrier serviced more than 3,500 Soviet communities and began branching out internationally in the 1970s.

A decade later, Aeroflot was the only carrier operating between Alaska and the Soviet Far East with a handful of charters. In 1989 and early 1990, the company used its standard cargo carrier, the Il-76, and the Tu-154 passenger jet to transport the first state chamber trade mission, game-processing equipment, a Soviet hockey team, Rotarians, and school students from Soldotna to Magadan. It explored a joint venture with the Alaska-based Northern Air Cargo in 1990 after Northern failed to secure government approvals and Aeroflot stepped in to deliver its cargo.

Aeroflot was most interested in the more heavily trafficked West Coast routes. In February 1992, it announced plans for weekly round-trip service between Moscow and San Francisco with a refueling stop in Anchorage. Round-trip coach seats were $2,600 for the nearly ten-hour nonstop flight. Most of the seats were booked for Moscow- and San Francisco–bound passengers.

Aeroflot soon followed the example of other carriers refueling in Anchorage. As longer-haul airplanes such as the Boeing 747-400 entered the market, they were able to fly over Anchorage's refueling stop, saving time and fuel costs. Action by the Gorbachev government in 1987 to open previously closed Soviet airspace also allowed international carriers to bypass Alaska.

DICK REEVE'S EARLIEST memory of Alaska-Soviet aviation ties was around 1943. On a visit with his dad to the US airfield in Galena in Alaska's Interior, the seven-year-old heard the drone of airplane engines in the distance. A flight of four-engine Soviet bombers soon appeared in formation overhead, headed toward Nome, where they acted as "pathfinders" during the Lend-Lease program to assist in the war against Germany. "It was awesome," recalls Reeve. "At that point, we were both on the same side."

Reeve's father, Robert, founded his airline company—what would become Reeve Aleutian Airways—in 1932. Son Richard became president and CEO in 1978. The company entered the Alaska-Soviet aviation market inspired by a vision.

In 1973, former Alaska Gov. Walter Hickel penned an article for *Reader's Digest* advocating his vision for the Arctic. It called on Americans to view the Arctic "on a schoolroom globe" with as much land as Western Europe, the continental United States, Japan, India, and China combined. "It is a vast, forbidding territory as mysterious as the moon, yet under its cover of ice and snow lies a unique opportunity for the future," Hickel wrote.

Two decades later, in the final year of his second term as governor, Hickel proposed a grand adventure to encapsulate that vision: a visit to fourteen cities in all eight arctic nations in seven days, including four stops in Russia. Dubbed the Circumpolar Expedition, the May 1994 trip attracted nearly eighty participants, each of whom paid about $7,000. Reeve Aleutian was selected to pilot one of the company's 727s for the trip.

Dick Reeve, who joined the trip as a paying passenger, said the expedition whetted his appetite for service between Alaska and Russia. Pinned down in Juneau by a legislative special session on subsistence hunting and fishing, Hickel missed all but the final leg of the trip—from Whitehorse, Canada, back to Anchorage.

After huge oil and gas reserves were discovered off the northeast coast of Soviet Sakhalin Island in 1977, international oil companies rushed in to capitalize on the bonanza. Alaska operators predicted the development would exceed Alaska's Prudhoe Bay oil and gas fields. Even though Alaska Airlines began passenger service to Sakhalin's capital city in 1997, Reeve calculated that there was plenty of business to be had supporting the oil companies.

For about three years, Reeve Aleutian operated combination passenger-cargo 727s to the island, ferrying in drilling equipment and the personnel to operate it. With heavy loads, Reeve's planes couldn't make the nearly three thousand miles between Anchorage and Yuzhno-Sakhalinsk nonstop, so the company refueled in Provideniya. Reeve also transported Alaska Gov. Tony Knowles and a large delegation of business officials to Sakhalin for a state trade mission in April 1997.

Alaska businessman Dave Heatwole (left) sold mining equipment to the Polyarni Gok mining complex on Chukotka's arctic coast in the early 1990s. By 1993, the mine was producing about 100,000 ounces of gold annually. COURTESY OF DAVE HEATWOLE

Open for Business

If Boris Yeltsin can stand on tanks in Moscow, we will accept rubles in Nome.

—NOME ALASKA-RUSSIA FRIENDSHIP ADVOCATE
JIM STIMPFLE, OCTOBER 25, 1991

DIRECT AIR LINKS between Alaska and the Soviet Far East were vital to the work of citizen-diplomats. The convenience of boarding a plane in Anchorage and four hours later meeting your business partner or cultural exchange colleague face-to-face in Magadan accelerated traffic across the strait.

Dave Heatwole estimates that he made the trip more than fifty times over nearly a decade in his pioneering efforts to establish profitable business ties. His first trip was the Alaska Airlines charter flight to Anadyr on March 1, 1989, to drop off members of the Bering Bridge ski and dogsled expedition. Although only on the ground long enough to take in a lavish Russian dinner and plenty of vodka, Heatwole was hooked.

Through his day job as vice president of public affairs at ARCO Alaska, Heatwole argued to his company brass that Soviet Far East reserves could help fulfill ARCO's needs for crude oil on the US West Coast. In 1990, Heatwole persuaded his boss to create an ARCO subsidiary, the ARCO Alaska Russian Exploration Company. It had one employee, Heatwole.

The position allowed the professional geologist to establish relationships with Soviet resource-development officials in Anadyr, Magadan, and Moscow. Two years later, ARCO consolidated its international exploration operations in the Lower 48. Rather than transfer out of Alaska, Heatwole resigned after twenty-seven years with the company.

The gregarious Heatwole quickly teamed up with Tom Austin, a Russian-speaking Alaskan, to form the Alaska Russia Company. Initially they focused on two opportunities in the Magadan region: gold mining and food sales. Heatwole's biggest business success was a 1992 deal to manufacture five 1.2-megawatt generators for a Magadan-area gold mine to replace the aging Soviet variety. He arranged for the generators to be assembled in Anchorage and air-freighted to near the Soviet mine site.

Heatwole's company later worked for the Anchorage wholesaler Carr Gottstein Foods Co. to sell food and consumer products in Magadan. To whet the local appetite, the company shipped cases of groceries to Magadan for an October 1993 food fair that attracted three hundred residents. Frozen strawberries, hams, and steaks were among the favorites of Magadan residents, who had long relied on high-priced products shipped in from Moscow, Europe, and China. Once they determined they could sell the products, shipping containers loaded with groceries were barged from Tacoma, Washington, across the North Pacific to Magadan.

Among Heatwole's biggest early challenges were a shaky Russian business law framework and currency-exchange problems. Instead of enforcing business agreements through a judicial system, most of Heatwole's early successes were based on the handshake of a business partner. He was approached by organized criminals who offered to expedite his equipment and food shipments through Soviet border control.

"I just said 'no' and they made it a little harder for me to get things through customs, but they never physically threatened me or any of my partners," he said.

With the Soviet ruble nonconvertible on the international currency market, getting paid required ingenuity. For gold mining and oil development, Russian companies were allocated US dollars to buy equipment. But for consumer products, Heatwole accepted rubles, which his Russian partners exchanged for dollars in the Russian banking system. The $1.7 million Heatwole received for his gold-mining generator deal required transfers between banks in Magadan, Moscow, New York, and Seattle before ending up in his Anchorage account three weeks later.

Heatwole was so bullish on Russia that he documented his many adventures with detailed personal accounts, including a thirty-five-page "love story" of how he courted and married an Irish flight attendant for Alaska Airlines. Initially captivated by her "warm and melodious" lilt giving landing instructions descending into Magadan in fall 1993, Heatwole married Margaret Daly six months later. He also proudly recounts shaking hands with President Gorbachev and posing with a wide grin and Russian fur hat in the ARCO company newsletter.

As the Ice Curtain melted, new US start-ups were guiding Alaskans through the complexities of the Soviet Far East. Both government and private-sector enterprises jumped into the "how to do business" business, setting up new companies and nonprofits and publishing guidance about the little-known region.

By January 1990, fifty-five Alaska companies had paid up to $1,000 to join Anchorage's World Trade Center, affiliated with the University of Alaska's Center for International Business. Membership included access to a global network of buyers and sellers linked through a dial-up computer modem offering goods ranging from Russian vodka to thirty-kilogram pieces of the Berlin Wall.

The trade center produced a monthly newsletter, *Soviet Far East News*, with summaries of the latest political and economic developments in the region along with notices of trade opportunities. The first issue in December 1991 included an appeal from a dilapidated machinery plant near Khabarovsk looking for partners to convert the production line to vacuum cleaners and microwave ovens, "which would then be available for export."

An Anchorage printer, Don Cromer, suddenly became a publisher with a new glossy magazine, *Russian Far East*. Relying on US and Russian writers, his debut issue in February 1992 featured thirty-two pages of Russian women in fur hats, articles about the Far East, and an eyebrow-raising profile of a Magadan company.

The Magadan company first tried to broker bank shares, then sold sewing machines, the magazine reported. "Now it has decided to contribute to the happiness of the 'better half' of the Russian Far East" by selling Russian-made "artificial phalluses." Quoting an unnamed source, the magazine said the product "doesn't ask for food and vodka and doesn't curse."

Anchorage engineer Kent Lee Woodman was so inspired by a trip to the Soviet Union with the Alaska Airmen's Association that he started a nonprofit dispensing advice about the Soviet Far East. His Center of Soviet-Alaskan Resources began in 1989 and three years later had 389 members. The group helped customize tours to the Soviet Far East, created a database of news clippings about Soviet developments, and produced a newsletter offering tips about doing business in the region.

The most well-regarded information source about the Soviet Far East was Elisa Miller, the University of Washington's Russia expert. With a doctorate in Russian studies, Miller began lecturing on Soviet trade issues in 1975. Alaska Airlines hired her to help with its efforts to fly to the Soviet Far East, and she accompanied CEO Bruce Kennedy to Provideniya for the run-up to the 1988 Friendship Flight and on the flight itself. She also worked with the University of Alaska's Gunnar Knapp on the earliest studies of Alaska-Soviet trade potential and with other private clients.

In 1991, Miller launched the *Soviet Far East Update,* a comprehensive monthly newsletter that covered the latest Soviet political and economic news and even offered travel tips about the best hotels and restaurants in the rapidly changing region. Beginning with just eighty-one readers, by 1999, when Miller sold it, the *Update* had nearly five hundred subscribers in the United States, Asia, Europe, and Russia who were paying up to $439 a year.

The *Soviet Business Journal,* another information source with a broader perspective, was a joint effort of Moscow and Seattle think tanks. The Moscow-based Center for US-USSR Economic Cooperation gleaned information from international publications and Soviet television to provide a digest of the latest economic and political developments in the rapidly changing Soviet Union. The center partnered with the Foundation for Soviet-American Economic Cooperation, a Seattle-based organization founded in 1989 by business consultant Carol Vipperman. The foundation operated for twenty-two years, providing trade tips and hosting conferences to link Pacific Northwest companies with the Soviet Union.

The Alaska media continued a drumbeat of accounts about Alaska–Soviet Far East business ventures, trade conferences, and Soviet visits. Anchorage television stations even included Soviet cities in their nightly weather reports.

Federal agencies readily made funding and expertise available to eager Alaska entrepreneurs. "I wouldn't have given a plug nickel" for business prospects with the Soviet Union two years ago, a US Agency for International Development official told an Anchorage conference in 1994. His said his tune quickly changed when he joined officials from the Small Business Administration, Overseas Private Investment Corp., International Trade Administration, and World Bank, all scrambling to connect Alaskans with Russian trade partners.

Numerous attempts were made to negotiate Alaska-Soviet joint ventures. An Anchorage company, Bering Sea International, announced a deal to import Provideniya-brewed beer. With the help of a $300,000 grant, the Arctic Slope Regional Corp., one of Alaska's largest Native corporations, studied the feasibility of building an oil refinery in the Soviet Union. The Kenai Peninsula Borough considered how to train workers and stage development for the proposed $10 billion oil development on Sakhalin Island. The operators of the Red Dog zinc mine in Northwest Alaska researched using Soviet icebreakers to expand the ocean-shipping season for exporting its mine ore.

Officials of the Alaska Commercial Company visited Magadan to consider importing Soviet products for sale in Alaska. Earl Romans, president of Alaska Battery, attempted to manufacture batteries in Magadan for international export. A Vladivostok lawyer and a Leningrad geologist seeking Alaska partners were keynote speakers at an Anchorage conference normally devoted to discussing in-state oil and gas development. Bering Straits Native Corp., based in Nome, and Anchorage mining consultant Ron Sheardown explored the feasibility of a gold-mining joint venture near Magadan.

In Nome, at the urging of the local Chamber of Commerce, many businesses tried to advance free trade when they agreed to accept rubles as payment for goods and services. The practice ran into trouble because Soviet law prohibited the export of rubles, and the Soviet currency was not convertible on the world market. Merchants calculated that their risk was relatively small; the average Soviet visiting Nome only carried about $40 worth of rubles.

"We're all willing to take this gamble in hopes we'll encourage national leaders to maybe look at one little Northwest Alaska community that's willing to develop international trade," said Nome Checker Cab owner Gary Hart, who charged four rubles for a $4 ride from the airport into downtown. To dispose of the Soviet currency, merchants such as music-store owner Leo Rasmussen packaged it for resale as souvenirs to US tourists, charging as much as $289 for a bundle of rubles. Other businesses pooled their Soviet currency for donations to Soviet charities.

In summer 1991, a shipload of Soviet cold-water swimmers from the Club of Walruses annoyed some Nome merchants. Dozens of the dollarless Soviets descended on local stores, aggressively trying to trade lapel pins, watches, and even bottles of vodka for Alaska T-shirts and baby clothes.

A few months later, the Soviet International Monetary and Economic Department fired off a letter to the Nome Chamber of Commerce demanding the practice of accepting rubles stop because taking Soviet currency out of the country was illegal. The directive was ignored.

CULTURAL AND EDUCATIONAL exchanges also flourished, many through sister-city connections. One of the earliest and most productive was between Alaska's second-largest population center, the Fairbanks North Star Borough, and Yakutsk, capital city of the Republic of Sakha. The relationship had its roots in World War II and the more contemporary movement to establish nuclear-free zones in the Far North.

Of the nearly fifteen thousand Lend-Lease aircraft shuttled from the United States to the Soviet Union between 1941 and 1945, more than half were flown over the Northwest Route with stops at Ladd Field in Fairbanks and in Yakutsk. In 2006, the Alaska city honored that historic link with a large bronze statue depicting American and Soviet pilots. US Secretary of Defense Donald Rumsfeld was among the dedication speakers.

In winter 1987, Juanita Helms, the Fairbanks North Star borough mayor, convened a handful of her constituents to consider an international sister-city program, with potential partners in China, Germany, and Japan. The idea of adding a Soviet sister city came from a local peace activist.

For two years, Fairbanks officials sent inquiries to the Soviet city and buttonholed contacts at conferences, without success. Finally, in summer 1989, Sister Cities International blessed the relationship, and three Fairbanks officials flew a circuitous route to Yakutsk, then numbering about three hundred thousand residents. Helms and her Yakutsk counterpart, Mayor Pavel Borodin, signed a Treaty of Friendly Relations on August 25, 1989. Sister-city pioneer Mimi Chapin has detailed the relationship's history since her first visit to the region with Helms.

Yakutsk is the capital of an India-size region in Siberia bordering the Arctic Ocean west of Chukotka. It was largely populated by Turkic Native people until the discovery of gold and other minerals in the late 1880s. Its population then swelled with Russians seeking high-paying jobs in resource development, including diamonds and oil and gas. Yakutsk is connected to Magadan by the nearly

1,300-mile Kolyma Highway, also known as the "Road of Bones" acknowledging the forced labor of gulag inmates who constructed it starting in 1932.

As a republic, Sakha has an elevated status within Russia's regional government structure. After its transition from an *oblast* (analogous to a state or province) in 1991, it was headed by a visionary veterinarian, Mikhail Nikolayev, who established close ties with Alaskans through the Northern Forum organization of northern regional governments.

Alaska communities that rushed to find Soviet sister cities tended to select those like themselves, as was the case with the Fairbanks borough and Yakutsk. Both are industrial cities built on permafrost located in their region's interiors on rivers— the Lena River in Yakutsk, the Chena and Tanana Rivers in Fairbanks. Both have widely varying subarctic climates where temperatures can exceed ninety degrees in the summer and drop to fifty below zero or lower in winter. Yakutsk boasts one of the coldest temperatures ever recorded, minus eighty degrees in 1838.

Universities also dominate the economies and cultures of the cities, so much of the sister-city relationship was centered on exchanges of scientists and scholars. In 1991, the University of Alaska Fairbanks and Yakutsk State University agreed to faculty exchanges and joint research. In 1993, UAF journalism professor Joy Morrison landed an $80,000 US Information Agency grant to bring eight Yakutsk journalists to Fairbanks for immersion into American-style journalism. Fairbanks journalists reciprocated the following year with a two-week training session in Yakutsk focused on both news reporting and how to run successful newspapers and television stations. Morrison said the exchange's success was in conveying the role of independent media to the Russian journalists whose livelihoods were tied to their government-owned media outlets.

"We have a very young democracy and it could easily be broken," said Yakutsk television reporter Katya Beznosova in a visit to Fairbanks. "We've shown ourselves to be effective organs of expression; people would be upset if they tried to take away the newspaper or the program."

Dozens of joint projects between Yakutsk and Fairbanks followed, including exchanges of police officers, Native artisans, ice carvers, artists, and Rotarians. One source of frustration, however, was an effort by Athabascan Indians in the Fairbanks area to connect with indigenous people from Yakutsk. The region's dominant indigenous group, Yakuts, comprised about half the population and their Turkic-rooted language was one of the two official languages. During early visits to Yakutsk, Alaska Natives complained of being kept at arm's length from local Russian Natives, who were hesitant to acknowledge their own heritage.

"It reminded me of the early days of white contact with our people when we suppressed our Native roots to avoid continued ridicule," said Fairbanks Native leader Miranda Wright. She complained that Yakutsk Native traditions, such as burial rituals and shamanism, were largely restricted to museums.

In 2010, Fairbanks and Yakutsk rejuvenated their relationship with video conferences between the mayors and schoolchildren and a visit to Fairbanks by a Yakutsk aviation historian who displayed Lend-Lease photos. The communities celebrated twenty years of productive relations in 2011 with music and dancing. Among the featured guests were Yakutsk-born Lena Shelt and her Fairbanks husband, Bruce, who had met on an exchange trip to Yakutsk.

At the celebration, sister-city pioneer Mimi Chapin recalled her first visit to Yakutsk with Mayor Helms. "It was midnight but still light out," she recalled, "and the two mayors started pretending to duel with each other with [shish-kebab] skewers, laughing about how America and Russia had always been enemies. They threw down their 'weapons' and drank a toast to friendship."

Like Fairbanks, Anchorage also jumped at the chance to improve relations with the Soviet Far East. In 1991, the city's Sister-City Commission asked Mayor Tom Fink to support establishment of formal ties with Magadan, the former USSR gulag prison city run by communists. Some were surprised when Fink got behind the proposal, given that five years earlier the Catholic, bow-tie-wearing insurance agent had been elected one of Anchorage's most conservative mayors in a generation. Fink served a term as speaker of the State House and twice ran for governor, advocating traditional less-government-is-better Republican principles.

Yet the mayor eagerly supported the sister-city relationship. He visited Russia three times in his final years in office and hosted his Magadan counterpart. He hoped his interactions with the Russians would encourage more free enterprise in Russia but "had the sense the local government officials in Magadan never had much control over anything."

One weekend, Fink tried to provide the visiting Magadan mayor an Alaska outdoors experience, spending time together at Fink's remote duck-hunting shack. Thinking it would be courteous to offer his guest a morning Bloody Mary, Fink produced a half gallon of vodka. His Russian colleague quickly drained the bottle.

Nearly a dozen other Alaska communities eagerly established sister-city relations, too. They included:

- Bethel and Anadyr, the capital of Chukotka, date unknown.
- Homer and the city and region of Yelizovo, Kamchatka, 2007: This relationship was founded on tourism exchanges.
- Juneau and the Lenin District of Vladivostok, 1991: Both communities are port cities, and the relationship focused on educational, business, trade, and cultural exchanges. It was among the most active in Alaska.
- City of Kenai and Okha, Sakhalin, 1991: This relationship began with an exchange of oil-industry officials and traditional dance groups.
- Kotzebue and the Chukotka community of Lavrentiya, 1989: Designed to advance social, cultural, and economic cooperation; the relationship was reconfirmed in 2003.
- Nome and Provideniya, 1988: This is the earliest such relationship established during the Ice Curtain era, having become effective the day following the Friendship Flight in June 1988.
- Point Hope and the village of Neshkan, Chukotka, 1993.
- Savoonga and Chukotka village of Sereniki, date unknown.
- Soldotna and the Kenai Peninsula Borough and Nogliki, Sakhalin, 1994: Oil and gas development were important to both communities.
- Unalaska and Petropalovsk-Kamchatsky, capital of the Kamchatka region, date of establishment unknown.
- Wasilla and the city of Mirnyy, Republic of Sakha, 1993: A delegation from Mirnyy visited Wasilla in June 1992 and the Wasilla City Council approved the relationship the following year.

FAIRBANKS INSURANCE AGENT Jack Randolph remembers the grim expressions of elderly residents of an old folks' home in Chita, an outpost on the Trans-Siberian Railway just north of the Mongolian border.

"It was an old, ugly building like a warehouse and the people just looked like they were going to die," he recalled of the disheartening visit in the early 1990s.

A year later, on his next visit, Randolph found the Russian seniors in a new, freshly painted building, ample bathrooms equipped with hot water, and sunshine streaming in the windows; "the people looked happy." The transformation, he said, was thanks to the Chita Rotary Club, one of about three dozen such clubs Alaskans organized across the Russian Far East and Siberia as the Ice Curtain melted.

Alaska Rotarians were among the business and civic leaders who first interacted with Soviets visiting their state in the late 1980s. Under the Soviet system, "community service" was a foreign term because the types of projects on which Rotary Clubs typically focus—public health, park improvements, college scholarships—were usually provided by the Soviet state. In 1989, Alaskans helped Magadan establish one of the first Rotary Clubs in the USSR.

By the time Randolph became Alaska's top Rotarian as district governor in 1995, the number of Russian clubs had expanded to about thirty-six. "A lot of the service work was with kids and old people, because under the communist system, that's who gets dropped," said Randolph, who visited Russian clubs thirteen times.

Dermot Cole, a longtime *Fairbanks Daily News-Miner* reporter and columnist, traveled across the Russian Far East in 1996 with an international Rotary delegation. In Nakhodka, an industrial port city near Vladivostok, he found thirty charter members of a new Rotary Club planning projects such as youth exchanges so that young Russians would have a better understanding of life beyond their borders.

"While many of them were once part of the communist elite, they are now pledging to follow the rules of Rotary and commit themselves to public service," Cole wrote. "[T]hey sang the Rotary song and talked of the four-way test of business ethics."

MARK DUDLEY NOTICED something strange. On August 19, 1991, he was taking a break from his duties as Magadan station chief for Alaska Airlines to show his visiting parents aspects of his life in the remote Soviet city. When they turned on the television looking for the regular morning news, Dudley was puzzled to find that it had been replaced with an endless stream of cartoons. So he decided to give his parents a tour of Magadan's air-traffic-control center. They arrived to find the tower in a frenzy.

Eleven time zones to the west, a handful of Communist Party hard-liners had suddenly disrupted the Crimean vacation General Secretary Gorbachev was enjoying with his family and placed him under arrest. A coup was under way to depose the most progressive Soviet leader since the 1917 revolution.

Thirty-seven hundred miles east of the Soviet capital, Magadan was rife with rumors: borders sealed, flights grounded, foreigners arrested. The televised cartoons were replaced by proclamations from the eight coup plotters, the State Committee for the State of Emergency.

Their ominous warnings were broadcast repeatedly on Soviet media: "We are addressing you at a grave, critical hour for the destinies of our Fatherland and our peoples. A mortal danger looms large over our great Motherland."

It turned out that the Magadan tower was the perfect place to ride out the coup attempt. Shortly after the plotters announced their intentions to restore order under a fortified Communist Party, the newly elected president of the Russian Federation issued his own appeal. Mounting a tank that had rumbled up to the Soviet White House in central Moscow, President Boris Yeltsin condemned the rebellion and exhorted soldiers to pledge their allegiance to his government instead.

Yeltsin's proclamation was distributed by hand to flight crews departing Moscow for the Far East. When they arrived in Magadan, Yeltsin's denouncement of the coup was read by air-traffic controllers to the local media. That convoluted relay system was the only way Soviets in the Far East could get news about the dramatic events under way in their national capital.

For three days, coup plotters controlled the nation's media. Soviet citizens outside Moscow and Leningrad had no idea that six hundred motorized vehicles and hundreds of soldiers in full battle gear had stormed into Moscow and surrounded the White House, where parliament was housed. An estimated half million Soviets joined protest rallies in the country's two largest cities.

In Moscow, citizens tried to erect barriers to prevent an attack on the White House. Skirmishes broke out near the US embassy, and three protesters defending the barricades were killed. It was not known until days later that the plotters had ordered a brutal attack on Russia's seat of government.

Nervous Alaskans, meanwhile, were glued to the news in Western broadcasts. They feared a return to the intolerable past. Would the melting Ice Curtain between Alaska and the Soviet Union, which had invigorated so many on both sides of the Bering Strait, be refrozen by a new hardline government and the United States' reaction to it?

Russian Far East villages such as Lorino, pictured here, were the focus of University of Alaska Anchorage efforts between 1993 and 2008 to help diversify local economies and partner with Alaska communities. PHOTO BY DAVID RAMSEUR

16

Beyond the Coup

Gorbachev was physically alive but politically dead, and so were most of the perestroika reformers.

—RUSSIAN JOURNALIST ARKADY OSTROVSKY, AFTER THE 1991 ATTEMPTED COUP AGAINST PRESIDENT GORBACHEV

VIC FISCHER WAS entertaining an extraordinary houseguest. The University of Alaska Soviet expert grew up in Moscow, where he attended an elite high school in the 1930s. Six decades later, one of Fischer's classmates tracked him to Alaska after stumbling across his picture in a book he discovered in a Moscow sidewalk stall. In August 1991, Vadya Popov made his first trip to Alaska to rekindle memories with Fischer and meet his wife, Jane.

The three clicked on the television in Fischer's Anchorage living room. They sat stunned as there in Moscow, where the boys had skied and played soccer and where Popov's father was later arrested and shot in Stalin's Great Purge, Boris Yeltsin climbed onto a tank and denounced the coup against Mikhail Gorbachev.

Popov anxiously called his wife in Moscow, who had heard nothing of the dramatic events under way just blocks away. Over the phone from Alaska, he relayed CNN's description of the upheaval.

Fischer and other Alaskans across the globe struggled to make sense of what they were watching during those three days in August. For them, the new freedoms Gorbachev tried to give his country helped melt the Ice Curtain along the only border it shared with the United States. Among the coup leaders and those they represented, Gorbachev's reforms were an erosion of their power and privilege. They feared the Soviet Union would break apart, reducing it to second-class world-power status. That was unacceptable to the Communist Party hierarchy and the well-entrenched military-industrial complex.

In the months leading up to the attempted coup, Gorbachev's *perestroika*-style government restructuring allowed legislative assemblies across the country to hold free elections with competitive candidates. That was in marked contrast to the single-candidate elections held after the revolution in which winners rubber-stamped Communist Party directives. Once elected in the early 1990s, the new reform candidates pushed for greater freedoms, including independence from Moscow. The process of breaking away from the Soviet Union began in the Baltics but quickly spread to the largest republic of all—the Russian Federation.

No one benefited from Gorbachev's reforms more than a construction worker from the Soviet heartland, Boris Yeltsin. Yeltsin rose through the ranks of his local Communist Party until he came to the attention of Gorbachev, who elevated him to the Politburo in 1986. Effectively the mayor of Moscow, Yeltsin was assigned to shake up the corrupt Moscow party apparatus. There he ran afoul of his benefactor by pushing aggressive reforms and even criticizing Gorbachev himself for the slow pace of change.

Forced to resign just two years later, Yeltsin then staged one of the most remarkable political comebacks in Soviet history. After being demoted to a lowly position as deputy minister for construction, he took advantage of competitive elections in 1989 to win a seat in the new Soviet parliament. From that high-profile post, he became one of his country's most outspoken voices against the Communist Party and an advocate for a market-based economy and free multiparty elections. Over Gorbachev's opposition, the parliament elected Yeltsin president of the Russian Federation in June 1991, just two months before the coup.

While Gorbachev remained out of sight under house arrest in the Crimea during those few days that warm summer, Yeltsin emerged from the palatial Russian White House to denounce the coup. "The clouds of terror and dictatorship are gathering over the whole country," he thundered from atop a tank. "They must not be allowed to bring eternal night."

Even though he demanded the safe return of Gorbachev, Yeltsin's actions were designed to empower himself. Three days after the coup began, it was over. Gorbachev returned to Moscow dramatically weakened while Yeltsin emerged boldly empowered.

The shaken Gorbachev addressed his country in a televised news conference, which Yeltsin repeatedly interrupted to bark orders suspending the Communist Party and demanding an investigation into its role in the coup. Later that day Gorbachev quietly resigned from the party for which he had worked his entire career and which rewarded him by trying to overthrow him.

Six months later, a demoralized and bitter Gorbachev stepped down as head of the USSR and handed over the nuclear-launch codes to his nemesis, Boris Yeltsin. On December 26, 1991, the Soviet Union passed into the history books. Gorbachev and Yeltsin never spoke again.

To Alaskans, the August coup attempt and demise of the USSR were both startling and stimulating. From his outpost in Magadan, Mark Dudley nervously anticipated Alaska Airlines flight interruptions, but none occurred.

Anchorage businessman Dave Heatwole was trolling for Alaska salmon during the coup and heard the news when he returned to the Seward boat dock. He postponed a trip to Magadan the next day but wrote in his diary, "The coup in the Soviet Union collapsed—the Soviet people threw the communists out! I knew they would, but I was surprised they were able to do it so quickly. The economic opportunities will open fast."

Natalie Novik was at home in the Northwest Alaska community of Kotzebue when her shortwave radio crackled with the news. The Soviet-affairs coordinator for the NANA Regional Corporation relayed developments to local officials who had been exchanging visits with their Soviet Native counterparts.

"For Chukotka, nothing has changed, except that the people there have shown their solidarity with Gorbachev and Yeltsin, as well as their commitment to democratic changes in the country," Novik reported. "For a few hours of the first day, they had the old fears haunt them."

For Vic Fischer, the economic impact of the Soviet Union's breakup was so devastating that he doubled down on his efforts to better conditions for his Russian brethren. Yeltsin's rip-the-bandage-off economic policies left the economy in shambles. Prices skyrocketed as the government lifted price controls on 90 percent of consumer goods. Bus and subway stops were filled with hungry, often elderly Russians selling anything they could find: a handful of cucumbers, a box of kittens, a rusty samovar. In the Far East, conditions were even worse as food and energy shipped to remote communities ran low.

IN THE DECADE prior to the mid-1980s, Alaska's interactions with the Soviet Union had been limited mostly to isolated scientific exchanges tied to the University of Alaska. As the Ice Curtain began to melt in fall 1989, a handful of university officials led by Lee Gorsuch, director of the Institute of Social and Economic Research (ISER), envisioned broader opportunities. Because of Alaska's burgeoning ties with the Soviet Far East, Gorsuch urged Fischer to look for potential federal support in Washington, DC. Fischer made the rounds of federal agencies but struck out. The State Department could not care less that Alaska and Russia were a mere two and a half miles apart; relations between the countries were appropriately managed in Washington and Moscow, he was told.

As pleas grew for the university's engagement with the Soviet Union, University of Alaska president Donald O'Dowd consolidated the disparate demands, found money in his office accounts, and named Fischer the university's director of Soviet relations in September 1989.

"The number of initiatives coming from Soviet sources are so great and varied that it's not possible for us to deal with them in the ad hoc manner that we've been pursuing to date," O'Dowd said.

From his ISER office in Anchorage, Fischer fielded a steady stream of exchange proposals, from geologists to marine mammal scientists, and slogged across the USSR to build his list of Soviet contacts. Before O'Dowd left the university, in 1990, he joined Fischer on two trips to the Soviet Union focused on scientific exchanges.

In part because of Alaska's ties with the Soviet Union, New York economist Jerry Komisar succeeded O'Dowd as UA president. The son of a Russian immigrant who had strong sympathies for the Russian Revolution, Komisar had traveled to the Soviet Union a decade earlier and "fell in love with the place."

Seeking to establish research relationships with Soviet Far East universities, Fischer and Komisar turned to a vital source of support, Senator Stevens, who shared their view of the merits of regional diplomacy and trade. Stevens had witnessed US-Soviet military cooperation nearly a half century earlier during the World War II Lend-Lease initiative. He left college in 1943 to join the Army Air Corps and earned his wings at age twenty. Stevens was immediately ordered to fly supplies over the Himalayan Mountains to China from Allied bases in India, one of the war's most dangerous assignments. More than four hundred aircraft and eight hundred men were lost flying "over the Hump." As a result of that experience, Stevens arrived in the Senate with a strong military orientation when he was appointed in 1968.

Stevens estimated that during his forty years in the Senate, he visited the Soviet Union ten times, becoming an advocate for citizen exchanges to help ease military tensions. So Fischer met a receptive audience when he appealed to Stevens in late 1990 to find funds for an Alaska-Soviet technical assistance effort designed to keep economic and political reform moving ahead.

"Alaska has much of the expertise and technology needed to help our Soviet neighbors deal with their critical problems, particularly in matters pertaining to functioning in and developing the North and remote regions," Fischer wrote. He detailed seven specific areas where federal funding could be useful: community infrastructure, economic development, environmental protection, government and public administration, housing, private enterprise, and telecommunications.

Stevens responded with a brief supportive letter and handwritten note: "I want to help as much as I can on this—it is a good idea." In addition to agreeing on the merits of advancing Soviet reforms, Fischer and Stevens shared a frustration with the Washington view that US-USSR relations were best conducted through the national capitals. Over the next fifteen years, the two irritated many federal officials by forcing millions of federal dollars across the Bering Strait.

A longtime member of the Senate Appropriations Committee, which writes the nation's spending bills, Stevens had been dubbed the "emperor of earmarks" by a fiscal-reform group. Never apologetic for the practice, Stevens directed nearly 1,500 individual spending projects to Alaska totaling $3.4 billion between 1991 and 2008.

The first Stevens-directed federal appropriation to the University of Alaska for Russian exchanges was $2 million through the US Information Agency. Fischer's two-member Soviet affairs office was not equipped to manage such large programs, so the university created a new entity to receive and administer the federal funds. When Jerry Komisar was recruited for the University of Alaska presidency, his search committee had been run by Charles Neff, a Yale-trained Soviet scholar and former administrator for international programs at State University of New York. Komisar suggested Neff to head the new entity, and in 1993 Neff moved to Anchorage to establish what would become the American Russian Center.

However, first Neff had to deal with the politically sensitive chore of sorting through two competing proposals for engagement with Russia. One came from a longtime University of Alaska Anchorage international affairs professor, John Choon Kim, who in 1984 had created the Center for International Business and landed a state endowment for operating funds. Kim envisioned an ambitious training center organized through his Korean-Russian contacts that could teach Western business practices to Russians across their entire country.

Fischer's competing vision was a narrower focus on technical assistance to the Russian Far East, particularly the Chukotka region, home to relatives of Alaska Natives. With help from Stevens's office, Neff had met with federal aid agencies in Washington before landing in Alaska and had a sense of what would fly with them. As the one with the ties to Stevens, Fischer prevailed. Thus the American Russian Center was created, its mission borrowing Kim's training concepts but focusing them on the Far East.

In addition to hitting up Stevens for funding, Fischer pitched Governor Cowper, who was in his final sixty days in office. Calling lack of money to support Alaska-Soviet activities a "crisis," Fischer asked for $257,000 in state funds to support an aviation exchange, production of a Soviet Far East "blue book" guide to the region, a dedicated phone line between Magadan and Alaska, support for a visiting Soviet professor, and funding for his own office.

"Lack of sufficient and timely funding is jeopardizing ongoing and future Alaska-Soviet interaction," Fischer wrote to the governor. The funding never materialized.

When the American Russian Center opened, I was finishing a four-month fellowship in Nizhny Novgorod, a Russian city I had never heard of before arriving there in spring 1993. Restless after working on a losing political campaign and looking to quench my thirst for Russian culture and language, I was advised by Fischer to explore this city, one of Russia's largest.

Stalin had renamed this city in the Russian heartland, 260 miles east of Moscow, Gorky in honor of locally born writer Maxim Gorky, an apologist for the Soviet dictator. Its original name restored by the time I arrived, Nizhny Novgorod was a manufacturing hub of Soviet MiG fighter jets and nuclear submarines. It had long had been closed to Westerners to protect state secrets. Fischer recommended it because a new generation of young upstarts were aggressively experimenting with *glasnost* reforms there.

One of those upstarts was its governor, a thirty-two-year-old physicist named Boris Nemtsov. I served as Nemtsov's volunteer media advisor under the auspices of the National Forum Foundation, an international democracy-building institute. With movie-star looks and boundless energy, Nemtsov came to power opposing construction of a local nuclear-power plant. As governor, he privatized hundreds of collective farms, beauty parlors, and grocery stores, and even issued a local currency, dubbed "Nemtsov-ski."

During my time there, journalists and international politicians, including Margaret Thatcher, descended in droves on a modest privatized cheese shop in downtown Nizhny. It offered a tasty contrast between failed Soviet socialism and the new reform capitalism.

My job included tutoring Nemtsov's staff on American-style media relations such as press-release writing and interview techniques. I also helped organize a regional media conference that attracted US foreign correspondents from Moscow and helped edit a pioneering English-language newspaper.

In my ample spare time, I dug into the city's history, including that of the fourteenth-century walled Kremlin overlooking the Volga River and massive public-works projects built by Nazi POWs. I was moved to tears in the tiny apartment where Nobel laureate Andrei Sakharov was exiled for six years until freed by Gorbachev in 1986. One of a handful of Americans among one and a half million Russians, I struggled to subsist on the rare banana, privatized cheese, and *kvass*, a summertime ale brewed from fermented black bread. My Russian-language tutor, Marina Grekova, did her best to help me blend in.

Governor Nemtsov was witty, brash, and as impatient about advancing his agenda as any politician I had ever seen. I remember the sheer terror I felt as a passenger in a car he insisted on driving to a TV interview at speeds that would rival a NASCAR driver. After leaving Nizhny Novgorod, I maintained distant connections with Nemtsov as he moved up the political ladder to Moscow before meeting a tragic end.

After returning to Alaska that summer of 1993, I was hired by the American Russian Center to administer the $2 million US Information Agency grant for cultural and educational exchanges. To broaden the reach across both Alaska and the Russian Far East, we solicited proposals for individual exchanges and received more than fifty. We funded twenty-five projects, ranging from Native leadership training and business journalism to marine mammal management and women's centers. We tried to target projects that complemented the American Russian Center's business-training efforts. Fischer received one of the largest grants, to help Russian Far East governments become more democratic. Hundreds of Alaskans and Russians participated in the exchanges with Russian communities from Chukotka to Vladivostok.

My duties included visits to Russian cities participating in exchanges. In Yakutsk, I saw public-school teachers inspire their students to participate in local elections after witnessing their Kids Vote counterparts in Fairbanks. In Magadan, I watched local journalists hone their reporting skills after interning with Alaska media.

Since Russia lacked a working banking system and credit cards were an innovation of the future, I resorted to carrying thousands of crisp US dollars hidden beneath my clothes for expense payments to our Russian partners. That practice, common among Alaskans crossing the strait, drove our receipt-obsessed university accountants crazy.

One of the more innovative exchange projects focused on an issue rarely discussed openly in Russia—women's reproductive health. For much of the Soviet Union's existence, abortion was the most common and effective means of family planning. The abortion rate in the remote Chukotka region at that time was reported at double the rate of births, 198 abortions per 100 births, with many Russian women having a dozen or more abortions.

An energetic Juneau organizer, JoAnn Grady, began working in the Russian Far East in 1989 to improve the plight of Russian women. Grady initially worked with the Moscow-based Foundation for Social Innovations. After witnessing the second-class status of many Russian women during nearly two dozen trips to the Soviet Union, Grady befriended a San Francisco philanthropist, Sally Lovett. Inspired by her own visits to the Soviet Union, Lovett committed thousands of dollars to a Petropavlovsk-Kamchatsky women's center. The Russian staff, including psychologists, ob-gyns, and a surgeon, all trained in Alaska before opening the Lovett Women's Center.

Grady was initially awarded $53,000 from the American Russian Center's federal grant to help organize Kamchatka women to combat problems of mental and reproductive health and domestic violence. Through an unprecedented collaboration between the Lovett Center and the local hospital, women received medical consultations and birth control. The project garnered considerable media attention, and Grady later transported her women's center model to Magadan, where it was enthusiastically welcomed.

Juneau's Tiffany Markey was among the young Russian-speaking Americans who managed the University of Alaska's American Russian Center business centers in the Russian Far East. Markey opened ARC's Magadan center in 1994. COURTESY OF RUSS HOWELL

University of Alaska Teaches
Capitalism 101

Millions in international aid flows though Alaska's "Capitalism U"
—ANCHORAGE DAILY NEWS, JULY 23, 1995

T HE UNIVERSITY OF Alaska's American Russian Center (ARC) came of
age at an opportune time. Two years into the Yeltsin government, in 1993,
the Russian economy was in chaos. Inflation was running at 12 percent a month
and continued decentralization meant significant economic and political authority were devolved to the regions where thousands of would-be Russian entrepreneurs were trying to cash in on the turmoil.

ARC director Charlie Neff noted that the two biggest cities in the Russian
Far East, Vladivostok and Khabarovsk, "probably have more people on the hustle
per capita than any city in the United States, including New York."

There's plenty of underground free market, he said, but what Russia needed
"is more regularity, the adoption of business practices that are compatible with
economic systems in the West, laws that work, more personal trust, more focus
on the medium to long run instead of the quick-ruble deal."

That was essentially ARC's mission. Quickly on the heels of the US
Information Agency grant for cultural and educational exchanges came millions more in federal dollars for small-business development and technical

training. The Anchorage center hosted hundreds of Russians who learned business management, including banking, accounting, computing, and marketing. It also opened seven business-development centers in the Russian Far East's larger cities—Vladivostok, Khabarovsk, Sakhalin, Magadan, Blagoveschensk, Yakutsk, and Petropavlosk-Kamchatsky. For the most part, the Russian centers were run in partnership with a local university and co-managed by an Alaskan and Russian.

After surviving stints working in the US Congress and Alaska State House of Representatives, Tiffany Markey embarked on a new adventure in late 1994. The twenty-seven-year-old Juneau native boxed up her computer, strapped $20,000 in cash to her body, and headed off to the gulag city of Magadan to open ARC's third Russian business center.

Markey earned her degree in Soviet studies and Russian language from Cornell University before returning to Alaska to work as Vic Fischer's Russian-affairs assistant. She showed off the Russian Far East to key federal officials, including a top aide to Senator Stevens and a State Department delegation that barely knew where the region was.

As a cold winter descended on Magadan, Markey and her cat, Max, lived for weeks in a one-bedroom flat with her Russian co-manager, his wife, and their two young children. After securing office space with the Magadan Pedagogical Institute, the center buzzed with local entrepreneurs trying to make sense of Western business practices. One Magadan flower shop owner wanted to expand and, at the suggestion of her Alaska instructors, asked the local bank for a loan. The bank demanded a bribe larger than the requested loan amount.

"Trying to convey American-style business was like teaching a foreign language," Markey said. "The biggest challenge trying to establish a market economy was lack of cash." Still, she said, the center helped connect Alaska-Russian joint ventures and established a well-received women's center.

The experience of Russians who received ARC training in Alaska varied widely. In spring 1994, twenty-one Russians from across the Far East trained in Alaska for ten weeks in the fundamentals of American-style small business. A Sakhalin woman who had produced one of her community's first English-language visitor guides wanted to capitalize on the influx of foreign companies rushing in for the island's oil and gas development opportunities. A Magadan commercial bank director hoped to start a new business importing medical supplies. A traditional Yakutsk wood carver needed training to supply a reindeer herders' village with consumer goods.

The Russian entrepreneurs usually spent the first six weeks in seminars learning accounting, management, and computer skills, and then a month as interns for Alaska and Lower 48 companies. After his Alaska training and internship with an Anchorage software firm, Yuzhno-Sakhalinsk businessman Aleksey Okhotnikov expanded his computer-assembly and sales company to employ thirty-one people. With Anchorage business training classes under his belt, Dmitry Vanyashkin opened an independent radio station in the Khabarovsk region broadcasting music aimed at twelve- to twenty-five-year-olds. He employed seventeen local Russians.

Ekaterina Ovchinnokova attended an ARC basic business course in Khabarovsk, looking for ways to introduce a new concept to the Russian Far East—credit unions, which could extend credit for personal needs at lower interest rates than Russian banks. After her training, she landed a Eurasia Foundation grant and opened two credit union branches, expanding membership from twenty-five to more than seven hundred.

Dr. Svetlana Kischenko was a teaching neurologist at Far Eastern State Medical University struggling to help Russian doctors transition from government employees to members of private clinics. After numerous ARC business courses and training at Alaska medical facilities, she returned to Khabarovsk to help train other doctors in family medicine.

ARC's operations, especially chaotic in Russia, were not without controversy. Senator Stevens was criticized by some of his Republican colleagues for spending US taxpayer dollars in Russia. Federal agencies continued to grumble about earmarks that steered funds from their programs to ARC for Alaska-Russian activities. They also complained about the high cost of the center's operations.

Many federally funded Russian aid programs of the era involved hiring American consultants, who showed up for a week to conduct a seminar and then moved on to the next city. ARC's model funded salaries and expenses for its employees who actually lived in the communities in which they worked.

A 2000 performance audit commissioned by the US Agency for International Development found that ARC's Russian business centers produced "impressive" results and had a significant impact on their host communities but "are not sustainable as currently managed and financed." It also questioned the 23 percent overhead the University of Alaska charged to house the ARC, although it was far less than that charged by other universities.

ARC was criticized within Alaska, too. For a training on banking, the center had to resort to hiring an Oregon banker when no Alaska bankers were available to participate, causing grumbling among Alaskans. A 1997 Alaska legislative audit reported several appearances of impropriety, including conflict-of-interest questions, lack of financial controls, and some questionable disbursements. The university president largely disputed the audit's findings and Charlie Neff and Vic Fischer attributed it to legislative politics.

Other evaluations of ARC's programs were generally favorable. A former State Department official and Stanford University evaluator, Chip Blacker of the Institute for International Studies, visited three ARC business-development centers in March 1998 to assess their performance. He told top officials at the State Department and National Security Council that the programs "are delivering considerable bang for the buck." They produced local jobs and taxes, helped grow Russia's private sector, and were essential to economic and political reforms outside Moscow, he said.

Edward Fiske, a former *New York Times* education reporter, was commissioned to evaluate the USIA exchange program to determine whether it served American foreign policy. After interviewing scores of participants in Alaska and the Russian Far East, he concluded that the exchanges produced a profound effect on individual Russians and Alaskans, restored faith in political institutions, encouraged a sense of volunteerism, and contributed to support for democratic institutions and a market-based economy.

"It is by no means clear that Russia will be successful in making the complex transitions from centralized political and economic systems to democratic institutions and market economies," Fiske concluded in 1998. "The USIA Exchange Program constitutes a limited but successful attempt to provide new visions and technical skills. What does seem clear is that, in the absence of outside assistance of this sort, Russia will find these transitions far more tortuous."

One of ARC's last and more controversial training programs originated with one of Alaska's most controversial political operatives, oil-patch entrepreneur Bill Allen. A onetime New Mexico welder, Allen expanded his multimillion-dollar company, VECO Corp., by cleaning Alaska beaches after the 1989 *Exxon Valdez* oil spill. He applied part of those proceeds to purchase the *Anchorage Times,* which he used to advocate for the state's oil and gas industry and expand his political influence.

In the late 1990s, Allen was frustrated with his inability to break into the lucrative oil and gas development under way on Sakhalin Island. So Allen sought help from Senator Stevens, his longtime political ally. Stevens earmarked $2.3 million for the US Department of Labor to train Russian Far East oil-field workers in project and logistics management and technical skills. The project was overseen by a four-person advisory council, which included a VECO executive. Fifty-five Russian managers were trained by University of Alaska faculty under ARC auspices between 2002 and 2003. According to an ARC final report, the training resulted in five joint ventures, five new contracts, and at least two hundred new US jobs.

In its fifteen years of operations, beginning in 1993, ARC took in $26.2 million, the vast majority from federal agencies: US Agency for International Development, US Information Agency, and the departments of education, labor, and state. About one-third of the total receipts were earmarks from Senator Stevens, according to ARC's second director, Russ Howell. Other funds came from IREX, an international nonprofit, and the Alaska Department of Labor.

The center supported as many as seventeen full-time and twenty part-time employees and up to twenty-four Russians. ARC detailed its accomplishments in a 2008 letter to Stevens:

- More than 62,000 Russian entrepreneurs, government officials, and non-governmental organization leaders received ARC training.
- Nearly 1,800 Russian business leaders traveled to Alaska to participate in 151 seminars and exchanges.
- More than six hundred Russians visited Alaska on thirty-two cultural and educational exchanges, and nearly two hundred Alaskans visited Russia through those programs.
- Seven self-supporting business development centers operated in the Russian Far East.
- More than one hundred Russian students received joint business administration degrees through the University of Alaska Anchorage and Russian universities.
- More than three hundred Alaska business officials participated in thirty seminars focused on business in Russia.

ARC's on-the-ground operations in Russia were all tied to local universities or institutes, which in turn benefited from sending their students to the University of Alaska Anchorage at in-state tuition rates. The relationships began in the late 1980s, when Fischer was still exploring opportunities for the University of Alaska.

In 1989, Fischer befriended a native of Kyrgyzstan named Asylbek Aidaraliev, who ran the Institute for the Study of Biological Problems of the North. The two negotiated the creation of a new Magadan-based international scientific center on northern issues called Arktika. Fischer and Aidaraliev became codirectors, with the center supported by the Soviet Academy of Sciences and the University of Alaska.

During a UA visit to Magadan the same year, Fischer and others worked with the Magadan Pedagogical Institute and Japan's Hokkaido University to form a new Northeastern International University. Several Alaskans, including Fischer and then–University of Alaska finance executive Brian Rogers, served on the board until dismissed by President Putin. The University of Alaska Anchorage partnered with Sakhalin State University in Sakhalin, with the Far Eastern State Transportation University in Khabarovsk, with Yakut State University in Yakutsk, and with Far East State University for Economics and Services in Vladivostok.

The center also helped attract more Russian students to the University of Alaska Anchorage than any other American university. Working with its Russian partners, the university created a joint degree program. At the same time, the University of Alaska adopted a policy that any student from an Alaska sister city could attend the university at in-state tuition rates. During the ten years starting in 2000, between 105 and 155 Russian students were enrolled at the university each year. Some Russian students resided in dorm rooms but most stayed with host families.

According to the late Cecile Mitchell, University of Alaska Anchorage's international student services director, finding housing for the Russian students was challenging. Many arrived expecting the independence of dorm life and sometimes clashed with host families. In 1993, Mitchell told her boss that three international students feared for their safety because of sexual advances from members of their host families.

Between 1991 and 2015, a total of 2,392 students from Russia attended the University of Alaska Anchorage, about 1,750 of them from the Russian sister cities Magadan, Petropavlovsk-Kamchatsky, Vladivostok, Yakutsk, and Sakhalin. Others went to University of Alaska campuses in Fairbanks and Juneau.

My tenure at the American Russian Center ended in late 1994 with the election of Tony Knowles as Alaska's new governor. A former oil-patch roustabout, restaurateur, and two-term Anchorage mayor, the moderate Democrat asked me to make a second tour in the Governor's Office as his communications director. I also doubled as Governor Knowles's foreign-affairs advisor. Just a few months into the new administration, I helped persuade the new governor to make his first trip to Russia for a mission that will haunt us both for the rest of our lives.

A statue of Vladimir Lenin is one of the few structures still standing just weeks after the 1995 earthquake that leveled the Sakhalin village of Neftegorsk. PHOTO BY DAVID RAMSEUR

18

Oil in Sakhalin, Flush Toilets in Chukotka

If ever once you visit Sakhalin,
the memories will be forever green.
The foggy voice of the boats,
the mountain's wild winter coat,
the avalanches, typhoons,
while my guitar gently croons.

—ALEXEY BAYANDIN, MUSICIAN AND PRESS SECRETARY
TO SAKHALIN GOV. IGOR FARKHUTDINOV, 1997

T HE COFFINS WERE the most disconcerting sight—flimsy plywood boxes stacked ten high to the roof of a wooden shed, waiting to be filled. The shed was among the few structures still standing. The nearby Soviet-style concrete-slab apartment buildings had collapsed quickly, their five floors stacked like deadly pancakes, compressing furniture, toys, bodies. Seventeen such buildings crumpled, killing more than two thousand Russians, about two-thirds of the town's residents.

Gov. Tony Knowles and I stared in quiet disbelief. We had just flown by helicopter to Neftegorsk, a village on the northern tip of Russia's Sakhalin Island. Weeks before, on May 27, 1995, a 7.5-magnitude earthquake had shaken the town apart.

Responding to an appeal from the state's new governor, Alaskans generously stepped forward to donate more than twenty thousand pounds of wheelchairs, prosthetics, and medical supplies. After securing federal approval to fly an

Alaska Air National Guard C-130 nearly three thousand miles to deliver the relief, Knowles decided to go along.

Shortly after landing in the nearest town with a hospital, Sakhalin Gov. Igor Farkhudtinov asked us to join him on the quick hop to ground zero. From the air, it looked like the stark desolation of a *Mad Max* movie. Row after row of dirt mounds were marked with tiny wooden crosses where the recovered bodies were hastily buried. A statue of Vladimir Lenin, ever present in the center of virtually every Soviet community, remained standing as if presiding over the tragedy.

After surveying the devastation, we slowly made our way back toward the helicopter. Suddenly, seemingly out of nowhere, scores of the remaining towns-people rushed in over the horizon surrounding the two governors, shouting angrily. They had been hunkered down in *dachas*, small shacks on the outskirts of town where they normally retreated on summer weekends to tend to gardens. With Knowles at his side, Farkhudtinov stood for an hour in a dusty field answering shouted questions.

"We finally buried everybody and now we don't have anything to do or any-where to go," said one woman whose daughter, mother, and niece all died in the quake. "We feel like we've been left behind."

Farkhudtinov tried to reassure the living that help from far-away Moscow was on the way. Knowles told the desperate residents of the medical supplies he had just brought and noted the special ties between Alaska and Sakhalin, a bond of geography and shared earthquake devastation. We later learned the government had already decided to bulldoze the remaining buildings, leaving only graves and a memorial where Neftegorsk once stood. The survivors were to be resettled before the fall snow.

More than a century earlier, in 1890, famed Russian author Anton Chekhov explored dismal penal colony conditions on Sakhalin Island and pronounced, "I have seen Ceylon, which is paradise, and Sakhalin, which is hell." A century later, this island just thirty miles north of Japan was the most visited and important Russian Far East destination for Alaskans.

AS KNOWLES MOVED into the governor's office in late 1994, Alaska's leading industry was ailing. Alaska North Slope oil production was in sharp decline, down more than five hundred thousand barrels a day from the 1988 peak. Prices also continued to slide, dropping to about $17 a barrel.

Once again, the oil industry looked west. Hoping to cash in on massive untapped oil and gas discoveries off Sakhalin's northeast coast, international giants such as Royal Dutch Shell, ExxonMobil, and Texaco prepared to invest $45 billion to extract Sakhalin energy for markets in China, Korea, and India. Alaska oil-patch service companies followed them in.

Lynden International, an air and freight-forwarding company, opened a Sakhalin office in 1994. "By the year 2000 or 2001, the amount of activity on Sakhalin should far exceed [Alaska's] Prudhoe Bay," predicted Lynden regional manager Rick Pollock.

To meet the island's housing shortages, especially for oil-field workers, Anchorage's Harry Pursell starting building oil-field camps. "There aren't many places in the world for our business so the slowing down in Alaska started our work here," said Pursell, president of Arctic Camps and Equipment. Reeve Aleutian Airways expanded its operations to Sakhalin, and the university's American Russian Center trained oil-field managers.

"It was natural for us to export our expertise because of Alaska's close relationship with Russia but also because Alaska oil-field services, building pipelines, and environmental protection were the state of the art in the industry," Knowles said.

As private companies from across the world tried to position themselves for the Sakhalin development, the regional government turned to Alaska for advice on how to handle the bonanza. On his way out of office in 1994, Governor Hickel signed an eight-point agreement with his Sakhalin counterpart, Gov. Evgeney Krasnoyarov. It called for cooperation on environmental protection, training oil-field workers, and setting up banking and insurance systems.

Inspired by the earthquake relief visit a year later, Governor Knowles and the new Sakhalin governor established a friendship that transcended business. Both had schooled in economics and local government as mayors; the two visited each other's homes and socialized with their families. Farkhudtinov reciprocated with an Alaska visit in late 1995 when he and Knowles created an Alaska-Sakhalin Working Group, which pursued joint cooperation between the regions.

As the Sakhalin development grew, however, the regional government was frustrated in its struggle to win Russian national parliament approval of how oil and gas proceeds would be divided through a production-sharing agreement.

The Communist Party–dominated Duma resisted laws guaranteeing protections for foreign investments while Farkhudtinov complained that delays cost jobs for local residents and revenues for sorely needed public services.

Alaska had little influence with the national government but enthusiastically assisted on regional and local issues. A parade of Alaska officials met with their Sakhalin counterparts to advise on issues such as environmental regulations, monitoring of marine mammals, and creation of a development bank modeled after Alaska's Industrial Development and Export Authority.

Two years after first visiting Sakhalin to deliver earthquake relief supplies, Knowles returned to Sakhalin on a Reeve jet with forty business leaders and state legislators for a two-day trade mission. The delegation included representatives from oil and gas, banking, aviation, telecommunications, and maritime transportation. The visit produced several agreements on oil-worker training, banking, environmental protection, education, and trade. The Alaska House speaker and Senate president joined the trip and signed their own cooperation agreement with their legislative counterparts.

At the concluding banquet, Knowles presented his Russian comrade with a pair of cross-country skis. Farkhudtinov gave Knowles a Russian 7.62-mm rifle, a type originally made for the czarist army. After returning to the state capital, the governor tried out the rifle at the Juneau shooting range. Never having used a scope during his Army service in Vietnam, Knowles sported a black "scope eye" for several weeks.

Meanwhile, the State of Alaska and the American Russian Center continued to look for opportunities for Alaskans in Sakhalin. In 2000, the state Division of International Trade and Market Development was awarded a $750,000 USAID grant to continue initiatives through the Alaska-Sakhalin Working Group "that assist Sakhalin to make the transition to a free-market economy."

One project explored the concept of a "Fund for Future Generations" modeled after Alaska's Permanent Fund, which saves a portion of state oil revenues. As part of that project, former Permanent Fund executive director Dave Rose led a three-day seminar for Sakhalin officials explaining how to manage natural-resource wealth.

"The group appeared unsure as to whether the anticorruption checks and balances used as international financial conventions would be accepted in their society," Rose told state officials. "Clearly, there was concern that the central government in Moscow must provide more legal and financial autonomy, otherwise Sakhalin is destined to continue to be a ward of the central government or fail in meeting the needs of the people."

Rose also conducted similar seminars in Magadan and Yakutsk. Each time he returned from Russia, he was debriefed by an FBI agent, according to his widow, Fran Rose.

Another project assisted Sakhalin's environmental agencies in preventing and cleaning up oil spills in arctic conditions. One weekend in March 1998, a panicked Bill Allen of VECO contacted Knowles at the governor's mansion. Allen was about to lose out in bidding on a large Sakhalin oil-field contract. At Knowles's request, I spent my weekend producing a series of letters for the governor's signature attesting to Allen's credentials and faxed them to various Sakhalin officials, including Farkhudtinov. Allen still lost the contract.

As Alaskans prospected for economic opportunities on Sakhalin Island and elsewhere in the Russian Far East, a type of political intrigue was under way in remote Chukotka that would rival the smoke-filled backrooms of Chicago. After the 1988 Friendship Flight, interaction between Alaskans and Chukotka residents blossomed as Natives from both sides reestablished long-lost ties. Hundreds of Alaska and Russian Natives crossed the Bering Strait without the requirement of visas, under the 1989 visa-free agreement between the two national governments.

In 1992, however, progress was largely stalled with the election of an old-school strongman, Aleksandr Nazarov, as Chukotka's governor. A founder of the Bear Party, Nazarov launched what a team of international researchers later termed the "Great Depression." Industries collapsed, unemployment skyrocketed, settlements were abandoned, and food shortages grew acute. Conditions were especially disastrous for Russian Natives, who were teetering on the edge of survival. Nazarov clamped down on exchanges between his constituents and Alaskans, sometimes sending delegations of his loyalists to Alaska meetings to which other Russian Natives had been invited.

Nazarov traveled to Alaska several times and rented office space for a consulate in downtown Anchorage to represent his region. In 1993, he emerged from a two-hour meeting with Governor Hickel. Nazarov pronounced Hickel to be Chukotka's "godfather" for his advice on how to manage local natural resources under Hickel's "owner state" concept.

"We can't allow a random development of capitalism here in Chukotka the way it's happening in most other regions of Russia," Nazarov told the *Evening Moscow* newspaper. "Local culture is unique and fragile. If we lose it to hazards of uncontrollable economy we will never be able to restore it."

Seven tumultuous years later, Nazarov was gearing up for a reelection campaign.

At the same time, in far-away Moscow, a handful of Russian industrialists were becoming enormously wealthy under President Yeltsin by manipulating lax regulations to acquire control of the nation's resources. Many sought seats in the national Duma, where holding office guaranteed them immunity from prosecution.

One was a shy young orphan from southern Russia named Roman Arkadyevich Abramovich. While still a student at Moscow's Auto Transport Institute, Abramovich established a small oil business that he parlayed into a seat on the board of directors for Sibneft, one of Russia's largest oil companies. He eventually took over the company and made billions selling it to the Russian gas company Gazprom. At the urging of Chukotka's Governor Nazarov in 1999, Abramovich won a seat in Russia's lower parliament representing the far-flung Far East region—about which he knew virtually nothing.

In Alaska, the University of Alaska's Vic Fischer remained frustrated by the deterioration in Chukotka, which he witnessed during frequent visits. In January 2000, John Tichotsky, a former American Russian Center staffer and Fischer confidant, met a leading Chukotka whaler at a meeting in Barrow. The two schemed to find an opponent who could beat Nazarov. They researched Russian law and were surprised to learn that a Chukotka governor only had to be a Russian citizen, not a resident of Chukotka.

Then they called the person they thought was the perfect candidate, a dual US-Russian citizen, a father of Alaska Statehood, and a former Alaska state senator: Vic Fischer. Fischer initially laughed off the idea but eventually took it seriously enough to consider his options. One of those he wanted to consult was Abramovich, whom Fischer thought could help underwrite his campaign, if it came to that.

At Fischer's urging, Governor Knowles invited Abramovich to Alaska. He arrived that summer of 2000 with his entourage in a chartered Boeing 707. As the governor's representative, I joined Tichotsky in welcoming the Russians to

This portrait was long considered to be of Vitus Jonassen Bering, the Danish explorer dispatched by Russian Czar Peter the Great in 1725 to determine if the Asian and North American continents were joined at what today is known as the Bering Strait. The 1991 discovery of Bering's remains and forensic reconstruction of his facial features raise doubts about the portrait.
ALASKA STATE LIBRARY PHOTO COLLECTION

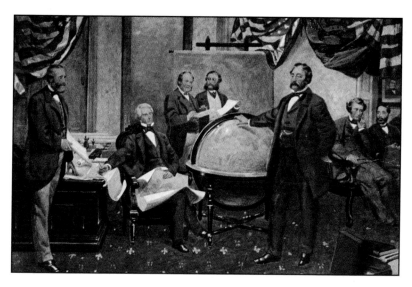

The signing of the Treaty of Cessation (Alaska Purchase), March 30, 1867, from a painting by Emanuel Leutze. Secretary of State William Seward sits at left; Russian ambassador Eduard de Stoeckl stands at the globe positioned on Alaska.
ALASKA & ARCTIC-RELATED ILLUSTRATIONS PHOTO COLLECTION, ALASKA STATE LIBRARY

Russian fur trappers were unable to match the hunting prowess of Alaska Native marine mammal hunters. So the Russians held Native women and children hostage while forcing the men to hunt sea otter. This engraving by Luka Vormonin is from a 1790 expedition to the Aleutian Islands.

Soviet and US military personnel gather under the wing of a Li-2 transport plane in Nome in September 1942 to celebrate the arrival of the first Soviet military mission as part of the Lend-Lease program. By the following summer, hundreds of Soviet crews were stationed at Alaska airfields in Fairbanks, Nome, and Galena. COURTESY OF US AIR FORCE

Dubbed "Alaska's gift to the Soviet Union" by the media, Alaska Performing Artists for Peace performed across the USSR in 1986 under the direction of Juneau musician Dixie Belcher.
PHOTO BY BOYD NORTON

Endurance swimmer Lynne Cox approaches a snowy beach on Soviet Big Diomede Island after swimming across the thirty-eight-degree Bering Strait in August 1987 to focus attention on the closeness of Alaska and the Soviet Union. PHOTO BY CLAIRE RICHARDSON

Alaska Siberian Yupik Darlene Pungowiyi Orr stands on Soviet soil in Provideniya for the first time in June 1988. She is joined by University of Alaska Fairbanks Native language professor Michael Krauss.
COURTESY OF DARLENE ORR

Governor Cowper (right) joins Provideniya Mayor Oleg Kulinkin (center) and Sen. Frank Murkowski during the Friendship Flight in June 1988 in Provideniya's House of Culture.
PHOTO BY WILBUR E. GARRETT, NATIONAL GEOGRAPHIC

Alaska artist Jon Van Zyle produced this special postage cache to commemorate the 1988 Friendship Flight, bearing cancellations from both Nome and Provideniya. The design also adorned the cover of a souvenir folder given to all flight passengers. COURTESY OF JON VAN ZYLE

Members of the US-Soviet Bering Bridge Expedition cross the frozen international date line between Alaska and the USSR in March 1989. US co-leader Paul Schurke is at far left.
COURTESY OF SASHA BELYAEV

Soviet "journalists" Anatoly Tkachenko (center) and Alexander Genkin (right) are led to an Alaska National Guard airplane for transport to Anchorage after they defected during the Bering Bridge Expedition crossing ceremony on Little Diomede Island.
COURTESY OF CAPT. REX "DUSTY" FINLEY

Governor Cowper (right) and the author, then Cowper's press secretary, in the Soviet Chukchi Sea village of Uelen during Cowper's 1989 Soviet Far East trade mission.
PHOTO BY DAVID RAMSEUR

Anchorage Daily News cartoonist Peter Dunlap-Shohl penned this cartoon in 1988 as exchanges between Alaskans and Soviets picked up steam.

Anchorage businessman Dave Heatwole visits an oil exploration drill rig in Chukotka. The chief driller (right) and crew lived at the site with their families and fished in nearby creeks. Heatwole, a former oil company executive, was one of the early Alaskans doing business in the Soviet Far East.
COURTESY OF DAVE HEATWOLE

Anchorage Daily News

VOL. XLIII, NO. 117 52 PAGES ANCHORAGE, ALASKA, TUESDAY, APRIL 26, 1988 PRICE 25 CENTS

TOP SOVIET SPOKESMAN CALLS AT LITTLE DIOMEDE

With the news media in tow, Gennadi Gerasimov walks in front of a one-word sign on the Little Diomede Store. The Russian word is "Peace."

Villagers give visitor warm welcome

Gerasimov makes no promises, but talks of melting the 'ice curtain'

By CLAIRE RICHARDSON
Daily News correspondent

Gennadi Gerasimov did not want to go to Little Diomede. At least, not when he first heard the idea from organizers of his whirlwind Alaska trip that took him through Juneau, Anchorage and Nome.

"That island is so far away," said Gerasimov, chief spokesman for Soviet leader Mikhail Gorbachev. The island is also known

for unpredictable weather that often strands visitors.

But when the weather cooperated Sunday afternoon, Gerasimov gamely boarded a chartered twin-engine plane and flew the 150-mile, 45-minute trip to the tiny island overshadowed by its Soviet neighbor, Big Diomede, almost three miles away.

The clouds hung low over the Bering Strait as Gerasimov's plane landed on the ice runway. The island's village perches pre-

cariously along its steep, rocky base. And while the residents of Diomede had no trouble scrambling up the slippery path to the school, Gerasimov and his entourage — surrounded by curious children — gingerly made their way up the ice steps.

Once inside the school gym, Gerasimov spoke to the villagers about opening the border between Siberia and Alaska.

"It's not an iron curtain," Gerasimov said, "it's an ice curtain."

He also pointed out that it was the FBI that in 1948 ended a 10-year agreement between the governments that allowed Eskimos to trade and visit with their neighbors across the Bering Strait.

"Of course, we also collaborated," Gerasimov added. "Now I think the Cold War years must be over, and with the Cold War over this ice curtain must melt and I

See Back Page, GERASIMOV

Noriega's foes may use force

Panamanian exiles aim for a 'knock-out punch'

By MELISSA HEALY
Los Angeles Times

WASHINGTON — Exiled opponents of the Panamanian government beginning next week will mount a series of economic, political and military actions designed to deal a death blow to the regime of Panamanian strongman Manuel A. Noriega, a leading opposition figure said Monday.

The announcement of the initiatives, which are to include armed actions coordinated by a newly formed, Washington-based military command, came as the Reagan administration considers softening its position demanding Noriega's immediate departure from Panama.

Juan B. Sosa, Washington envoy of the ousted government of Eric A. Delvalle, contended that economic sanctions imposed by the United States against Panama have been "very successful" and said the measures were

See Back Page, PANAMA

Crash into fire burns boy, then father in rescue

By LARRY CAMPBELL
Daily News reporter

A father and his 10-year-old son were critically burned in Tok last week when the boy crashed from a three-wheeler into a raging bonfire and his father dashed into the flames to rescue him.

The boy, Billy Wertz, was reported in critical condition Monday at Fairbanks Memorial Hospital. He is isolated and sedated, suffering from second- and third-degree burns over about 60 percent of his body, said Dennis Rogers, physician's assistant at the Tok Clinic. Jake Wertz was listed in serious but stable condition, with burns to nearly 30 percent of his body, Rogers said, mainly to his front torso, arms and hands.

The accident happened about 8 p.m. Thursday while the Wertz family, including wife and mother Sandy, were attending a birthday party for a friend, Candy Troupe. Tok is a rural community on the Glenn Highway about 200 miles northeast of Anchorage.

A small bonfire was blazing, about five feet

See Back Page, BURNED

Soviet spokesman Gennadi Gerasimov was so moved by his 1988 visit to Little Diomede and its proximity to his homeland that he worked inside the Kremlin to approve efforts to melt the Ice Curtain.

Kamchatka Peninsula English teacher Janna Lelchuk, surrounded by her Juneau high school students, first visited Alaska on a 1991 education exchange. Twenty-five years later, thanks to her influence and her nationally used textbook, hundreds of American students speak Russian.

Alaska Gov. Tony Knowles and Sakhalin Gov. Igor Farkhudtinov grew close after Knowles led an effort to provide medical relief supplies following a devastating 1995 earthquake in Sakhalin, Russia. COURTESY OF GOVERNOR TONY KNOWLES

Alaska meat processor Doug Drum spent years and millions of dollars trying to help Russian Native herders better manage and process their reindeer, only to get taken to the cleaners. Here Drum tastes a slice of reindeer horn in the Sakha Republic in 1991. COURTESY OF ANDREW CROW

Chukchi Native dancers welcome Alaska visitors to the Russian Bering Sea village of Lorino in summer 2016. Village elders encourage youth to participate in Native dance, walrus-ivory carving, and skin boat races to help preserve the Native culture. PHOTO BY LOURDES GROBET

Juneau's JoAnn Grady helped organize one of Kamchatka's first-ever women's conferences in 1993 titled "Imagine—An International Collaboration of Women." It was held in the capital city of Petropavlovsk-Kamchatsky in conjunction with the opening of the Sally Lovett Women's Center.
COURTESY OF TERI TIBBITT

Former Chukotka Gov. Roman Abramovich, one of Russia's wealthiest oligarchs, remains popular in the region although he left office in 2008. In 2016, this campaign poster adorned the cash window at the public *banya* in Uelen, Russia's northeasternmost community. A poster for Abramovich's successor, Gov. Roman Kopin, is below. PHOTO BY DAVID RAMSEUR

Larry Khlinovski Rockhill, a teacher from Alaska, caught the Russia bug so severely that he relocated to Russia and married Magadan genetics researcher Lena Khlinovskaya. COURTESY OF LARRY ROCKHILL

Elena Kostenko-Farkas first met Alaskans during a teacher exchange to Magadan in 1988. She moved to Alaska four years later and helped found America's first Russian-language immersion program for non-native speakers in Anchorage public schools.
PHOTO BY DAN JOLING

Anchorage-born Catholic priest Michael Shields was called to "go pray in the camps" and moved to Magadan in 1994 to minister to survivors of the nearby gulags. Father Shields plans to be buried on the grounds of his Church of the Nativity of Jesus on the outskirts of Magadan.
PHOTO BY DAVID RAMSEUR

Russian Big Diomede Island can be seen on the eastern horizon from the abandoned Chukotka village of Naukan, at the northeasternmost point of the Asian continent. About fifty-four miles away to the left of Big Diomede is Paavik Mountain in the Alaska mainland village of Wales. PHOTO BY DAVID RAMSEUR

Anchorage. In blue jeans with his standard three-day-old scruffy beard, one of the world's richest men was so soft-spoken I could barely hear him or extract more than one-word responses to my attempts at casual conversation. In his meeting with Governor Knowles later that week, Abramovich was polite but equally elusive.

Fischer and Abramovich met several times during his visit, and Fischer reported the Russian to be chagrined at conditions in Chukotka. The two discussed Nazarov's reelection prospects, but Abramovich never encouraged Fischer to run. A few months later, the youthful oligarch declared himself a candidate for governor. He coupled his announcement with a shipment of food aid to Chukotka's coastal villages, a Black Sea holiday for 3,300 of the region's schoolchildren, and the founding of a new newspaper that praised his generosity. About ten days before the election, Nazarov was summoned to Moscow by federal tax authorities and soon after dropped out of the race. Abramovich was elected governor with a reported 99 percent of the vote.

ALASKANS WERE SO elated with Abramovich's election that Governor Knowles sent a state delegation to his January 2001 inauguration in Anadyr, Chukotka's capital. Debby Sedwick, then commissioner of the Alaska Department of Commerce, led the state officials and noted that the Alaskans were singled out for VIP treatment. Sedwick, a former real-estate agent, recalls that Abramovich inquired about buying a home in Anchorage from which he could preside over Chukotka. The new governor set up the Pole of Hope charity managed by his cousin, Ida Ruchina, to direct his own money and aid from Moscow into the hard-hit region.

Among the other Alaskans at the inaugural was ARC's John Tichotsky, who had hit it off with Abramovich during the latter's Alaska visit a couple months earlier. Within a few weeks, Tichotsky had signed on with one of Abramovich's off-shore companies as a foreign and economic policy advisor to the governor. He also taught at one of Alaska's private universities, Alaska Pacific University.

A few months earlier, before Abramovich's election, Fischer had buttonholed Senator Stevens at an Anchorage reception and filled him in on the dismal situation in Chukotka. Stevens responded with another earmark, $5 million from USAID. It went to a new UAA entity Fischer created, the Alaska Chukotka Development Program.

To help run the program, Fischer hired Andrew Crow, an interpreter with considerable experience in the Russian Far East. With a degree in Russian from New Hampshire's Trinity College, Crow was working as a New England tour guide for visiting Soviet groups in the late 1980s. Through a friend, he was introduced to Tichotsky. In August 1989, Crow moved to Alaska and within weeks joined Tichotsky to help interpret on Governor Cowper's trade mission across the Soviet Far East.

Fischer's new Chukotka initiative focused on social problems such as rampant alcoholism, strengthening indigenous organizations, and encouraging local entrepreneurs. It helped local marine mammal hunters secure quotas to hunt whales, assisted reindeer herders to improve their herds, trained Chukotka residents to repair their boats and motors, and helped Uelen ivory carvers market their work internationally. Crow and Tichotsky met often to coordinate efforts between the university and Abramovich's new administration.

Within the university, Fischer's new earmark was not enthusiastically welcomed in all quarters. ARC managers complained that the project arrived without their knowledge, undermined their relationship with USAID, and lacked measurable results—and its connection to a controversial oligarch raised eyebrows in the United States and Russia.

Fischer's staff bristled, complaining about ARC's bureaucratic management and months-long delays in reimbursements to subcontractors. After about a year of butting heads, administration of the program was moved from ARC to the think tank Fischer had helped established decades early, the Institute of Social and Economic Research.

As governor, Abramovich made regular visits to Chukotka and built a house in Anadyr. He directed executives of his Sibneft oil company to "volunteer" to leave their families in Moscow while they spent weeks at a time in Chukotka to ensure that improvements were under way. He brought in Turkish and Canadian companies to renovate and build schools, houses, hospitals, and roads. Public-sector workers were paid on time, consumer products reappeared in shops, and the Chukchi language and culture were reintroduced into the local school curriculum.

Between Abramovich's investments and Fischer's federal funds, eighteen new schools, twenty-eight medical facilities, and hundreds of new, brightly painted houses with hot water and flush toilets were constructed in Chukotka between 2001 and 2008. Abramovich's photograph occupied a hallowed spot in many Chukotka homes, where some residents even considered him a deity worthy of prayer.

Although less godlike in Moscow, Abramovich maintained his influence at the highest levels of the Kremlin. By the late 1990s, President Yeltsin was ruling Russia, relying on a close group of advisors known as "The Family." Along with fellow oligarch Boris Berezovsky and Yeltsin's youngest daughter, Tatyana, Abramovich was among those on the inside.

"What is not in doubt is that the young oil man won the trust of the Yeltsin family," wrote two British authors in their biography of Abramovich. "Their faith in him was such as that he was given responsibility for their financial affairs and eventually became known as 'the cashier.'"

In his final year as Russia's leader, Yeltsin's health was failing and his government was in shambles. He had replaced his prime minister five times in seventeen months. On New Year's Eve 1999, Yeltsin surprised the world by announcing his immediate resignation, six months earlier than he was scheduled to leave office. The Family, including Abramovich, advised him on a successor. As Russia's new president Yeltsin selected a former KGB officer named Vladimir Putin.

Doug Drum and Andrew Crow of Alaska work with Russian Native reindeer herders in the Sakha Republic in 1991. COURTESY OF ANDREW CROW

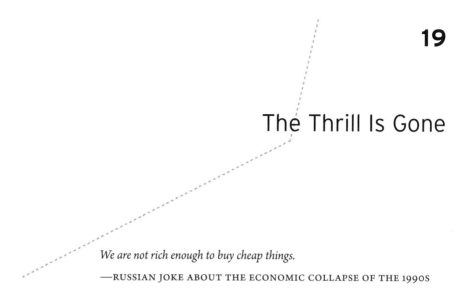

The Thrill Is Gone

We are not rich enough to buy cheap things.

—RUSSIAN JOKE ABOUT THE ECONOMIC COLLAPSE OF THE 1990S

T HE GROCERY CHAIN Carr Gottstein was among the Alaska companies that had succeeded in threading the obstacles to doing a profitable business in the Russian Far East. The company got its start in 1915 selling supplies to railroad workers living in a tent city along muddy Ship Creek near what is now downtown Anchorage.

Eighty years later, Carr Gottstein's hot dogs were so popular in the former gulag city of Magadan that they had to be ordered months in advance, according to the company's Russia agent, Dave Heatwole. By the late 1990s, Carr Gottstein was profitably selling enough container loads of consumer products barged from Tacoma, Washington, to merit setting up a food warehouse in Magadan.

That all changed on August 17, 1998. On that day, the Yeltsin government floated the ruble, exposing it to the whims of international currency rates. The value of the Russian currency immediately plummeted from the Moscow-set rate of about five rubles to the US dollar to twenty-seven. Within a week, Carr Gottstein's Magadan warehouse inventory was worth about 75 percent less.

After the burdens of language barriers, shipping challenges, and ignorance about Western business practices, that was the final straw. The company left the remaining food to its Russian partners and gave up on Russia. The debacle prompted a lawsuit between the company and Heatwole over who was at fault. It was eventually settled out of court.

Across Russia, the Yeltsin government's attempt to bring order to its erratic economy scared off American investors like Carr Gottstein. By the mid-1990s, Russia owed $60 billion in old Soviet debt to other countries. The wages of the Russian workforce had dropped by half, and 60 percent of workers weren't paid what they were owed. In the first seven months of 1998, the Russian stock market lost 75 percent of its value.

Watching their nation's resources leave the country on the private jets and yachts of billionaire oligarchs stuck in the craw of average Russians. Under Yeltsin, Gorbachev's vision to privatize state-owned enterprises evolved into a new Russian slang term, *prikhvatizatsiya* ("grabification") It reflected the widespread belief that state resources went only to those with insider connections.

"The crisis of August 1998 did not only undermine Russia's currency and force the last reformers from office . . . it also seemed to erase any remaining Western hope that Russia would successfully reform its economy," concluded two US scholars of Russia.

Two months after the ruble crisis, Dennis Mitchell landed in Sakhalin's capital city to check on the operations of his company, Lynden, Inc. The Anchorage-based freight-shipping company had been so bullish on Russia that it opened a Moscow office in 1993 and quickly expanded to the Far East, where it delivered equipment for oil drilling in Sakhalin and timber harvesting in Khabarovsk.

The Alaska Airlines MD-80 on which Mitchell arrived that October day had just turned around and was lifting off for its return flight when a horrific noise startled everyone in the terminal. One of the plane's engines blew, forcing the pilot to ground the plane and reverse thrusters to keep it from careening off the runway.

It turns out that Yuzhno-Sakhalinsk's runway was constructed from concrete blocks. As the blocks separated over time, airport maintenance crews poured tar into the cracks, melting it with a blow torch to seal the openings.

"I remember when we taxied in, the guys out on the runway with one of those weed burners waved at us, but I didn't think anything of it," Mitchell said.

"But when the plane took back off, the wheels picked up some hot tar and shot it into the engine, which just destroyed it."

The incident caused a multiday standoff between Alaska Airlines and Yuzhno airport authorities. The Russians deemed the mishap an aviation accident and demanded the aircraft's emergency-monitoring black boxes. Alaska Airlines resisted a Russian investigation and scrambled to get its plane back home.

Without a spare engine at the airport, Alaska was forced to charter one in at considerable expense on a Lynden Hercules freighter. When the engine arrived, mechanics discovered that the airport lacked a forklift to move it. So a half-dozen men, including Mitchell, were recruited to pull the huge engine from the Herc, chain it to the back of a pickup truck, and drag it across the runway, metal grinding on concrete. Working through the night, the mechanics got the replacement engine attached as the Russians threatened to arrest them and seize the plane. The Herc and the Alaska jet quickly took off, leaving debris and a huge pool of oil on the runway.

Days later, in October 1998, Alaska Airlines ended all its service to the Russian Far East. The decision was made by Alaska CEO Ray Vecci, who seven years earlier had proudly announced his company's inaugural service to the Soviet Union before an enthusiastic crowd at Anchorage International.

Alaska Airlines' departure was among the most significant factors in the slowdown of business and cultural exchanges across the Bering Strait. Reeve Aleutian maintained its service to Sakhalin for two more years, and Bering Air continued charter flights to Chukotka. But getting from Alaska to the other major Russian Far East population centers suddenly became much more expensive and time-consuming.

The most direct route took about twenty-four hours through Seoul and required connecting with unpredictable Aeroflot flights to Vladivostok, Khabarovsk, and Magadan. Some airplane seat–tolerant Alaskans opted for the virtually round-the-world option through New York to Moscow and then all the way across Russia to the Far East.

A handful of Russian carriers—including Mavial (Magadan), Yakutia Air, Vladivostok Air America, and Volga-Dnepr Airlines—sporadically flew between Anchorage and a few Far East cities between 1999 and 2015. All but Yakutia eventually discontinued service for lack of passengers.

The ruble collapse affected Alaskans trying to do business in Russia in different ways. In addition to representing the grocery-store chain, Heatwole sold equipment to Magadan gold miners. That business continued for a while because the mining companies were allocated US currency for such purchases.

Dennis Mitchell of Lynden happened to visit the Yuzhno-Sakhalinsk casino the week of the crash and hit it big at the roulette wheel, walking away with a thick stack of rubles. When he tried to convert the Russian money, he learned that a chaotic run on the bank meant no US dollars could be had on the island. So he used his ruble winnings to pay employee salaries.

Alaskan Dave Parish had launched a Sakhalin business advising companies how to win lucrative contracts in the island's oil and gas development. He was scheduled to fly to Sakhalin the week of the ruble collapse but thought twice about it when a US State Department advisory warned against travel to Russia. Parish decided to keep the business going to demonstrate his commitment to the Sakhalin government. Some clients walked away.

"It had the unintended effect of giving all our Russian employees significant pay raises because we still paid them the same in terms of US dollars but Russia had knocked a couple of zeros off the ruble," Parish said.

THE CONTINUED UNCERTAINTY in Russia sent a chill through those in Alaska's business community who had pursued joint ventures across the strait, or were thinking about it. It refreshed the sour memories of the high-profile case of an Alaskan who tried to work with the Russians for all the right reasons but ended up the victim of international collusion that cost him millions of dollars.

Doug Drum acquired his passion for meat processing while growing up on a Michigan farm. He immigrated to Alaska in the mid-1960s to run grocery-store meat departments and trapped and hunted in Prince William Sound. In the foothills overlooking Turnagain Arm, about twenty miles south of Anchorage, Drum built a cedar home and later added a meat-processing plant specializing in processing salmon, moose, and other game for locals to preserve their harvest. By the late 1980s, he was grossing more than $3 million a year from his Indian Valley plant, turning Alaska reindeer into mouth-watering sausages for consumption by Alaskans and mail-order customers across the world.

As the Ice Curtain melted, Drum was asked to provide snacks at a reception for visiting Soviets. Used to gristly, fat-laden sausage, the Soviets were so impressed with the quality and variety of his sausage samples that they couldn't believe it was reindeer. Hearing reports of the eight hundred thousand reindeer estimated to roam across the Russian Far East and how primitively they were harvested, Drum tasted opportunity.

Accustomed to working with Alaska Natives, Drum was also moved by the plight of Soviet Natives, some of the country's poorest peoples. For centuries, nomadic Chukchi and Koriak followed great reindeer herds across the Russian northern tundra, subsisting on the meat and making clothing and shelters from the hide. After the Russian Revolution, the Soviets attempted to "urbanize" these Native peoples, forcing them onto state collective farms to produce food for local consumption.

In fall 1988, Drum met one of the earliest delegations of Soviet officials to have visited Alaska. They were immediately taken with his plainspoken, often profanity-laced manner. That spring, Drum made his first visit to the Soviet Union to explore the possibility of a joint venture in reindeer processing. After joining up with regional agricultural officials in Magadan, they traveled to the desolate village of Chaibukha, about three hundred miles to the northeast and reachable only by air or the occasional barge.

At the site of the dilapidated Parenskii state farm founded in the 1930s, Drum and his Alaska interpreter, Andrew Crow, were shocked at the primitive processing and wanton waste. Thousands of reindeer were slaughtered in the fall, their carcasses suspended in open-air buildings during the winter, where they hung frozen stiff. Sometimes they couldn't be processed by spring so farm workers were forced to bulldoze into the tundra up to twenty thousand rotting corpses and the buildings in which they were stored.

Some reindeer hides were turned into clothing, but many were wrapped around aboveground water and sewer lines for insulation. Very little of the meat ended up as local sausage; the rare Russian sausage that made its way to Chaibukha usually came from other parts of the country.

Drum's vision was to teach the Soviets his style of reindeer meat processing. His altruistic motive was improving the desperate lives of local Natives. His capitalistic motive was a 10 percent commission on the supplies he provided—sausage casing, spices, processing equipment. His compensation was based on the most valuable part of the reindeer, its horn.

When sliced wafer thin, reindeer horn was cherished in Korea as an aphrodisiac and natural medicine. The most valuable horn is *panti*, gorged in blood and blanketed in velvet. In the early 1990s, *panti* was worth more than $40 a pound in Seoul. Drum envisioned having an endless supply of horn because reindeer sprout new ones each year.

In an annual ritual akin to nineteenth-century cattle branding in the American West, Native reindeer herders cut the horn in early summer. In small tracked vehicles called *vezedkhod,* or "go anywhere," the herders and their families crossed about one hundred miles of tundra to their summer base camp.

Herding up to five hundred animals close together, the herders lassoed individual deer with a lariat and pinned them to the ground. They then cut the horn close to the head and wrapped a rubber tubing tourniquet around the wound to slow the bleeding. The still-warm horn rack was propped upside down to keep the blood in.

After harvesting hundreds of pounds, the herders took a break to enjoy a local delicacy—fresh *panti*. After burning the velvet off in the campfire, thin slices of chewy horn were passed around. One reporter described it as tasting like a crunchy carrot.

Drum and his Soviet partners formed a joint-venture company, Magal, a combination of Magadan and Alaska, and negotiated a complex business deal. Here's how it was supposed to work: the Soviets would harvest the reindeer horn, which was then shipped to Korea. Drum would negotiate a horn price with Korean buyers, who would deposit payment in a Korean bank. The bank would then wire the money to an Alaska bank. Drum would take a percentage of the cost of setting up sausage-making equipment on the Soviet state farms. The processed sausage would be consumed both locally and across the Soviet Union.

Drum and Crow went to great lengths to ensure adherence to terms of the arrangement, insisting on export licenses and letters of credit and making visits to the USSR to check on operations. When Drum flew eighteen tons of sausage-making equipment to Chaibukha and assembled it in three days, one hundred state farm leaders and dignitaries flew in from across the country to praise him as a Russian hero. The *Washington Post* profiled Drum as "among the most creative" Alaska entrepreneurs who negotiated successful joint ventures with the Soviets.

As the deal came together in fall 1990, Drum, Crow, and their Soviet partners all traveled to Seoul to meet the Korean buyers. The Soviets seemed more interested in partying and shopping than negotiating. The Koreans provided each Soviet with $2,000 in spending money.

In the initial months of operations, Magal worked fairly smoothly. Drum built a bunkhouse and classroom next to his Alaska processing plant to accommodate visiting Soviets. Early horn sales generated more than $1 million in deposits to the Anchorage bank.

By summer 1991, however, the venture began to unravel. In the midst of the ruble crisis, the Russian government froze hard-currency accounts and issued new ruble bills. Drum's Russian partners stopped making bank deposits and payments to the state farms. They cut out the Alaskans and began dealing directly with the Koreans. The Russians were naïve about Western business practices, and when they failed to insure the revenues from the sale of the horn, the money largely disappeared.

At a showdown meeting in Magadan in June, much of the $3 million generated from horn shipments to the Koreans could not be accounted for. That was the end of Drum's vision of setting up eight to ten processing plants across the region to provide local jobs and a market for the reindeer.

When Magal failed, the Native herders were the biggest losers. They were doing the hardest work yet seeing none of the profits and few of the basic consumer goods that they hoped the joint venture would yield them. The herders returned to scratching out a meager subsistence existence under the failed socialized model imposed on them.

In spring 2016, the usually energetic and upbeat Drum had been hobbled by a stroke, frustrated by a slow shuffle and difficulty uttering more than one-word responses to questions. The Indian Valley office above his busy meat-processing plant was still cluttered with Russian memorabilia: brightly colored sausage casings embossed with a Cyrillic Magal logo, his dusty 1990 Exporter of the Year trophy from the State of Alaska, stack of dried sliced reindeer horn.

Drum says he lost a couple million dollars in Russia. More costly was the wasted time he could have invested in building his own Alaska-based family business. After the failed joint venture, Drum spoke to business groups and warned them how such good intentions could so quickly go awry.

Gov. Tony Knowles convened Russian Far East governors and hundreds of business leaders for a 2002 US West Coast–Russian Far East Working Group conference to focus on business opportunities. Knowles is third from the right, with Sakhalin Gov. Farkhudtinov to his right.

COURTESY OF GOVERNOR TONY KNOWLES

20

Mercy Mission to Magadan

In Kolyma, winter lasts twelve months; the rest is summer.

—POPULAR ADAGE IN THE RUSSIAN FAR EAST

D OUG DRUM'S EXPERIENCE and the difficulty of flying to the Russian Far East in the late 1990s dampened Alaskans' enthusiasm for continued overtures across the Bering Strait. For many Alaskans, the novelty of interacting with Russians on cultural exchanges also grew thin.

In the early days, hundreds of Alaskans eagerly hosted Russian visitors in their homes. We showed up at airports in the dead of night to collect our curious guests, feeding and entertaining them through language and cultural barriers. When they arrived with little money, we bought them clothes, appliances, and liquor and transported them across Alaska.

Many Alaskans were forever touched when Russian guests broke down in tears at our grocery stores, overwhelmed by the routine selection of fruit or shampoo. A few Russians even dismissed such displays of capitalistic extravagance as a Potemkin village, referring to fake communities said to have been created to hide poor conditions during Empress Catherine II's visit to Ukraine and Crimea in 1787.

Federal earmarks, the lifeblood of the University of Alaska's efforts in the region, also slowed as the US government refocused its economic aid on a new international hotspot, Afghanistan. Within Russia, the chaotic aftermath of the ruble collapse continued to take a toll on average Russians. Nowhere was that more dramatic than the Russian Far East.

From those who continued to brave the long, roundabout flights to the region, Alaskans began to hear of terrible hardships plaguing their western neighbors: food and energy shortages, rampant joblessness, increasing despair. Children of the region were forced to wear mittens to bed in heatless apartments and teachers went on strike to protest below-freezing temperatures in their classrooms. One-third of the Magadan-area population abandoned the region over a ten-year period.

"All of Russia is hurting economically but the Far North, which is especially dependent on state spending, is hurting most of all," reported *U.S. News and World Report*.

Few Alaskans knew Magadan better than Gretchen Bersch. A gregarious professor of education at University of Alaska Anchorage, Bersch began hosting Magadan students in her Anchorage home in 1989. She was so taken with the region and its people that she bought an apartment there and visited at least annually—more than twenty times in all—starting in 1991. She remembers the winter of 1999 being cold in Alaska but more so in Magadan: no hot water, limited electricity, average apartment temperatures of forty-two degrees and outside temperatures of thirty below.

"Parents can't feed children so they are dropping them off at orphanages in record numbers," reported a fact sheet distributed across Anchorage.

Bersch joined forces with local church leaders, sister-city activists, and Anchorage's mayor to launch Operation Magadan, an effort to collect and donate tons of warm clothing and food to Magadan. In just four days, thirty thousand pounds of clothing piled into grocery stores, churches, and city hall. Bersch spent hours at a collection center helping bundle the donations, only to discover her own coat with a cherished Swiss Army knife in its pocket had been mistakenly shrink-wrapped into the shipment.

On Christmas Eve 1998, 156 boxes of clothing, blankets, and baby formula were air freighted to Magadan for free by Mavial, the regional Russian airline. Thousands of pounds of additional clothing donations followed. Thanks to a federal grant, twenty thousand tons of coal from Alaska's Usibelli Mine was shipped to Magadan, where icebreaking ships were required to clear the way through the harbor to the power plant.

Four years earlier, Anchorage Mayor Rick Mystrom had been invited by his Magadan counterpart to honor their sister-city relationship by celebrating the end of World War II. After his three days in Magadan in fall 1995, Mystrom was especially struck by the food disparities and proud patriotism. In the grocery stores, he and his wife, Mary, saw row after row of largely empty shelves. Yet in the evenings they were guests of political leaders at some of the most lavish dinners he'd ever seen.

"I realized in that egalitarian society some people are a lot more equal than others," Mystrom said.

He also remembered the honor paid to local veterans of what Russians call the Great Patriotic War, which cost the Soviet Union more than twenty million people. Magadan's chilly streets were crowded with aging, medal-wearing veterans of World War II and the citizens who honored them.

With those images still fresh from his Magadan visit, Mystrom got solidly behind the relief mission to Anchorage's sister-city. The second phase of Operation Magadan was a food drive.

In 1999, Anchorage residents purchased more than fifteen thousand thirty-seven-pound boxes of staples—rice, sugar, flour, oil, powdered milk, tea, and candles—through the local Carr Gottstein grocery chain. Families making donations wrote notes expressing empathy to Magadan recipients. The food was barged and air freighted, with help from the Alaska National Guard.

Dave Heatwole coordinated with Magadan churches to ensure that relief supplies got to those who needed them. Even one of Alaska's leading cynics, *Anchorage Daily News* columnist Mike Doogan, sorted donated clothes and praised the initiative.

Despite the ruble crisis–driven damper imposed on Russian business prospects, governments and advocacy groups continued to advocate for cross-strait ties. In summer 2000, Governor Knowles invited an old college friend, US Deputy Secretary of State Strobe Talbott, to see Alaska-Russia relations firsthand.

In the late 1960s, Knowles and Talbott attended Yale University, where Talbott honed his expertise on the Soviet Union. Talbott and another ambitious college student named Bill Clinton were Rhodes Scholars together at Oxford University, where Talbott translated Khrushchev's memoirs into English. After working as *Time* magazine's resident Russia expert, Talbott was recruited by President Clinton to manage US policy on the Soviet Union's demise.

As Governor Knowles's foreign-policy advisor, I joined Talbott and Knowles on a three-day whirlwind trip across northern Alaska. On St. Lawrence Island, close to the Russian mainland, Talbott was struck by seeing cigarette packs that had been tossed aside by Russian military scouts on unauthorized visits.

Talbott praised Alaska's assistance to a hard-hit Russia, including Knowles's efforts to secure federal approval to ship six thousand tons of canned salmon to needy Russian families. "Just as Alaska was out front for America in times of war in the twentieth century—hot war and cold—Alaska is out front for peace in the twenty-first," Talbott told the Alaska World Affairs Council.

In September 2002, to help keep Alaska-Russia activities alive, Governor Knowles assembled the largest collection of top Russian Far East officials in Alaska since Governor Cowper's Northern Regions Conference twelve years earlier. A dozen governors and other senior officials gathered to discuss business and cultural ties. Among those making return trips to Alaska for the summit were Sakhalin Governor Farkhutdinov and Chukotka Governor Abramovich. Others included Alexander Vershbow, President George W. Bush's ambassador to Russia, and a top administrator of the US Agency for International Development, which had funded much of the activity across the strait.

The top officials convened as part of the seventh annual meeting of the US West Coast–Russian Far East Working Group, an entity spun off from a 1993 summit between Presidents Clinton and Yeltsin. The two presidents had established a joint Commission on Economic and Technological Cooperation cochaired by Vice President Al Gore and Russian Prime Minister Victor Chernomyrdin and widely known as the Gore-Chernomyrdin Commission.

The working group focused on business and cultural exchanges between the West Coast and Russian Far East. Its secretariat was housed with the Seattle-based Foundation for Russian-American Economic Cooperation (FRAEC) and staffed by Ginna Brelsford, who had pioneered Alaska-Soviet relations under Governor Cowper.

The Anchorage conference attracted about three hundred participants, including officials from Washington, Oregon, and California. Knowles and the Russian governors signed a broad "declaration of regional cooperation" pledging a focus on "economic, political, and people-to-people relations across the Russian-U.S. border." Knowles also signed individual continuing cooperation agreements with the governors of Chukotka, Sakhalin, Kamchatka, Khabarovsk, Koryak, and Buryatia.

The Alaska governor played up the special historic kinship between Alaska and Russia, such as the same sense of independence from each country's capital and desire to solve problems locally.

"Here in Alaska, Russian influence from the times of Bering and Baranov remains strong, in language, family names, religion, enjoyment of certain foods—for me especially, salmon caviar," Knowles said. At a breakfast meeting of the governors, the Alaskan hosts served reindeer sausage.

As business and cultural connections between Alaska and the Russian Far East cooled, a handful of eccentric visionaries worked to keep alive their dream—a ground transportation link beneath the strait explored by Vitus Bering nearly three centuries earlier. The idea was a sixty-mile tunnel under the international date line. Under proposals advanced by various US and Soviet thinkers, the tunnel would house railroad tracks, a highway, and possibly even oil and gas pipelines.

"Compared to the billions of dollars annually spent by the United States and Soviet Union on the instruments and personnel for bloody war, the cost of this peace-promoting venture which would materially aid the economies of North America, Eurasia, and Japan is not only manageable but small in comparison," wrote Anchorage advocate Joseph Henri.

The idea of connecting Asian and North American rail lines dates to the late nineteenth century when Russian finance minister Sergei Witte visualized a railroad across the span of his country from Moscow to Vladivostok. His vision was largely fulfilled in 1906, when thousands of Russian soldiers and prisoners toiled in some of the planet's most unforgiving conditions to build the Trans-Siberian Railway. Two decades later in 1923, President Warren Harding pounded a golden spike in the Alaska Interior community of Nenana to signal completion of the Alaska Railroad.

The Bering Strait tunnel idea died with Stalin in 1953 but was brought back to life in the early 1990s. Today, connecting the Trans-Siberian Railway from Vladivostok to the Bering Strait for a crossing would require about 2,500 miles of new line. On the Alaska side, some 1,300 miles of new track would have to be laid just to connect with the Alaska Railroad. In 2001, the cost of building a tunnel was estimated at $50 billion.

Despite the price tag, numerous studies, summits, and speeches were undertaken to advance the concept. Conferences were convened in Fairbanks and Novosibirsk in 1994, producing new market analyses. They forecast that crude oil would comprise up to 35 percent of the railroad shipments through the tunnel, with grain, automobiles, and containerized cargo making up the rest. Passenger traffic was estimated at up to one thousand riders a day "primarily for tourist travel and work access."

One advocate envisioned a "world-class hotel" with a spectacular view of the confluence of the Pacific and Arctic Oceans built on Alaska's Little Diomede Island, serviced by an elevator connecting to the train below the Bering Sea. A Russian visionary, director of the government's Center for Regional Transport Projects, estimated the railroad would shorten the shipping time for cargo across the Pacific by up to two weeks and would create thousands of jobs.

"If presidents signed the deal, you could start buying tickets for the train that will be ready to depart in twenty years," said Victor Razbegin, whose Moscow office telephone doubled as a model-train car.

Former Governor Hickel endorsed the project. In 2001, Kremlin transportation officials said the tunnel could be part of an overall eastern Russian rail expansion effort.

VLADIMIR PUTIN'S APPOINTMENT as Russia's president in 2000 was broadly welcomed in the international business community as a promise of stability in the Russian economy. To a significant degree, the timing of his ascension was plain good luck. After nearly a decade of unstable chaos, President Yeltsin's efforts to transform Russia's economy were finally taking hold. By 1997, about 70 percent of Russia's gross domestic product was generated by the private sector, and two years later Russia's economy was growing at better than 6 percent annually. The new President Putin continued to push market reforms with a flat tax, streamlined the creation of small businesses, and allowed the sale of agriculture land, which had been prohibited since communist days.

Yet Putin also sent a shiver through the Western business community by reversing Yeltsin's decentralization policies. The highest-profile act was his confiscation of Russia's largest and most successful company, Yukos Oil, which led to a wave of renationalization of Russian companies. Putin reined in Gorbachev-era policies to encourage joint ventures with non-Russian companies and ended the free elections of regional officials, instead appointing hardliners loyal to him.

"Finally somebody was in charge of a country that had become very dys-functional," said Alaska entrepreneur Dave Parish. "But from a democracy and freedom-of-speech standpoint, they stepped backward."

With the cooperation of the national parliament, Putin also made it more difficult for nonprofit and citizen organizations to operate in Russia. The Duma in 2015 put twelve private democracy-building and civil rights organizations on a "patriotic stop-list" and ordered the prosecutor general to deem whether they were a threat to national security and subject to arrest and jail. News stories reported the arrest and deportation of Western scholars undertaking seemingly innocent research in Russian libraries and archives.

Moscow's crackdown was felt in far-away Alaska. Russ Howell was a West Point infantry officer who wanted to become a specialist in the Middle East. But when the training slots for that region were full, he opted for Russia instead after a supervisor noticed he had studied the language at the US Military Academy. After earning a master's degree perfecting his Russian, he was eventually trans-ferred to Alaska in 1987.

Following his retirement five years later as a lieutenant colonel, Howell became the deputy director of the university's American Russian Center. He oversaw the expansion of ARC's Russian Far East business-development centers, traveled extensively across the region, and was promoted to ARC director in 1997.

Six years later, on another routine trip to the Far East, Howell landed in Khabarovsk and noticed that no passengers were getting off the plane. Suddenly he felt a tap on his shoulder by a federal agent, who flashed a badge and informed him his visa was not in order. After a four-hour interrogation in Russian late into the night, Howell was released: "That was the most scared I have ever been in my life."

Two months later, Howell traveled twenty-four hours from Alaska to Moscow for a US Agency for International Development conference. Presenting his passport and visa to Russian customs at Moscow's Sheremetyevo International Airport, Howell was detained and refused admission to Russia. He was marched to the departure area and forced to buy a new ticket, and flew back to Alaska. He received no explanation and never returned to Russia.

Andrew Crow traveled between Alaska and the Russian Far East dozens of times, starting in 1989 as an interpreter for Governor Cowper and program officer for the University of Alaska, working to improve life for average Russians. Around 2004, he fielded a call from the Russian consulate in Seattle informing him of a "glitch" with his multiple-entry Russian visa. The consulate demanded that Crow send them his passport, which contained the Russian visa. But rather than risk seizure of his passport, the suspicious Crow declined.

Crow questioned the timing of the request, which coincided with Putin's angry reaction to the Orange Revolution in the Ukraine. Late that year, the Kremlin-backed president of the Ukraine was deposed by a challenger supported by the West. Putin charged the United States with orchestrating the overthrow and reacted by cracking down on US organizations doing civic work in Russia.

Crow, who knew of other Americans encountering Russian visa problems at the same time, has no interest in returning to Russia. "Why would I pay to go to a place to get arrested?" he said.

Always Keep Talking

The sable was still running along the Bering Strait, balancing on the ice floes and risking falling into the water. The sable had no idea that invisible bridges were being built on both shores.

—DIVIDED TWINS, YVEGENY YEVTUSHENKO & BOYD NORTON, 1988

A FTER GOV. TONY Knowles's second term expired in December 2002, I was relieved to end nearly weekly commuting to Juneau and returned to Anchorage to contemplate my next career move. That spring, a young Anchorage-born businessman and local-government activist decided to make a third run for Anchorage mayor, after losing two prior efforts.

Mark Begich was one of four sons of Nick Begich, an educator and former Democratic state legislator who was elected to Alaska's sole US House seat in 1970. Running for reelection in October 1972, Congressman Begich, along with House Majority Leader Hale Boggs of Louisiana, boarded a twin-engine Cessna in Anchorage for a late-evening flight to a Juneau fund-raiser. They never arrived. Their disappearance prompted the largest search-and-rescue operation in Alaska history. Three months later, Begich, Boggs, and two others on the plane were officially declared deceased. Mark Begich was ten years old.

The young Begich grew up with a disdain for politics, largely because it had cost him his father. Instead, Begich pursued business—a teen night club, vending machine company, real estate—and helped his widowed mother raise his

The author visits the makeshift memorial for slain Russian opposition leader Boris Nemtsov in March 2015. Nemtsov was shot in 2015 just off Moscow's Red Square, and thousands of Russians offered flowers and memorials in his honor. RAMSEUR PERSONAL COLLECTION

five siblings. In 1981, Begich was working in a city health department back office when he was summoned to city hall by Mayor Tony Knowles. Knowles needed a driver and gopher; the Anchorage-born Begich knew every back alley in town. He quickly perfected his skills at retail politics. Seven years later, at age twenty-six, Begich was elected the youngest member of the Anchorage Assembly, where he served three terms including as its chairman.

In 2003, Begich ignored the advice of his closest advisors and jumped into the mayor's race against incumbent George Wuerch, a decorated Marine officer and former oil-company executive. I knew Begich socially and from his occasional visits with Governor Knowles, who had appointed him to the University of Alaska's Board of Regents. Begich's campaign manager recruited me to critique his presentations at campaign events. He was animated and well versed in municipal minutiae but often long-winded and disjointed. I ended up volunteering on his campaign, writing talking points for speeches. To the surprise of most political insiders, Begich won, avoiding a runoff by fewer than two dozen votes. After I managed his transition into the mayor's office, he brought me into city hall as his chief of staff.

In Alaska, Anchorage mayor is the one of the highest-profile political posts in the state, second only to the governor. Begich willingly took on legislative Republicans and, in his second term, Alaska's new governor, Sarah Palin. He actively participated in high-profile national organizations such as the US Conference of Mayors and debated climate change with environmentalist Robert Redford.

At my urging, Begich also plunged into international affairs, raising Anchorage's profile with an international organization of mayors of northern cities. We welcomed to Anchorage mayors from Russia, China, Greenland, Canada, Korea, and Japan. Begich and I traveled to Greenland and South Korea to focus on global warming and best practices in winter cities, ranging from snow removal to public health. In 2005, Begich and Sergey Abramov, vice mayor of Anchorage's Russian sister city of Magadan, raised a new Russian flag to rededicate Sister Cities Plaza next to Anchorage's city hall.

In 2008, in his final year as mayor and again against the advice of political oddsmakers, Begich challenged incumbent Sen. Ted Stevens. Months after Begich entered the race, Stevens was indicted for failing to report gifts from Bill Allen, the same contractor who secured Stevens's help getting work for his company in Sakhalin, Russia.

Despite Begich's double-digit lead in the polls when he entered the race, the final results were so close he wasn't declared the winner until nearly a month after Election Day. Begich was the first Democrat elected to Alaska's three-person congressional delegation in nearly thirty years. His election—and that of Minnesota Sen. Al Franken—gave Democrats a sixty-vote majority to pass landmark legislation such as health care and Wall Street reform.

Within weeks, I was packing my bags for Washington, DC. Senator-elect Begich asked me to help open and staff his Senate office as chief of staff. Lobbyists, military brass, and ambassadors lined up at our door for a few precious minutes with the forty-seven-year-old who got his political start as a driver for his hometown mayor.

As chief of staff, one of my biggest challenges was fending off countless distractions while trying to keep our operation focused on Alaska-specific issues. Still, I took advantage of the many opportunities to sate my foreign-policy interests, regularly participating in chief of staff–only foreign-policy seminars, dining with ambassadors, and joining trips to Cuba, Jordan, Croatia, and Israel.

I also continued my focus on Alaska's neighbor to the west, welcoming various Russian officials to our offices in Washington and Alaska and interjecting our office into Russian issues. At the Russian embassy, I joined experts to explore renewed aviation links between Alaska and the Russian Far East.

A high-profile Russian issue at the time was the case of a Moscow lawyer and whistleblower, Sergei Magnitsky. In 2005, Magnitsky worked for British-based businessman William Browder and unveiled Russian government corruption. Arrested in 2008, he was held nearly a year without trial in a Moscow prison where he was tortured and ultimately beaten to death. Magnitsky's plight became a rallying point in Washington against the broader Russian crackdown on civil society.

At my urging, Begich cosponsored Senate legislation named for Magnitsky that imposed sanctions on Russian officials implicated in civil-rights abuses. At the request of dissident groups, we issued press releases calling for reforms and pointed out Alaska's close ties with the Russian Far East. The Magnitsky bill was signed into law by President Obama in December 2012. Russia reacted angrily by barring Americans from adopting Russian children.

One of the periodic Russian visitors to Washington was Boris Nemtsov, a leading opponent of the Putin government whom I had first met nearly fifteen years earlier, when he was the reformist governor of Nizhny Novgorod. By 2010, Nemtsov had become a leader in Solidarnost, Russia's United Democratic Movement. I set up meetings between Nemtsov and my boss and hosted workshops for him with other Senate foreign-policy staffers. Nemtsov swept into Begich's Washington office with the same energy I remembered, a gorgeous Russian model on his arm. A Russian journalist and fellow dissident, Vladimir Kara-Murza, accompanied Nemtsov.

"Your commitment to the issues of democracy, human rights, and rule of law in Russia has been long-standing, but it was especially important (and uplifting) for me to hear your clear expression of moral support and solidarity while I was being held in prison," Nemtsov wrote Begich after our meeting.

Begich was defeated in his bid for reelection in the 2014 sweep when Republicans picked up six Senate seats. After six years of commuting between Anchorage and Washington every few weeks, I happily returned to Alaska.

In March 2015, I traveled to Moscow for the first time in two decades. The occasion was the Dartmouth Conference, a weeklong below-the-radar meeting between former high-level US government officials and our Russian counterparts. Launched in 1960 at Dartmouth College, the initiative was designed to strengthen the relationship between the United States and Russia through informal channels. The conference convened nearly every year through the Cuban missile crisis, Cold War, Moscow Olympics boycott, and Russian invasion of Afghanistan. But ours was the first full-fledged session since 1990.

Our twenty-three delegates included President Clinton's ambassador to Russia, former top State and Defense Department officials, industry representatives, medical and religious leaders, and journalists. The twenty-member Russian delegation was equally diverse: former senior government officials, an Oscar-winning film director, a top Russian Orthodox Church priest. The Ohio-based Kettering Foundation, which promoted international democracy building, underwrote the US participation.

One of the biggest surprises came before we even departed for Moscow. At a Washington, DC, briefing with a senior State Department official, we learned that communications between our countries had eroded to virtual silence. Relations were so bad between the two strongest nations on earth that Russians and Americans refused to speak to each other, except for occasional calls between our presidents and top foreign ministers. We were shocked and demoralized and flew to the Russian capital energized to try to improve on that.

Most of our conference took place in Suzdal, one of Russia's most historic and picturesque villages dotted with scores of centuries-old churches and monasteries. The 140-mile bus ride was a four-hour journey back into feudal Russia. Today's Moscow is bustling and energetic, its skyline a mix of gleaming skyscrapers and brightly colored onion-domed churches. Young Russians dress in the latest European fashions and sip $6 lattes in crowded multistory shopping malls outside the gates of the Kremlin.

As we fought bumper-to-bumper commuter traffic northeast toward Suzdal, Soviet-era high-rise apartment buildings gave way to latticed wooden hovels slowly sinking into muddy fields. The dark-windowed Mercedes SUVs common in the capital were replaced by aging Ladas, their bumpers dangling by wire from rusty car bodies.

On the first morning in Suzdal, the eleven-hour time difference with Alaska had me wide awake at three a.m. At first light, I ventured out for a run down Suzdal's main boulevard. The ever-present Lenin statue presided over the town square as a hunched babushka brushed away a couple of inches of new snow with a straw broom. From the tenth-century walls of Suzdal's Kremlin fortress, the Kamenka River snaked to the horizon, frozen in time like this village from which Russia was once ruled.

Despite the idyllic setting, our conference soon erupted into fireworks over Russia's "invasion" of Ukraine and the West's imposition of sanctions in retaliation. Our Russian hosts cited Ukraine's affiliation with Russia since Catherine the Great and noted that eight million Ukrainians were killed fighting the Nazis alongside the Soviet Army in the Great Patriotic War. We agreed to set aside such intransigent disputes and focused instead on issues where the two countries share common goals: arms control and disarmament, combatting Middle East–grown terrorism, and the impact of climate change on the Arctic.

I recapped the successful melting of the Ice Curtain between Alaska and the Russian Far East that had produced decades of productive relations. Even with today's heightened tensions and mistrust, I argued that such citizen diplomacy could produce breakthroughs again.

ON THE EVENING of February 27, 2015, less than a month before our Dartmouth conversation convened in Russia, Boris Nemtsov and his twenty-three-year-old Ukrainian girlfriend were walking to his Moscow apartment after dinner. About halfway across the Bolshoy Moskvoretsky Bridge, just below St. Basil's Cathedral in Red Square, up to eight gunshots rang out. The fifty-five-year-old was hit four times—in the head, heart, liver, and stomach. He died almost instantly.

Nemtsov's assassination occurred just two days before a march he had organized to protest Russian intervention in Ukraine. Two suspects from the North Caucasus region were arrested two weeks later.

The bridge remained a stirring memorial when I paid my respects on a sunny day three weeks after Nemtsov's death. Bundles of red and white carnations and roses were laid knee-high; candles flickered in the cold breeze amid pictures of the slain activist and hand-scrawled messages to his memory. Thousands of Russians made a pilgrimage to the site, pausing to reflect beneath fur hats, the Kremlin's red brick guard towers just a stone's throw away.

I struggled to extract meaning from Nemtsov's death, and of the destructive detour in US-Russian relations. Initially I had immersed myself in Russia—toiled to learn its language, labored through its literature, baked its black bread—for novelty and adventure. Slowly, Russia got under my skin. From my perch in government, I participated in modest improvements in the lives and attitudes of Alaskans who shared a unique bond across the Bering Strait.

Nemtsov exemplified hope for ending a futile Cold War as Alaskans and Russians of the Pacific worked to melt the Ice Curtain. With his death, Russia's struggling democratic movement was set back even further as US-Russia relations deteriorated even more.

A Russian Chukchi woman hangs freshly caught salmon for drying at a remote Bering Sea hunting camp in summer 2016. PHOTO BY LOURDES GROBET

Detained on the Bering Strait

Over the last decade in Russia, the Federal Security Service (FSB), the modern successor of the Soviet secret police (KGB), has been granted the role of the new elite, enjoying expanded responsibilities and immunity from public oversight or parliamentary control.

—*THE NEW NOBILITY, 2010*

MAJOR POLOSIN WAS not smiling. The stern border guard officer—a member of the notorious Federal Security Bureau (formerly the KGB)—confronted us in the remote Bering Sea village of Lavrentiya demanding our documents. That's when our sixteen-hour detention, hearing, and sentencing began.

For more than two weeks in the summer of 2016, I joined eight other adventure travelers for a hands-on look at the isolated Russian Native villages across the international date line from Alaska's northwest Seward Peninsula. In eighteen-foot aluminum skiffs, we logged about 330 miles on the frigid Bering Sea, encountering spouting gray whales, an occasional walrus, and once-thriving villages abandoned at the height of the Cold War.

My purpose was to document the post-Soviet changes in this region since I last visited in 1988 with Gov. Steve Cowper. I wanted to assess the impact that nearly thirty years of contact with Alaska had on these remote peoples, and whether they were eager for more.

As the Ice Curtain began melting, Alaska and Soviet Far East residents were giddy to reunite long-separated Native families and take advantage of new

Gorbachev *glasnost* reforms sanctioning interactions with Westerners. At the time, most of these communities were thriving with Soviet collective enterprises such as dairies, reindeer-hide tanneries, fox farms, and ample subsidies from Moscow. Western Russians and those from Soviet republics such as the Ukraine and Kazakhstan happily migrated east for high salaries and generous benefits.

After the Soviet Union collapsed in 1991 and support for collective enterprises dried up, the population of the Russian Far East and Siberia plummeted from more than eight million to about two million. Most of those leaving Chukotka were non-Natives. "But the Native people had nowhere to go; this was their land, where their ancestors were buried, and where they now had to live in new and unusual conditions," said a 1998 study. It pronounced the Chukotka economy "in crisis."

Chukotka Natives found post-Soviet relief from two sources: Alaska and Chukotka Gov. Roman Abramovich. Beginning in the early 1990s, Alaskans poured thousands of dollars into the region from federal aid and private sector investments. Shortly after becoming governor in 2001, Abramovich steered millions of rubles into infrastructure and economic development across the region.

In 2016, we observed villages making a challenging transition back to their traditional subsistence ways. Many Native adults worked as marine mammal hunters and berry gatherers while their children shuffled along dusty village streets surfing the Internet on their cell phones. The population had stabilized, thanks to national policy encouraging families to produce multiple children along with generous federal subsidies, such as assistance to take in orphans. Still, inadequate housing remained the top concern facing local residents, along with a lack of jobs, alcoholism, and preserving cultural identity. Past interaction with Alaska remained a pleasant memory of productive accomplishment while renewed connections were burdened with bureaucratic red tape and prohibitively expensive.

Our expedition included a mix of Alaskans: Etta Myrna Tall, a Native traditional healer from Little Diomede hoping to find long-lost relatives; Diddy Hitchins, a retired University of Alaska Anchorage political science professor; retired civil engineer Steve Shrader; and *Alaska Dispatch News* reporter Kirsten Swann. Trip organizer Tandy Wallack, president of Circumpolar Expeditions, was a frequent Chukotka visitor and the recipient of a National Park Service grant to reunite Alaska and Russian Native relatives.

Three award-winning Mexican filmmakers—Lourdes Grobet, cinematographer Xavier Grobet, and sound engineer Juan Cristobal Perez Grobet—made their first trip to the region to document the reunification of Alaska and Russian Natives.

Nervous with anticipation, we gathered at Nome's Airport Pizza for our last American supper of pepperoni pizza and beer. After encountering drunken boat crews on earlier trips, Wallack wisely imposed a ban on alcohol consumption once we arrived in Russia. In 1995, five prominent American and Russian researchers and thirteen local Natives were killed outside Provideniya when their walrus-skin *umiat* mysteriously capsized. Equipped with mandatory life jackets, an emergency satellite phone, and the booze ban, we weren't taking chances.

The adventure and expense of travel in the Russian Far East began long before the trip. Deemed a high-security "border zone" because of its proximity to the United States, this region requires both a $300 Russian visa and a special permit listing each destination likely to be visited, no matter how tiny the outpost. That's how we ran afoul of Major Polosin.

During the heyday of Alaska-Russia exchanges, flying to the Russian Far East was nearly as easy as to the Lower 48. Yet in recent years, Nome's Bering Air had been the only carrier offering occasional charters to Provideniya and the Chukotka capital of Anadyr. A Russian airline, Yakutia Air, provided weekly flights during a six-week summer period between Anchorage and the Kamchatka Peninsula and Yakutsk in the Sakha Republic.

After reporting to Bering Air's spacious hangar, we were subjected to the "hurry up and wait" standard for air travel in this part of the world, but exaggerated in Russia. Provideniya is twenty hours ahead of Nome, essentially four hours earlier the next day. The flight routine requires waiting until after noon in Nome to call the Provideniya tower when it opens at eight a.m. (Russian time) for a weather report. Provideniya's cloud ceiling standards—2,800 feet—are higher than in most of Alaska, so flying weather must be near-perfect. If the Chukotka fog doesn't blow out by around noon (four p.m. in Nome), Bering pilots are forced to cancel the flight and wait for another day. We just slipped through the window, departing Nome about three thirty p.m.

On our descent, the turquoise blue waters of Provideniya Bay sparkled in the bright arctic sun. Instead of the Cold War nervousness of my first visit, I was stunned. In 2016, Provideniya looked like Beirut after its 1980s civil war. The scores of barracks and military buildings along the road into town were abandoned. Concrete and steel rubble, broken utility lines, and rusting equipment cluttered the tundra.

Even in the city center, many of the multiple-story apartment buildings were eerily empty, their windows and doors sealed shut with thick steel plates and covered with Cyrillic graffiti. Foot-tall patches of yellow dandelions hid broken vodka bottles and the remnants of sidewalks.

In the 1980s, this self-described "gateway to the Arctic" was bustling with nearly daily cargo-ship port calls, production of consumer goods such as fresh milk and vegetables, and optimism for a promising collective future. Now only about two thousand residents remained—fewer than half the population during the final years of the Soviet Union. About one-third of them were Russian Chukchi who moved to this regional hub from more remote villages for health care and to join relatives. Many of the others were multigenerational Provideniya natives whose families immigrated here in search of salaries many times those available in the western Soviet Union.

The weather-beaten toll on Soviet-era buildings still in use was masked by red, yellow, and blue metal siding that brightened the long winter landscape. Locals proudly told us these panels were installed during the administration of Chukotka's former governor, oligarch Roman Abramovich. Inside, apartments were warm and comfortable with Russian brands of microwaves and color televisions, guarded by thick metal doors equipped with multiple locks. Scores of dogs of every possible mongrel mix—Siberian husky to dachshund—wandered unpaved streets, sniffing for an open apartment building for a warm napping spot.

One of my first stops was the community hall on Dezhneva Street. This gravel street was named for the seventeenth-century Russian explorer Semyon Dezhnev, who in 1648 sailed around the continent's northeasternmost point that now bears his name. Dezhnev's report of his trip lay buried in Russian archives for nearly a century, so Vitus Bering got credit as the first European to discover the region in 1728.

In June 1988, this hall hosted the joyous reunions of Alaska and Chukotka Native relatives during the daylong visit of the Friendship Flight. Its plaza was mobbed by flag-waving children trading lapel pins and candy bars with Alaska visitors as Vladimir Lenin presided over the commotion from a large portrait.

Lenin's picture was gone but his bust remained in the town square, framed by two whale ribs. The building now housed an elementary school, a sign welcoming students featuring critters a long way from the Arctic—an elephant and a smiling monkey. We were invited into a crowded back room for a Native dance performance to welcome the single Alaska Native in our delegation. We sampled homemade Chukchi fry bread and were fascinated by Chukotka throat singers, whose guttural art form was foreign to Alaskans.

At city hall, we were granted an audience with Provideniya's deputy administrator, Vladimir Paramonov, a fifth-generation Provideniyan. Guarded and bureaucratic, he said his region's future lies in the same gold, silver, and copper extraction pursued for the past half century, although little mining was under way in 2016. His community welcomes well-heeled cruise-ship passengers who make rare visits. But when asked about facilities to attract those tourists—restaurants, hotels, even a dock to get them off the ship and into town—Paramonov said there were too few visitors to justify the investment.

Partly in response to an Alaska initiative in the 1980s, in 2013 Russia's central government created five parks in Chukotka, collectively comprising the Beringia National Park. The remote parks feature spectacular scenery protected from development and employ several dozen rangers and administrators, most of them Natives. Despite efforts to attract visitors, only about eight hundred tourists made the trek in 2015, said director Vladimir Bychkov, an English-speaking former Provideniya mayor who earned his college degree in Alaska.

One of our favorite destinations was the town bakery, a bright blue metal-sided building with a warm baked-bread aroma. It churned out a staple of the Russian diet, tall bricks of white bread that the locals buy daily. A government-subsidized loaf cost fifty-two rubles, about eighty cents.

Surprisingly, the bakery's shelves and frozen-food lockers were stocked full of offerings, from birthday cakes to German beer. Supply ships from Vladivostok arrive about eight times a summer, but not at all between September and May when the sea is frozen. Air connections with Anadyr run twice weekly in the summer but only every other week in the winter, weather permitting.

After three days in Provideniya, we were antsy to get up the coast. We hoped to reach Eurasia's northeasternmost point, where we might see the western side of Russian Big Diomede, and perhaps even Alaska's Little Diomede next door.

The voyage began on the local bus, actually a dump truck with the dump box replaced with a passenger cabin of stiff metal seats. We hit every pothole on the twenty-five-mile gravel road to the nearby village of New Chaplino, stopping once to take in the barren rocky scenery and check our dental work.

During my last visit, in 1989, this village was just thirty years old, established by Soviet decree. Beginning in the late 1940s, as the Cold War brought on fear and paranoia, the Soviets closed dozens of northern Native villages, moving the residents to new consolidated sites. The original village of Chaplino was perched on an ocean spit, with easy access to the whales and walrus on which the residents subsisted for thousands of years. It and at least three other villages were merged into New Chaplino in the late 1950s and moved to an interior bay about ten miles from the open ocean. The bay remained frozen longer into the spring than the ocean, distancing the residents from their major food source.

Now New Chaplino bore witness to the improvements by former Governor Abramovich. Virtually all the original wooden shacklike houses had been replaced with blue, metal-sided, square individual homes connected to village water and sewer. Each was perched on a steel frame supported by about a dozen jacks, which can be adjusted to keep the house level as the permafrost beneath it settles. Drying black whale meat and red salmon hung from clotheslines.

The eighty children among the nearly five hundred residents attended school in a multistory modern building, equipped with a gym, cafeteria, and computer lab. The houses and school were designed by Canadians. Both held up well in the winter's ninety-mile-per-hour winds and snows that can drift as high as the roofs.

Despite modern appearances, New Chaplino worked hard to preserve its ancient roots. Beringia park ranger Andrei Kaininan, a fifty-five-year-old Yupik and lifelong resident, invited us to "harpoon" a buoy from about fifteen feet as his hunters must do in rough seas to feed the village. We all missed.

To help instill Yupik culture, New Chaplino was preparing to host regional skinboat races and Native sports events such as the high kick and stick carry. The school also offered Yupik language classes, but Kaininan was resigned to the sad reality that fewer and fewer students could speak Native languages, preferring Russian or even English. In the computer lab during summer break, local teens stood in line for a chance to kill attacking robots in video games. One of the students showed off his walrus ivory carvings of seals and polar bears. His favorite was a large menacing dragon carved from a walrus penis bone with detachable whale-bone wings.

The next day we met the Chukchi hunters who would take us across nearly 350 miles of the Bering Sea beyond the northeastern tip of Asia. They were from Lorino, a village some ninety miles north. With assistance from Alaska, the Lorino Natives in 2009 formed a marine mammal hunters' association to supply subsistence foods to the community. We hired three association boats with three crewmen each.

As the crews ran their boats onto the gravel shore, they appeared stunned at the mountain of gear we expected them to haul. We were requested to limit ourselves to a waterproof duffle and small backpack each but no one complied. We heaved in plastic bins stuffed with oatmeal, coffee, Pilot bread, and peanut butter; multiple layers of long johns, rubber pants, and ski masks; and three hundred batteries for the film and recording equipment.

I was assigned the seat against a fifty-five-gallon barrel of gasoline, just in front of Capt. Valentin Yatta and his two young crew members, Aleksei Ettyn and Eric "Eddie" Kuyapa. All three smoked incessantly the entire trip, taking a breather only to siphon gas from the drum into smaller tanks. Attempting conversation in my rusty Russian, I tried to convey why we had paid more than $6,000 each to risk our lives on this precarious adventure.

Our nervousness about these tiny open boats was quickly allayed by climate change. The Arctic is experiencing some of the warmest weather ever and we launched as its happy victims. With temperatures in the seventies, twenty hours of bright sunlight, and glassy seas, we stripped off jackets and slipped on sunglasses for a pleasure cruise.

Rocky low rolling hills define the coastline is this area at about sixty-five degrees latitude; some beaches were still covered with thick blankets of the past winter's snow. The occasional whale spout broke the surface of the smooth sea. Arctic marine birds common in Alaska—black cormorants, yellow-billed puffins, snow-white gulls—dove beneath our boats as we clipped along at about twenty-five miles an hour.

About an hour up the coast we were surprised to make out the silhouette of a large building on a coastal plateau—the hospital in the tiny village of Yanrakynnot. The community is home to nearly four hundred mostly Chukchi, about one hundred fewer than in Soviet times. As we pulled up on the beach, two teams of thick-furred sled dogs tied to rusting machinery noisily announced our arrival.

As was the case in every village we set foot, a uniformed border guard officer met us at the shoreline to examine our documents. Sometimes we had to produce our passports; others settled for an explanation of our expedition from our interpreter and guide, Oksana Yashchenko, the Beringia Park's deputy director. With a 2013 master's degree in cultural anthropology from University of Alaska Fairbanks, Yashchenko was a model of patience with a disarming smile and reassuring British lilt.

LATER WE STROLLED through Yanrakynnot, whose name comes from Chukchi meaning "detached, firm land." The quaint village is perched between the sea and a lagoon, beyond which roam large reindeer herds. The village's marine mammal hunters trade whale and walrus meat for reindeer hides.

Yanrakynnot boasted new "Abramovich houses" along Soviet Street and a hospital seemingly too large for this community. We were told it should have been built in the larger Lorino but never got the full explanation. A new television and cell phone tower was being erected to deliver round-the-clock, government-controlled Moscow news and Russian game shows to village homes.

As we continued up the coast, the hills swelled to steep cliffs that dove into the sea. Our captains steered us so close to a bird rookery that we winced at the pungent odor of years of guano dripping down the rocky face.

For a pit stop, we pulled into the long-abandoned village of Mechigmen along a sandy beach just south of Lorino. For centuries, we were told, this was a whale harvesting and trading site. Hunters meticulously assembled whale bones into large pits to store whale meat, which they traded with reindeer herders from the distant foothills. Hundreds of years of amassed whale bones had created overgrown ridges two stories high.

A row of erect whale ribs remained upright for securing overturned whale boats. I stumbled over a fresh reindeer antler covered by arctic stink weed. Silent but for the rustle of tall grass in the breeze, the place had a mystical air like Stonehenge. When asked about a spiritual connection, Capt. Vladimir Piny shrugged and made an eating motion; it was all about whale meat, he seemed to say.

We finally eased onto shore at Lorino, strategically situated on a high plateau overlooking the sea. Our crews had alerted their families by cell phone of our pending arrival, so dozens of wives and children streamed down narrow paths to the beach. As a couple of toddlers played chase around a rusting ship partly submerged in the tide line, we were honored with Chukchi welcome dances by teenage girls in brightly flowered *kuspuks*. An unusually chatty local border guardsman attempted friendly conversation in rapid Russian while his wife took iPad pictures of our passports.

Lorino felt like a village making a successful transition from the Soviet era. Of the approximately 1,500 residents, 1,272 were Chukchi Natives, according to a census provided to us by Mayor Victor Kalasnikov, a Ukrainian who had lived there for twenty-three years. In communist days, Lorino had an additional one thousand residents, many of them Russians, Ukrainians, and Azerbaijanis lured by the Arctic's high salaries to operate the dairy, chicken, greenhouse, fox, and vehicle-repair collectives.

"In Soviet times, life was like a boiling kettle. Everything was working," said the mayor in his tiny office adorned with regional maps and an authoritative picture of Vladimir Putin. Lorino, he said, offers the lifestyle mix residents want: rich subsistence hunting in a spectacular setting with the modern conveniences of cell phone service, hot running water, and a well-equipped school.

During the long sunny evening after our arrival, Lorino's dirt streets were teeming with kids kicking soccer balls, chasing dogs, or strolling hand-in-hand with their parents, including several of our boat crew. There were none of the Abramovich houses we saw in New Chaplino; most residents lived in aging three-story apartment buildings decorated with huge murals of walrus, polar bears, and whales. The village's main store and bakery offered essentials from microwaves to linoleum flooring. We stocked up on the first apples and oranges we had seen in Russia.

Like much of Chukotka, Lorino was full of children, encouraged by federal policy to reverse Russia's plummeting population. The number of Russians peaked in the early 1990s at about 148 million. The country's population is projected to drop 20 percent to 111 million by 2050, due to a combination of early death rates, frequent abortions, and low immigration.

Families receive a national subsidy of 500,000 rubles—about $7,600—for a second child and another 130,000 rubles for a third, our Beringia host told us. Additional subsidies are granted for taking in foster children. After President Putin banned American adoption of Russian orphans in 2013, local families willing to raise orphans also got top priority for apartments.

The lack of adequate housing topped the list of local problems in most villages we visited. Mayor Kalasnikov was trying to accommodate 160 people awaiting housing or upgraded apartments. The last new apartment building was constructed in 2005, so the city issued bids for two new buildings in 2015. Unexplained complications resulted in the award of only one contract, for a sixteen-unit building. Funding came from the Chukotka regional government while Lorino provided land and utilities.

Like all the subsistence villages we visited, Lorino was struggling to preserve its Native culture in the face of challenges from modern technology and climate change. In the cramped offices of the marine mammal hunters' association, director Alexey Ottoy explained how his members follow traditions handed down by elders.

Nearly an elder himself, with graying moustache and no-nonsense air, Ottoy said the association shared boats, outboard motors, an industrial refrigerator, and harpoons and rifles to harvest fifty-six gray whales and three hundred walrus annually. It encouraged its young people to learn hunting and boating skills through skin-boat competitions and dogsled races. Women also help feed the village by gathering plants and berries.

In a ramshackle hut housing the village's walrus-ivory-carving operation, up to six craftsmen carved on commission, filling orders from Moscow and Vladivostok. Our host, Alexey Ryrultet, began carving as a boy and was now qualified as a master. He admitted it was challenging to entice Lorino's youth to enter the craft, saying too few have the necessary artistic vision.

Ryrultet showed off a walrus skull with the tusks attached, intricately etched with scenes of hunting and village life. Its sale price in Russia would be around $500, he said. We estimated such a piece would easily get five times that in Alaska. An international treaty prohibits importing ivory across most national borders, but Lorino carvers admitted that some of their work ends up in China.

Ottoy and others said the impacts of climate change were wide-ranging. Winters are definitely warmer, changing animal migration patterns and ice conditions. Recently, walrus had hauled out near Lorino for the first time in memory, but Yanrakynnot had gone two years without seeing walrus. A warming Arctic also opened Bering Strait waters to more ship traffic, including lucrative cruise ships.

The Chukchi marine mammal hunters speculated that smaller cruise ships a decade earlier had frightened walrus from their shores. Still, they welcomed the cash infusion that well-heeled tourists might provide their communities with shore visits.

Lorino was one of just two Bering Sea villages still with a working fox farm; the other was in Inchoun on the arctic coast. In Soviet times, such farms generated thousands of pelts for fur coats, producing a healthy source of village income. Western groups such as Greenpeace protested the practice, claiming that the Soviets overharvested whales to feed their fox industry.

Lorino's farm, on a high bluff overlooking the sea, once housed ten thousand animals and spanned hundreds of square feet. Now, most of the cages once suspended on tall wooden stilts had collapsed onto the tundra. I guessed just a few dozen cages still held blue foxes, barely visible through my telephoto lens. The farm was surrounded by a tall fence, and the operators declined our request for a visit.

The wire cages where the animals spent their lives measured about four feet square, open to the air so waste drops to the ground. They were fed leftover whale meat, we were told. When the wind died, I could detect a haunting wailing from the cages.

Barely a day after arriving in Lorino, our boat crews opted to take advantage of continuing good weather and head north for Uelen, about seventy-five miles around the tip of Asia. While the crews loaded the boats, their children rushed to the water's edge as clouds of eight-inch-long skinny silver fish sloshed against the tideline. We guessed they were hooligan, a type of smelt commonly known in Alaska as candlefish because when dried their oily bodies burn like candles. Two giggling kids tossed slippery fish at each other as a dog plucked them fresh from the sea for a late breakfast.

As we ventured outside the protected waters of Mechigmensky Bay, we quickly came to appreciate the skills of our boat captains. Entering the Bering Strait with nothing between us and the North Pole except open ocean, we were buffeted by large white-capped waves rolling in from the northeast. We scrambled to pull on rubber pants and ski goggles. One boat took the lead, with the others following fifty yards in its wake. This shielded us from the direct onslaught, but we were quickly drenched in frigid spray, hanging on to the aluminum rails with a death grip.

Suddenly, our engine stopped cold, our boat tossed wildly in the waves. Cinematographer Xavier Grobet and I exchanged worried glances. Our crewmen casually flicked their cigarettes overboard and switched gas cans. We were soon under way again.

As we began the longest open-water crossing of the trip across the mouth of Lavrentiya Bay, we could barely make out the outline of the hub community of Lavrentiya to the west. I tried to envision Captain Cook sailing through here on the feast day of Saint Lawrence in 1778. My thoughts were quickly redirected to more immediate business: making it across the seventeen-mile expanse.

Our boats repeatedly eased to the top of waves before quickly nosing into the next trough, the salty spray making it hard to see through goggles designed for powder skiing, not a Bering Sea shower. Suddenly, from the top of a wave we made out the hazy outline of what looked like a large tabletop on the eastern horizon. After a few more roller coasters, our captain confirmed the sighting: Big Diomede Island. Minutes later, a small mountain beside it appeared from the sea—Little Diomede.

None of us had ever seen this view. We ignored the heaving sea long enough to circle our boats and hear a quick prayer of thanks from Etta Tall. She had spent her first nineteen years on Little Diomede yet was banned by the US and Soviet governments from crossing the two and a half miles to Big Diomede.

"It was so emotional for me," Tall said later. "I couldn't believe Big Diomede was so close but we couldn't go there." As a young girl, Tall picked up Russian music on her grandmother's radio and occasionally ventured across the frozen strait with family members to meet Russians at the date line to exchange candy and cigarettes.

On this trip, Tall carried a three-inch-thick printout of her grandfather's handwritten recollections of life in the Diomedes in the 1920s and '30s. She pulled it from her backpack in each village we visited, hoping to rekindle memories of Russian Natives whose ancestors were forced off Big Diomede nearly seventy years earlier. A few moments after our poignant interlude, a gray whale spouted and flipped its tail, perhaps a welcome for us Alaskans so close to home.

Just short of East Cape, the northeasternmost point of Eurasia, we spotted three bleached whale ribs standing erect on the hillside. They marked the abandoned village of Naukan. Once home to as many as 350 Naukanski Yupik Natives, the village prospered for centuries with its bird's-eye view of food in the sea and proximity to the Diomede Islands and Alaska mainland. In 1948, Soviets forced villagers living on Big Diomede to Naukan. A decade later, Naukan was ordered closed and its residents relocated to three villages to the south.

We landed on the gravel beach to find Naukan an eerie ghost town, the rocky foundations of the homes of banished residents clinging to the grassy slope. We were surprised to encounter the first humans we had seen on the Bering Sea outside a village, a half dozen mostly elderly Natives huddled around a campfire. Visiting from Lavrentiya, a few of the women were born in Naukan and were visiting the site with an American researcher. We left them at peace and made our way up the steep hill through the remnants of the village, careful to avoid stepping on the wood scraps of old houses as if in a cemetery. Whale bones were scattered everywhere; I plucked a three-inch piece from a small bone pile and slipped it into my pocket as a keepsake.

In the distance, a crumbling lighthouse perched on a hill. Climbing to it, we were struck by the irony that the structure doubled as a monument to seventeenth-century Russian explorer Dezhnev, who beat Bering through this region by eighty years. It was dedicated in 1955, about the same time the Soviet government was banishing many of its country's indigenous peoples from their homeland. From Dezhnev's monument against a sparkling clear blue sky, we could easily see Big Diomede Island. Just to the north of it rose Paavik Mountain—the tallest hill in the Alaska mainland community of Wales, just a fifty-four-mile seagull flight away.

Unsettled after reflecting on Naukan's fate, we silently proceeded around the eastern tip of Russia through the Bering Strait into the Chukchi Sea. In less than an hour, we landed on the gravel beach at Uelen, Russia's northeasternmost village. Fresh walrus carcasses sloshed in the tide as the community's water truck drove onto the beach to haul our gear to an empty room in the ivory-carving institute for what became our home for the next three days.

My only memory from a brief visit to Uelen in 1989 was the exquisite ivory and bone carving by local craftsmen. Now we got to spend hours admiring a century's worth of masterpieces in the carving school and museum, founded in 1931.

Wearing sweatpants from Kotzebue, Alaska, local master carver Stanislov Nuteventin fired up an electric drill to show how he shaped a small block of walrus ivory into the tiny paws of a sled-dog team. His demonstration interrupted by his ringing cell phone, Nuteventin showed off a shoe box of ivory pieces produced by his students. Happy to make a few sales to his visitors, Nuteventin said the rubles would be welcomed by the local families. Most of his students, he acknowledged with resignation, do not stick with ivory carving because it doesn't pay well compared to government jobs—if available—and it's not prestigious.

Uelen's school faced similar challenges instilling the Chukchi culture in its two hundred students. National government policy requires Russian students to study two foreign languages, including English. In Uelen, Chukchi was the second language offered, but a shortage of qualified teachers limited classes to just twice a week for only about fifty students, explained thirty-three-year Chukchi language teacher Tatyana Zhukovskaya.

In Soviet times, speaking Chukchi was forbidden; today, few parents urge their kids to learn it. To encourage student interest, Zhukovskaya's classroom was a celebration of the Chukchi culture, jammed with drawings of famous Chukchi, intricate beadwork crafts, and the names of marine mammals translated into the consonant-laden language.

About halfway into our stay in Uelen, the public-works department decided to clear the village water lines. That's when the industrial sink shared by the ten of us and our nine boat crewmen started spitting out what looked like chunky chocolate milk. We persuaded the operator of the village *banya,* or sauna, to stay open late so we could sweat out the dirt. A campaign poster of former Governor Abramovich, with his trademark three-day whiskers, greeted *banya* visitors. Walking back to our temporary quarters, we spotted a 1978 blue-and-gold Alaska license plate nailed to the door of an aging house.

After our third night on the school's hard floor, we awoke to low clouds and a brisk wind. But even our patient boat crews wanted to head south. The normal practice for launching these boats involved laying eight-foot whale ribs like railroad ties at the tide line and pushing the boats across them into the sea. But that day Uelen's surf was too rough. The crew managed to get one boat afloat, minus gear and passengers, and then pulled the others through the waves with a long rope. In the pitching sea, we transferred bags and climbed nervously between boats, a preview of the trip ahead.

We all had layered up—long johns, rain pants, stocking hats, rubber gloves—but were quickly soaked in Chukchi Sea spray. As we rounded Cape Dezhnev heading south into the Bering Strait, waves from Alaska rolled at us. Soaked and shivering after about eight hours in rough seas, we finally arrived back in Lorino. One of our crewmen took pity on us and arranged for the town *banya* to stay open late.

Relieved to be on solid ground for a few days, we commandeered the city bus for a day trip to Lavrentiya, the regional hub village of two thousand about twenty-three bumpy road miles from Lorino. Our plan was to visit the government archives to aid Etta Tall in her search for distant relatives. Descending the final hill into town, we passed a deserted radar station. Like the DEW Line radar network built across Alaska and Canada during the Cold War, we were told this site warned against incoming hostilities from Alaska.

When I last visited Lavrentiya, the city had boasted a richly diverse population topping three thousand. Sixty years earlier, the Soviets had established a "culture base" there to ensure the forced acculturation of Chukchi and Yupik peoples. As the government closed smaller villages during the Cold War, many residents were moved to Lavrentiya. Now it had the only airstrip north of

Provideniya and was headquarters for federal services, including a court and border guard station.

OUR BUS RUMBLED to a stop just past the dusty city square anchored by two statues: Lenin and what Americans know as a Billiken, a chubby Buddha-like figure supposed to bring good luck. The Billiken must have been out of order. Waiting for our arrival were two armed border guard officers who directed us to remain in our bus seats while they demanded the special "border zone" permits required for travel in this part of Russia. None of us had ever seen such a permit; our interpreter and guide, Oksana Yashchenko, had wisely held them for each of us to lessen the odds that someone would lose their permit. However, Yashchenko had mistakenly left them in Lorino.

The senior guardsman called his superiors in the capital of Anadyr while Yashchenko had copies of our permits faxed to the border guard headquarters. After a tense standoff, the guards decided that Russian justice must run its course.

Ordered to the guard station on the industrial outskirts of Lavrentiya, we were paraded into a conference room decorated with intimidating panels detailing the history of the KGB. It was now the Federal Security Bureau, the umbrella agency of the border guard. In one picture, Putin forcefully marched into an arctic snowstorm, surrounded by uniformed border guards.

As we killed hour after hour, two baby-faced guards brought in tea, candy, cookies, and Russian magazines. Escorted to Major Polosin's office one at a time, we were forced to acknowledge the charges against us. On his wall a poster demonstrated arctic hand-rescue signals. I memorized the one for "help," hoping it might come in handy in a remote gulag.

Six hours after our arrival in Lavrentiya, we were ordered across town to the courthouse to answer the charges before a federal judge. One at a time, we were summoned into the courtroom and seated at the defendant's table, the chair bumping up against a prison cell made of thick construction rebar. From the prosecutor's table across the courtroom, Major Polosin scowled.

A redheaded judge in black robes burst into the courtroom. In the fastest Russian I've ever heard, she recited the charges against us and demanded a plea through our interpreter. In hopes of expediting the process, we had agreed among ourselves not to dispute the charges. Each of us confessed to failing to have the special permit with us in Lavrentiya. It took nearly an hour each to process the nine of us.

The verdict: guilty. The penalty: a five-hundred-ruble fine, about $8 each. Just before four a.m.—sixteen hours after our arrest—we were released into the bright arctic daylight. Displaying my string-bound conviction paperwork, I relished the experience, posing for a picture next to the federal courthouse sign.

Over the few final days in Chukotka, I tried to assess the impacts of three decades of renewed interaction between Alaskans and residents of this region. Thanks to the 1989 visa-free agreement between the US and Russian national governments, nearly five thousand Soviet and Russian Natives had crossed the strait to visit Alaska since then. Thousands of Alaskans also made the trip.

Among the Russian Natives was Uelen Mayor Valentina Kareva, whose Chukchi dance group traveled to several Alaska villages on multiple cultural exchanges. Kareva cherished her reunions with Alaska Natives and welcomed more. But visits today require three months' worth of paperwork, she said, and few Russian Natives can afford air fares without Alaska assistance. A more productive means to improve US-Russia relations should be directed at the national level. "That's where the problem is," Kareva said, the ever-present President Putin on her office wall.

We saw evidence that business and nonprofit practices advanced through University of Alaska assistance and other Alaska entities continue to pay dividends in the Russian Far East. For example, marine mammal associations in Lorino and New Chaplino were inspired by Alaska's North Slope Borough and federal agencies such as the National Park Service and National Oceanic and Atmospheric Administration. Some marine mammal harvesting equipment supplied by Alaskans remains in use.

Living conditions appeared to have improved over the past three decades, with many aging Soviet-era wood houses replaced with more modern weather-resistant metal homes connected to running water and sewer. Most of those improvements came from the regional government during Abramovich's tenure. Capitalism also had gained some favor, as most of the single state-run stores of Soviet times were supplemented by multiple shops offering a broad mix of consumer goods.

Some Russian Far East officials remained less enthusiastic about the benefits of renewed ties across the strait. "No iron curtain ever existed between Alaska and Chukotka; it was probably between our national governments," said Provideniya city official Paramonov. His region would benefit from broad international contacts, such as cruise-ship passengers, and not just from Alaskans "who are just like us."

Just a month after our trip, the 820-foot *Crystal Serenity* made history as one of the largest cruise ships to ply the Arctic. It departed Seward, Alaska, with nearly 1,200 passengers paying up to $120,000 each for a thirty-two-day voyage. It sailed northeast through the Bering Strait to the Canadian Arctic and Greenland en route to New York. Although the *Serenity* did not stop in Russia, three of its passengers flew from Nome to Provideniya for lunch.

"The era of active relations between Alaska and Chukotka has passed and it probably will never come again," the dour Paramonov speculated.

On our final day on the Bering Sea, we made gifts of our gear and medical supplies and posed for snapshots with our crewmen, who had kept us safe and introduced us to some of the most spectacular scenery and gracious hospitality many of us had ever experienced. As billowy clouds cast evening shadows on the barren rocky hills, the boatmen started north for home, leaving three identical wakes across a glassy Bering Sea.

Children play on insulated utility ducts in the Russian Bering Sea community of Provideniya in summer 2016. PHOTO BY DAVID RAMSEUR

A Special Alaska-Russia Affinity

I am sure that if constancy and loyalty are to fail anywhere, the failure will not be in the states which approach nearest to the North Pole.

—WILLIAM SEWARD, AUGUST 12, 1869

FOUR YEARS AFTER surviving a brutal knifing during the Lincoln assassination conspiracy and two years after signing the treaty consummating the US purchase of Russian America, William Seward delivered those words in Alaska's territorial capital.

Addressing the few hundred American settlers eager to hear what life under the American flag might mean for them, Seward shared his vision. The fervent expansionist foresaw an essential role the new territory could play in advancing American global interests. This included a key partnership between the two nations—America and Russia—that had just crafted one of the biggest real-estate deals in US history.

The sixty-nine-year-old Seward had stepped down as secretary of state a few months earlier and wanted to see in person the new American possession that was one of his proudest accomplishments. In June, he and his son Frederick traveled west as some of the first tourists on the just-completed Transcontinental Railroad. From San Francisco, they sailed aboard a private steamer to the territory that helped fulfill Seward's belief in Manifest Destiny, the nineteenth-century conviction that the United States was destined to control North America from the Atlantic to the Pacific.

In Sitka, Seward continued to preach national expansionism. He noted that during his lifetime, twenty new states had been added to the United States.

"I now see, besides Alaska, ten territories in a forward condition of preparation for entering into the same great political family," Seward said. His forecast was nearly a century ahead of its time: Alaska finally achieved statehood in 1959.

Seward also visited the Chilkat Indian Village of Klukwan at the northern end of Alaska's Southeast Panhandle, about twenty miles north of current-day Haines. There he was received by the fearsome six-foot-tall Tlingit leader, Koh'klux, whose name translated as "hard to kill."

During Seward's visit, a total solar eclipse darkened the sky, silencing birds and insects and terrifying the Tlingit, who hid in their houses. That is, until Seward alleviated their fear by explaining the mysterious astronomical phenomenon with an orange and an apple in front of a cabin light. Seward so impressed Koh'klux that the great chief had the statesman's name tattooed on his arm.

As he departed Alaska, Seward stopped at Fort Tongass, an American military post near the Canadian border about sixty miles south of current-day Ketchikan. There the Tongass tribe of Tlingit Natives threw a potlatch—a large celebration—in his honor, and even fashioned special totems to recognize Seward and the slain President Lincoln.

Seward's interaction with the Tlingit served as a premonition for attitudes a century and a half later. Koh'klux objected to the "sale" of the Alaska territory. Only Russian-owned commercial assets could be sold, the Tlingit leader contended, not the Alaska landmass that neither Russia nor the United States owned.

Tongass chief Ebbit, offended that Seward failed to bring gifts to his own potlatch, ordered the secretary's ears and nose painted bright red on his totem as a sign of shame. The original of that pole and a replica carved in the 1930s are believed to have been "returned to the earth," as is the traditional practice. Another copy of the pole was being carved in late 2016.

Resentment toward Seward's actions persist today. They even complicated plans to mark the 150th anniversary of America's purchase of Alaska in 2017. Alaska's Lt. Gov. Byron Mallott, himself a Tlingit and a leader in planning the state's sesquicentennial, insisted the event be termed a "commemoration" instead of a "celebration."

"It's not like no one has ever said we shouldn't commemorate the event," Mallott said. "Everybody says, 'Let's do it,' but be sensitive to the reality so it doesn't turn into a one-sided, Eurocentric event."

Despite the flack Seward encountered after his brief visit to America's newest territory, it helped confirm his belief that a strong Alaska-Russia relationship advanced America's global interests. The nation, he wrote, must inevitably "roll its restless waves to the icy barriers of the North." During his negotiations with the Russian foreign minister over the Alaska purchase, Seward imagined a US-Russia alliance that would limit England's global influence while strengthening the bond between Alaska and Russia.

Since Seward's time, that relationship has fluctuated broadly. During World War II, the US-Soviet Lend-Lease partnership was designed as a strategic military alliance yet it also fostered broader cooperation and understanding across the Bering Strait. The Cold War that followed aroused new suspicions, threatened the world with nuclear annihilation, and erected an Ice Curtain across the only border shared by the United States and the Soviet Union.

After forty years of isolation, the strait's indigenous peoples helped demolish that obstruction by pursuing a millennia-old way of life with long-separated relatives. Melting the Ice Curtain ushered in a three-decade heyday of productive relations, an era instructive for today.

Some dismiss this period as a historic flash in the pan, a temporary confluence of circumstances in which people in a little-noticed part of the world were allowed to practice harmless citizen diplomacy. Yet the 1988 Friendship Flight and other high-profile initiatives in the region helped end the Cold War, preceding East Germany's dismantling of the Berlin Wall by two years.

The pioneering efforts to warm Alaska-Soviet relations faced significant national and local resistance. At least initially, both the Reagan administration and Gorbachev's Kremlin only gave lip service to such overtures until persistent citizen-diplomats refused to back down. Early Alaska advocates for easing Cold War tensions, such as Dixie Belcher, Gov. Steve Cowper, and Jim Stimpfle, were branded communists or kooks.

Today, the special Alaska-Russia affinity can help explain Russia's complexity beyond the Bering Strait. Americans roll their eyes at Vladimir Putin tossing a judo opponent to the mat but are perplexed by his saber-rattling directed at the United States. At the same time, most Russians support their iron-fisted president and resent the second-class status with which many Americans treat Russia.

Even at the highest levels, Americans seem befuddled by Putin's Russia. After a cooperative Boris Yeltsin, President Bill Clinton found his handpicked successor, Vladimir Putin, cold and troubling. President George W. Bush looked into the eyes of the former KGB agent to get "a sense of his soul," but their relationship quickly deteriorated. President Barack Obama took office eager to "reset" US-Russia relations. Obama's initial optimism produced progress with then-President Dmitry Medvedev, but Putin's resumption as Russia's leader refrosted relations.

The surprise 2016 election of Donald Trump was enthusiastically welcomed in the Kremlin, at least publicly, for Trump's pledge to engage in "constructive dialogue." During his campaign, Trump echoed Putin's agenda: acceptance of Russia's annexation of Crimea, skepticism of NATO, and relaxation of Western sanctions. American intelligence agencies concluded that Russian cyberspies hacked into the US election on Trump's behalf, which Trump as a candidate even encouraged. Now many experts foresee Putin simply capitalizing on disarray in the West to help Russia return to its former glory before the breakup of the Soviet Union. With Russia no longer widely considered a superpower, Putin's intervention in Syria and the Crimea, disinformation campaigns in Europe, and unchallenged crackdowns on internal opposition demonstrate that military might is unnecessary for global influence.

The Trump-Putin "bromance" provides a unique opportunity to reset the worst relations between the United States and Russia since the 1962 Cuban missile crisis. While the West won the Cold War, Putin's Russia has successfully redefined that victory in recent years. The US and Russia begin a new era with their leaders bearing remarkably similar traits. Neither are indebted to a political party or financier for their quick rise to power, freeing both men to do and say largely what they want regardless of the consequences. Both are adept at using unconventional means of communications to make blanket assertions regardless of the facts. And both see their nations as inadequate yet destined for renewed greatness.

As a model for future US-Russia relations, the Trump administration would be wise to look to Alaska. Its three-decade-long era of successful diplomacy with Russia based on shared experiences, direct personal contact, and mutual benefit can serve as a blueprint for making both nations great again.

This approach does not naïvely expect that a few well-meaning Rotarians or Natives connecting with would-be business partners or distant relatives can set policy in Moscow or Washington. Certainly, future cooperation between America and Russia will remain challenging, but not impossible. Based on the nearly three decades of recent productive relations between Alaska and Russia, here are some specific ways that special connection can ease tensions and rebuild trust between our countries.

Avoid Diplomatic Slights

The United States and Russia began the twenty-first century poised for cooperation. After the September 11, 2001, terrorist attacks on the United States, Putin offered Russia's support and even contemplated closer ties with the West through Russian membership in the North Atlantic Treaty Organization (NATO). But a series of actions and pronouncements by both sides quickly exacerbated misunderstanding and resentment. For example, NATO added seven new members along Russia's borders in 2004. And popular rebellions in Moscow in 2011 and 2012 and Ukraine's 2013 revolution, which Putin believed were instigated by the West, increased his paranoia.

A breakthrough appeared on the horizon in 2009, when the Obama administration and Russia outlined an ambitious collaborative agenda. As term limits forced Putin to temporarily vacate the presidency, Obama and then-President Medvedev formed a comprehensive US-Russia Bilateral Presidential Commission. It focused on nineteen specific areas of cooperation, ranging from arms control to education. Working groups and subcommittees began fleshing out detailed policy recommendations with assistance from sixty American and Russian government agencies. Even eighteenth- and nineteenth-century Russian documents stolen and offered for sale by American auction houses were returned to Russia as a sign of good faith.

Yet just five years later, Obama exacerbated Russia's inferiority complex by dismissing it as a "regional power." He continued the diplomatic slight when he excluded Russia from a White House conference to strengthen arctic security with five Nordic nations. Relations quickly deteriorated further after Russia's 2014 incursion into Ukraine. The United States reacted by suspending all Bilateral Commission activities and imposing sanctions on Russia.

Today, as Russia has increased its international clout on issues from Syria to the European Union, the impact of those sanctions is negligible. The West needs to rethink policies designed to further isolate Russia or continue pressure in the belief it will suddenly transform into a cooperative democracy. To encourage more acceptable Russian behavior, the new American president should consider carrots instead of a stick, such as restarting the presidential commission initiatives. What better place for a US-Russian presidential summit to launch this new era in US-Russia relations than its former fur colony of Russian America?

Science Can Help Overcome Politics

During the Cold War, cooperation between Alaska and the Soviet Union was largely in the form of scientific exchanges focused on fish and wildlife management, climate, and rural health. Today, even with strained national relations, some scientific collaboration between Alaska and Russian scientists and institutions continues.

Joint research already under way ranges from subsea permafrost and Bering Sea fisheries to endangered Native languages and arctic ecosystems. In 2016, Alaska and Russian biologists announced a cooperative effort to produce a database of historic walrus haul-out locations along the Bering and Chukchi Seas. Yet that cooperation is threatened by years of Russian neglect of science, the isolation of its research community, and petty harassment of Western scientists by Russian security forces.

Native Links Need Stronger Bonds

Reuniting long-divided Bering Strait Native peoples was a chief catalyst in melting the Ice Curtain in the mid-1980s. Now the children of both Alaska and Russian Native elders who had close relatives separated across the strait lack the same personal connections as their parents and grandparents. Despite efforts on both sides to preserve Native cultures, the continuation of those traditions appears endangered.

In the Chukotka region, indigenous languages are offered in schools, but classes are limited by lack of resources and dwindling interest. Fewer Russian parents encourage their children to speak Native languages at home as interest in activities to preserve indigenous culture, such as ivory carving and dance, declines. The Alaska experience is similar, with linguists predicting some Bering Sea Native dialects will be gone in another generation.

The 1988 Friendship Flight, said retired University of Alaska Fairbanks linguist Michael Krauss, "failed to stop the loss of the Yupik language in Alaska and failed to regenerate any long-term interest in reviving the language in Chukotka. For the life of the language, I cannot say the flight had any long-term effect."

His colleague, UAF professor Lawrence Kaplan, said Native languages in both countries "are overwhelmed by a sea" of English and Russian from television, the Internet, and printed publications.

Isolated efforts struggle to keep the culture alive. In summer 2016, thirty-one Russian Natives traveled to Savoonga on Alaska's St. Lawrence Island for two weeks of cultural renewal, tea drinking, and Native dancing. Organized by local activist John Waghiya with $50,000 from the National Park Service Beringia Program, the Alaska and Russian Natives successfully communicated with each other mostly through Siberian Yupik. Waghiya termed travel logistics "ridiculously difficult," including the cost of flying US Customs officials to St. Lawrence to process the Russians. But he said that will not prevent him from organizing future visits.

"That's my passion in life," Waghiya said. "If I'm going to leave a legacy, that's going to be it. I'm compelled to keep the connections alive. These are the very same people that we are composed of, same language, same culture, same dances. I hope that once we are gone, the young people will keep doing what we do."

The 1989 US-Soviet agreement for "visa-free" travel for indigenous peoples helped thousands of Alaska and Russian Natives reunite. Nearly three decades later, such exchanges remain bureaucratic and expensive. Despite reforms adopted in 2015, some Chukchi and Alaska officials complain about the months-long process to complete and exchange the paperwork for what was envisioned as streamlined visa-free travel.

The Arctic Is the Best Opportunity for Cooperation

The area of greatest potential cooperation between Alaska and the Russian Far East is managing a changing Arctic. Nearly half of the world's Arctic falls within Russia, 40 percent of arctic residents are Russian, and the Russian Arctic generates about 30 percent of that nation's overall exports. In the United States, Alaska is the only reason America is an arctic nation, which has produced enormous benefits for the nation. For example, Alaska's North Slope accounted for a quarter of US domestic oil production at its 1988 peak, although today that output is down significantly.

President Obama made his first extended visit to Alaska in September 2015 as the United States assumed its two-year term as chair of the international Arctic Council. His administration followed up by sending nine cabinet secretaries or their deputies to Alaska to maintain a focus on arctic concerns and proposed a $6 million down payment on a new $1 billion icebreaker.

Today, many northern nations fear Russian "militarization" of the Arctic. Russia announced plans to reopen fifty mothballed Soviet-era military bases, and its air incursions over the Arctic have increased threefold. It currently boasts forty icebreakers and is building more. In 2015, Russia launched a massive arctic military exercise to demonstrate its combat readiness in the region.

Russia says its heightened military presence is designed to protect transportation routes and develop resources in an increasingly ice-free Arctic. What it does not say openly is that it also is troubled by China's arctic presence. China is building its own extensive fleet of modern icebreakers to assist in shipping goods and resources, skirting Russian transit fees in the process. During Obama's Alaska visit, Chinese warships appeared off the state's coast.

To accommodate a changed Arctic, especially Russia's dominance of the region, the Arctic Council should consider changes to how it operates. The thoughtful Washington, DC, think tank Center for Strategic and International Studies advanced three areas for Arctic Council reform.

First, expand the council's jurisdiction to include military and national-security issues. Ironically, at American insistence when the council was created, those issues were deemed outside its jurisdiction.

Second, based on the Alaska-Russia model of joint ventures, the council should focus more on economic development and remove barriers to cross-border business. Under Canadian chairmanship in 2013–2015, the council created an Arctic Economic Council. Yet at the same time, Russia adopted a law prohibiting payments from Western companies to Russian entities unless they register as "foreign agents." That's a step few are willing to take. The conflict needs to be resolved to allow more commercial links.

Third, while Alaska and Russian scientists actively cooperate, the Council should adopt an Arctic-wide agreement that prohibits barriers for more scientific cooperation and joint ventures.

Even with these reforms, some believe the Arctic Council's current structure and jurisdiction is simply inadequate for a rapidly changing Arctic. This is driven by Russia's increased muscle flexing and the growing number of entities seeking more arctic involvement. By 2016, nearly three dozen countries and organizations had won Arctic Council "observer" status, as distant from the Arctic as India and Italy.

An entirely new arctic management entity could have a broader mandate over economic, security, and human issues more relevant to the four million people who live there. But such a new entity would be costly to create and likely to meet resistance from the eight arctic nations that are currently members of the council.

The most direct US-Russia interactions occur in the Bering Strait, a vital marine shipping route for both nations and others seeking to capitalize on a melting Arctic. A Brown University institute proposed two US-Russia actions specific to operations in the strait: bilateral oil-spill response and search-and-rescue exercises, and establishment of a "joint maritime domain-awareness center" for better ship traffic management.

When it comes to arctic management, a distinct American disadvantage is its failure to ratify the 1982 United Nations Convention on the Law of the Sea. The treaty grants to those nations that are a party to it jurisdiction over issues such as navigation and territorial claims. Nearly 170 nations have ratified the convention. Conservative Republican opposition in the US Senate, which believes the convention is a threat to American sovereignty, has prevented its approval.

Countries such as Russia and Denmark have made territorial claims on the Arctic under the Law of the Sea. But the United States lacks the jurisdiction to weigh in because of its failure to join the convention.

Personal Relationships Matter

Situated nearly equidistant from their national capitals and burdened with similar northern climates, residents of Alaska and the Russian Far East enjoy a special affinity. After nearly three decades of active engagement across the Bering Strait, far more Alaskans and Russians know of Anchorage and Magadan than of Akron and Murmansk.

"My colleagues and I were very interested to learn about Alaska's experience to address issues such as a market economy, government regulation, resource management, relations with the federal government, and interactions with indigenous people," former Magadan Gov. Vyacheslav Kobets recalled nearly thirty years after initial contacts with Alaskans. "We are close by our historical, cultural, and even family ties, because the Russian explorers discovered and even mastered Alaska."

That's why a dozen sister-city relationships were established between communities in Alaska and Russia and why Rotary Clubs, churches, and youth organizations engaged in civic and cultural contacts. Today, virtually all Alaska-Russia sister-city relations are dormant. Only the Fairbanks-Yakutsk connection remains active. Both Alaskans and Russians who participated in earlier exchanges express interest in resuming, but high hurdles stand in the way.

One significant barrier remains the lack of regular air service. Charter flights from Nome on Bering Air remain the only efficient option to Russia's Chukotka region, but increased prices put those flights out of reach for average Alaskans and Russians.

Another deterrent is Russian persecution of both Western visitors and domestic dissenters, from petty harassment to murder. Some of Alaska's most experienced and well-meaning Russia experts are now prohibited from returning to Russia. The detention of me and my fellow travelers by border guards in 2016 certainly makes us think twice about returning to Russia. The media regularly report of Western scholars engaged in innocent scientific research in Russia being harassed, arrested, or worse.

"Since the collapse of the Soviet Union, murder has been an unfortunate reality in the business and political life of Russia," reported Radio Free Europe, documenting nearly fifty murders or suspicious killings of government officials, journalists, and business leaders in Russia between 1994 and 2006. That list included Magadan Oblast Gov. Valentin Tsvetkov, shot dead in Moscow in 2002 while trying to crack down on crime in his region's gold and oil industries.

More recently, the *New York Times* detailed a crackdown on those who challenge the Russian government under Putin. "Muckraking journalists, rights advocates, opposition politicians, government whistle-blowers, and other Russians who threaten that image are treated harshly—imprisoned on trumped-up charges, smeared in the news media and, with increasing frequency, killed," the paper reported.

At a minimum, the national governments of the two countries, which have the weapons to destroy each other many times over, need to keep talking. In advance of traveling to Moscow in summer 2015 for the Dartmouth Conference with our Russian counterparts, our US delegation received a State Department briefing on the current state of US-Russia relations. We were shocked to hear from the agency's senior Russia expert that there was virtually no ongoing communications between the two nations.

To its credit, Alaska continues to try to talk to Russia. In 2016 Gov. Bill Walker directed that his state rejoin the Northern Forum, a federation of northern regional governments launched nearly three decades earlier by Governors Cowper and Hickel. A sizable contingent of Russians from Siberia and the Far East gathered in Anchorage for several days to discuss best practices and the changing Arctic.

Alaska and Russian Citizen-Diplomats Keep Relations Alive

Despite the barriers, personal interactions between Alaskans and Russians continue. Scores of Russians who first stepped foot in Alaska to help melt the Ice Curtain remained to build new lives and advance Alaska-Russia understanding. Some Alaskans were similarly inspired to relocate permanently to Russia. Here are the stories of four of them.

JANNA LELCHUK was born and raised on the isolated Kamchatka Peninsula, long closed to Westerners because of military sensitivity. As a local English teacher, she helped coordinate the first Alaska delegation to her hometown of Petropavlovsk-Kamchatsky in 1991 and reciprocated with her first visit to Juneau six months later. Lelchuk was invited back to help Juneau high-school students learn Russian. During her first day in class, the principal was so impressed by Lelchuk's enthusiasm and skills that he asked her to start a Russian-language program in Juneau public schools.

Twenty-five years later, hundreds of American students speak Russian and appreciate Russian culture because of Lelchuk's influence. Her textbook, *I Want to Speak Russian*, is used nationally. Six of her Juneau students took first place at the state's Russian Olympiad and were rewarded with a trip to Moscow. Another served as a Russian interpreter at the Sochi Olympic Games. Lelchuk has expanded her influence into adapting computer technology for more engaged learning by her students, earning her a 2016 technology teacher of the year award.

Lelchuk's three sons are successful products of Juneau public schools. She volunteers with Russian visitors to Alaska and helps new arrivals adjust to American culture. "I love living in our community where people know each other and are always ready to help," Lelchuk said.

LARRY KHLINOVSKI ROCKHILL is among the few Alaskans who fell in love with Russia and stayed. As a ten-year-old child of the Cold War, Rockhill was so mesmerized by the mysterious Soviet Union that he tuned in to Radio Moscow on his Zenith short-wave radio. As an educator with an interest in anthropology, Rockhill migrated to Alaska in 1970 to work with Native students at Mt. Edgecumbe High School in Alaska's old territorial capital. There he developed a passion for Alaska's shared heritage with Russia.

Teaching on the Kenai Peninsula in the late 1980s, Rockhill designed an Alaska-Soviet studies program in which his students exchanged pen-pal letters with Magadan's School No. 1. After hearing of the first large Soviet delegation planning to visit Anchorage in 1989, Rockhill invited some Russian teachers to join the group. He made his first reciprocal education-exchange visit to Magadan later that year. He took a two-year leave from his Alaska school district to become the first recent American to live and teach in Magadan through a partnership between University of Alaska Fairbanks and North Eastern State University.

During those early years in Magadan, Rockhill was introduced to a local genetics researcher, Lena Khlinovskaya. They recently celebrated twenty-five years of marriage and divide their time among Magadan, Moscow, and England, where they are both associates at Cambridge University. The two have organized international photo exhibitions, and Rockhill is finishing a memoir about his life in Russia.

"I am a totally different person because of my experiences in Magadan," Rockhill said via Skype from outside Moscow. "Some of my very best friends are Russian. I used to get a kick out of saying to Alaskans that some of my best friends are commies. The melting of the Ice Curtain began [by] believing we could make a difference in each other's lives, and I think we did."

ELENA KOSTONKO-FARKAS grew up in Magadan, where her first interaction with Alaskans was a 1988 teacher exchange with educators from the Kenai

Peninsula. Three years later, Farkas accompanied a group of her students to Alaska to assist with their musical performances. She married an Alaskan in 1992 and moved to the state, where she had a daughter and showcased Russian culture through the Russian from A to Z book and gift store in Anchorage she operated for a decade.

As Alaska interest in Russia grew, Russian was a popular foreign-language option in Anchorage high schools. With a federal grant, Farkas helped expand the Russian offerings to three junior high schools. In 2003, she helped develop the first Russian-language immersion program in the country for nonnative speakers.

In 2016, Farkas's first group of sixteen students who began learning Russian twelve years earlier graduated from high school. The ceremony was attended by Patricia Eckert, a retired State of Alaska international-trade specialist, who adopted two Russian children. There wasn't a dry eye while each graduate delivered a heartfelt speech in Russian about the close connections they had developed through their immersion experience, Eckert said.

Susan Kalina, a former professor of Russian at University of Alaska Anchorage, called Farkas "an impresario" for her ability to inspire her students, their parents, and Alaska's Russian community through language and the celebration of Russian culture, including cooking, dance, and music. Farkas is the first person Kalina always introduces to new Russian arrivals eager to learn their way around Alaska.

FATHER MICHAEL SHIELDS volunteered to accompany his boss, Archbishop Francis Hurley, to Magadan in 1989 after others from the Archdiocese of Anchorage declined the trip. Despite broad local interest in the Gospel—"Christianity was the newest show in town," said the Alaska-born priest—Shields decided service in the former gulag city wasn't for him. Then two years later he undertook a forty-day spiritual retreat seeking an answer to the query "what God wants for my life."

"I heard from the very depths of my soul, where I heard my own call to the priesthood, which is the deepest part of myself: 'go pray in the camps,'" said the sixty-seven-year-old Shields during a brief respite in Anchorage's Lady of Guadalupe Parish. "I knew that meant Magadan, I knew that meant forever, and I knew I had to go."

As early as age seven, Shields had heard the call of the church. Hearing it again in 1994, he moved to Magadan full-time and was still there in 2016. The son of a federal aviation official, Shields spent his childhood in Alaska, in the then-rough Anchorage neighborhood of Spenard and in Talkeetna, gateway to international climbers scaling North America's tallest peak. Shields himself summited Mt. McKinley (later renamed Denali) just before his first visit to the Soviet Union.

Shields's initial Russian ministry focused on survivors of the scores of prison camps built on the barren tundra within a few hundred miles of Magadan starting in the 1930s. After he issued an invitation on the local radio, more than eighty camp survivors showed up weekly at the public library. "Little by little they trusted me, and little by little I found out their stories," said Shields, a frequent smile breaking out from above his graying goatee.

This sharing of memories resulted in two books published for their families, including *Martyrs of Magadan*, which was translated into English. Shields didn't speak a word of Russian until landing in Magadan but now he preaches and counsels parishioners in their native language.

Most of the camp survivors, he said, "have gone to heaven." So Shields began to work with parentless children or those left home while their parents work or suffer from alcoholism, the elderly, and pregnant young women struggling with the decision of motherhood or abortion. The Church estimates that the average Russian woman has five abortions in her life and that for every ten births in Russia, there are thirteen abortions. As national policy seeks to increase the Russian population, the number of abortions is declining.

After the post-Soviet population exodus in the Russian Far East, Shields said life in Magadan is "more settled," although the economy remains in decline. Turnover is steady in his ministry because many of his parishioners spend their working lives in Magadan and then retire to warmer, less challenging Russian cities in the west, taking their extended families with them. After a brief spiritual renewal in Alaska, Shields headed back to Russia, where he intends to be buried on the outskirts of Magadan at his small Church of the Nativity of Jesus.

The special affinity between Alaskans and residents of the Far East remains, Shields said. But it is challenged by new "realities" between the United States and Russia that some forecast as a return to the Cold War.

"It's a painful political time," the Father said. "There's going to be this freezing of relationships, but hopefully there will be finding compromise and looking at how we can live together in this global community. The radical proclamation that we're losing contact with each other, that's just not true."

ON MY LAST day in the Russian Far East in the summer of 2016, I was up early, nervous about the flying weather. After two fascinating yet frustrating weeks along Russia's remote Bering Sea coast, I was ready for American normalcy. Russia always has this effect: it is irritatingly unpredictable while there, but I'm always eager to return. The low clouds hanging over Provideniya had us anxious about missed connections and messed-up lives back home.

With nothing to do but wait, I headed out into Provideniya's dusty streets for a few last-minute photos. On the crumbling concrete steps of the community hall that twenty-eight years earlier had been ground zero for melting the Ice Curtain, I remembered the elation among the Alaskan and Siberian Yupiit who had reconnected after four decades. I remembered the enthusiasm of the business leaders who envisioned new markets for Alaska services and new Russian resources ripe for development. I remembered my own relief that everyday Soviets were not the red menace of my childhood but instead pretty much like us.

As I stood there feeling glum over the passing of an era of such high expectations, a local Russian rushed up, interrupting my thoughts. Recognizing me as a foreigner, he asked in broken English where I was from. When I told him Alaska, he pointed at the eastern horizon and with a wide grin gave me a hearty thumbs-up.

Epilogue

It's hard to find anyone—Russian or American—whose life was not permanently and positively affected by their involvement in melting the Ice Curtain. For virtually everyone contacted for this book—who visited Alaska or Russia, who hosted an Alaskan or Russian in their home, or who in any way interacted with an Alaskan or Russian counterpart—the experience remains among the highlights of their lives.

Despite today's logistical and political challenges, many continue their relationships across the Bering Strait through social media, personal and professional contacts, and even occasional visits. The 150th commemoration in 2017 of Russia's sale of Alaska to the United States is already stimulating a renewed interest in Alaska-Russia relations.

Thousands of Alaskans and Russians helped melt the Ice Curtain. Here, in the order in which they appear in this book, is a brief accounting of some of the key players and events in this era:

Honest John—More than seven thousand of the Honest John rockets of the type my father learned to arm with nuclear warheads in New Mexico were produced during the Cold War. The last Honest John was discarded by the National Guard in 1982.

Steve Cowper—In 1989, Alaska's sixth governor announced he would not seek a second term in the same news cycle as the *Exxon Valdez* running aground in Alaska's Prince William Sound. Cowper has returned to Russia several times as a director of the Northern Forum, with the Northeast Asia Economic Forum, and to work on fisheries issues. He lives in Austin, Texas.

Eduard De Stoeckl—The Russian diplomat who negotiated the sale of Alaska to the United States received $25,000 for his work and an annual pension of $6,000 (about $300,000 in today's dollars) from Czar Alexander II. He resigned two years after signing the 1867 treaty and died in Paris in 1892.

William H. Seward—After Lincoln's assassination, he remained secretary of state under President Andrew Johnson and traveled the world, including to Alaska in 1869. He died at his New York home in 1872.

Charles Maultsby—The US Air Force captain whose U-2 spy plane flew into Soviet airspace in 1962 was later banned from flying near the North Pole or Chukotka Peninsula. He died of prostate cancer in 1998.

Russian airplane intercepts—Between 1961 and 1991, 306 Soviet aircraft flights were intercepted along Alaska's coastline with the Soviet Far East. Today, those intercepts continue at an average of about five a year.

Leo Rasmussen—After a half century as a Nome merchant, volunteer fireman, and mayor, Rasmussen retired to Fairbanks.

Jim Stimpfle—The early advocate for a revival in Alaska-Russia relations still sells real estate in Nome, advocates for the legalization of cannabis, and tries to keep up with his granddaughter.

Dr. Ted Mala—The retired physician, Native public-health advocate, and early Alaska-Soviet Union pioneer has a new family that divides its time between Hawaii and Alaska.

Dixie Belcher—After celebrating her seventy-sixth birthday in 2016, Belcher embarked on an around-the-world trip. Her public-policy focus has shifted from Russia to environmental protection in the South Pacific.

Gennadi Gerasimov—After working as Gorbachev's spokesman, Gerasimov served as Russian ambassador to Portugal for five years. He died in 2010.

Lynne Cox—Living in California, Cox has written six books about the power of swimming and travels as an inspirational speaker.

Gunnar Knapp—Retired in 2016 as director of the University of Alaska's Institute for Social and Economic Research, he is working on a book about Alaska fisheries.

Mead Treadwell—Starting in 2010, he served a four-year term as Alaska's lieutenant governor, then lost in the Republican primary for the US Senate in 2014. He is an Anchorage businessman.

Frank Murkowski—The twenty-one-year US senator was elected Alaska's eighth governor in 2002, losing his reelection bid four years later. Murkowski and his wife, Nancy, are retired in Wrangell, Alaska.

Bruce Kennedy—The Alaska Airlines CEO stepped down in 1991 to pursue Christian humanitarianism. He was killed piloting his own single-engine airplane in 2007, at age sixty-eight.

Jim Rowe—The founder of Bering Air is largely retired in Michigan, although he remains involved with the company, which is run by his children.

Ginna Brelsford—The former Alaska international-trade specialist married her Bering Bridge Expedition teammate, Sasha Belyaev, in 1991 and moved to Seattle, where they have two children. She works to provide educational opportunities for girls in Afghanistan.

Michael Cowper—After her divorce from Steve Cowper in 1991, Alaska's former first lady returned to practice law in Santa Barbara, California, where she died of cancer in 2015.

Gov. Walter Hickel—The former US interior secretary was elected Alaska's governor a second time in 1990. He died in 2010 at age ninety and reportedly was buried in Anchorage standing up facing east toward Washington, DC, with which he frequently battled.

Capt. Terry Smith—The longtime Alaska Airlines pilot who flew the 1988 Friendship Flight between Nome and Provideniya retired in 2007. In August 2010, he was piloting a de Havilland Otter that crashed on a fishing trip near Dillingham, Alaska. Smith was killed, along with US Sen. Ted Stevens and Bill Phillips, a longtime Stevens aide who had explored fisheries business opportunities in the Soviet Far East in 1989.

Alaska Airlines Friendship No. 1—The Boeing 737 jet that made the historic flight in 1988 and delivered members of the Bering Bridge Expedition to Anadyr the following year is on display at Anchorage's Alaska Aviation Heritage Museum. It bears the name of its captain, Terry Smith.

Darlene Orr—The Yupik and Russian speaker originally from St. Lawrence Island lives in Sitka, Alaska, and continues to study Alaska-Russian Native connections.

Michael Krauss—The retired University of Alaska Fairbanks Native language linguist lives in Fairbanks.

Friendship Flight gifts—The exquisite walrus ivory carving and two sealskin Eskimo figures presented to Governor Cowper in Provideniya in June 1988 seem to have disappeared. The US Fish and Wildlife Service seized them when the flight returned to Nome. Cowper requested that they be displayed at the University of Alaska Museum of the North in Fairbanks. Neither the museum nor the federal agency can locate them.

Vic Fischer—The preeminent pioneer in Alaska-Russia relations celebrated his ninety-second birthday in 2016 and lives in Anchorage with his wife, Jane Angvik.

Garrey Peska—The former chief of staff to Governor Cowper is retired with his wife, Karen, in Juneau.

Vaycheslav Kobets—The former Magadan governor is retired in the Crimea, making summer visits to Magadan. He remembers the Friendship Flight as "an incredible event for the Magadan region and the country as a whole."

John Handeland—The former mayor of Nome is a manager at Nome's Joint Utility System and the son-in-law of another Nome mayor, Leo Rasmussen.

Stas Namin—The Moscow rock-and-roll musician, born Anastas Alekseevich Mikoyan, continues to push boundaries, producing music and cultural festivals in Russia and elsewhere. He once proposed taking Lenin's Tomb on tour, with the proceeds going to those harmed by the father of the Soviet Union.

Paul Schurke—The American co-leader of the Bering Bridge Expedition continues to lead wilderness trips from his home in Ely, Minnesota.

Dmitry Shparo—The Russian Bering Bridge Expedition co-leader was awarded the Order of Lenin, the Soviet Union's highest honor, and continues to work to encourage youth to experience the outdoors.

Rex "Dusty" Finley—The former National Guard captain involved with the Little Diomede defections is the Force Management Division Director for US Army Alaska and pursues his interest in Alaska military history.

William Wortman—The ranking Alaska Army National Guard officer on scene during the Little Diomede defections is retired in Anchorage. For nearly twenty years he has coordinated the Dancing Bears annual dance camp.

Diomede defectors—Not long after leaving Alaska in 1989, the Soviet defectors disappeared from public view.

John Schaeffer—The first Native adjutant general of the Alaska National Guard died in August 2016, just days after the US Coast Guard aircraft hangar in his hometown of Kotzebue was named after him.

Dave Heatwole—The former oil-company executive and businessman is a part-time consulting geologist. He and his wife, Margaret, whom he met in Russia, travel the world searching for fine wine.

Mark Dudley—The former Alaska Airlines Magadan and Vladivostok station chief is the Seattle-based director of Interpacific Aviation and Marketing, Inc., which operates summer air service between Petropavlovsk-Kamchatsky and Yakutsk and Anchorage.

Charlie Neff—The first director of the University of Alaska Anchorage's American Russian Center is retired in Seattle, where he writes novels and plays trumpet in a local jazz band.

Russ Howell—The second director of the American Russian Center helped transition the center into a new UAA Office of International Support, which helped open a campus Chinese Confucius Institute and established an English as a Second Language center for Korean students. Federal funding for ARC's Russian programs ended in 2008, and the center closed the following year. Howell is retired in Eagle River, Alaska.

Cecile Mitchell—The former UAA admissions director who eased the transition to Alaska for hundreds of foreign students, including those from the Russian Far East, died in September 2015.

Tony Knowles—The former two-term governor of Alaska and two-term Anchorage mayor is retired in Anchorage and still shoots his Russian rifle.

Igor Farkhudtinov—The former Sakhalin governor was among nineteen people killed in a helicopter crash in August 2003 after leaving a meeting of regional governors on the Kamchatka Peninsula. He was fifty-three.

Roman Abramovich—The former Chukotka governor left office in 2008 and lives primarily in London, where he owns the Chelsea soccer team. *Forbes* magazine named him the world's fifteenth-most wealthy billionaire, worth $23.5 billion.

Doug Drum—The owner of Indian Valley Meats continues to work in his reindeer- and meat-processing plant south of Anchorage.

Andrew Crow—The longtime Russian interpreter who helped launch UAA's assistance efforts in the Russian Far East works in cooperative business development at the university and maintains friendships in the Russian Far East.

JoAnn Grady—The early advocate of relations between Juneau and Vladivostok and Petropavlovsk-Kamchatsky operates an environmental mediation firm between Juneau and Ashland, Oregon, and still maintains ties with the Lovett Women's Center in Magadan.

John Tichotsky—The economist and longtime Russian interpreter was appointed an economic advisor to Alaska Gov. Bill Walker in 2016.

Mark Begich—The former Anchorage mayor formed the Northern Compass Group consulting firm after he was defeated in his bid for reelection to the US Senate in 2014. He divides his time between Anchorage and Washington, DC.

Vladimir Kara-Murza—The prominent member of Russia's political opposition and close colleague of the late Boris Nemtsov was the subject of an apparent poisoning attempt in 2015. He survived, continues his work for the Open Russia movement, and lives in Moscow and Washington, DC.

Appendix

Friendship Flight Passenger Manifest

This is the official list of passengers on the June 13, 1988, Friendship Flight between Nome, Alaska, and Provideniya, USSR, as compiled by Alaska Airlines.

State of Alaska

Governor Steve Cowper

Michael Cowper—first lady

Walter Hickel—former governor

David Ramseur—Cowper press secretary

Ginna Brelsford—international-trade specialist

Willie Hensley—state senator

Al Adams—state representative

Gunnar Knapp—University of Alaska professor

Robert Wagstaff—Alaska Bar Association

Congressional Delegation

US Sen. Frank Murkowski

Nancy Murkowski

Mr. and Mrs. William Bittner (representing US Sen. Ted Stevens)

Leo Rasmussen—former Nome mayor (representing US Rep. Don Young)

John Handeland—Nome mayor

Jessica Gavora—Sen. Frank Murkowski administration assistant

State Department
Bob Clarke

Nome List
Jim Stimpfle—chairman, Nome chamber Committee for Cooperation, Commerce
    and Peace

Bernadette Alvanna-Stimpfle—Nome bilingual teacher

Ian Stimpfle—then two years old

Neil Colby—Nome City Council and Alaska State Chamber of Commerce

Dr. Michael Krauss—former director, UAF Alaska Native Language Center

Dan Johnson—Northwest College media director

Edna Apatiki—Siberian Yupik bilingual teacher, Gambell

Willis Walunga—performer, Gambell

Nancy Walunga—performer, Gambell

Louis Iyakitan—Gambell

Vivian Iyakitan—Gambell

Anders Appassingook—performer and bilingual teacher, Gambell

Luceen Appassingook—Gambell

Darlene Orr—Yupik, English, and Russian speaker, originally from East Cape

Tim Gologergen, Sr.—performer, Savoonga and Nome

Anna Gologergen—dancer, Savoonga and Nome

John Waghiyi, Sr.—Savoonga and Nome

Nick Wongittillin—dancer, Savoonga

Lucille Wongittillin—dancer, Savoonga

Ora Gologergen—dancer, Savoonga

Pat Omiak, Sr.—performer, Little Diomede

Leah Weyapuk—grandparent from Siberia

Mike Saclamana—King Island performer

Francis Alvanna—performer, King Island and Nome

Gabriel Myktoyuk—performer, King Island

John Kiminok—performer, King Island

Earl Mayac—performer, King Island

Chet Waluklewicz—carrying postage cancellations to commemorate flight

Franklin Kaningok, Sr.—Siviquag, Inc. president, Gambell

Caleb Pungowiyi—Kawerak, Inc. director, Savoonga and Nome

Jane Antoghame—Gambell

Alaska Airlines
Bruce Kennedy—chairman and CEO
Jim Johnson, Sr.—vice president, public affairs
Ray Vecci—chief operating officer
William MacKay—regional vice president

Alaska Airlines Guests
Robert Giersdorf—president, Exploration Cruise Lines
Elisa Miller—University of Washington professor
Mead Treadwell
John Van Zyle—artist
Frank Ashida—vice president, Holland America-Westours
Bill Garrett—chief executive, *National Geographic*

Alaska State Chamber of Commerce
George Krusz—president

Alaska Performing Artists for Peace
Dixie Belcher

Alascom
George Shaginaw—president and CEO

Media
Terry Drinkwater—CBS News
Robert Dunn—CBS News
Todd Pottinger—KTUU- TV
Peter Cyril—KTUU-TV
Laura Spaan—KIMO-TV
Kimberly Cason—KTVA-TV
Clare Richardson—KNOM Nome radio
Jeff Berliner—UPI
Arthur Schmitt—UPI

David Foster—AP
Rob Stapleton—AP
Hal Bernton —*Anchorage Daily News*
Dan Saddler—*Anchorage Times*
Holly Reimer—*Tundra Times*
Sandra Medearis—*Nome Nugget*
David Postman—*Time* magazine
Carrie Dolan—*Wall Street Journal*
Jerry Reeves—ABA
Jay Matthews—*Washington Post*
Steve Raymer—*National Geographic*

Waiting List
Mildred Irrigoo
Clarence Irrigoo
Grace Cross
Lena McAlpine
Howard Slwooko

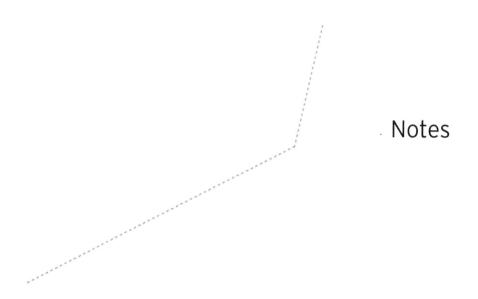

Notes

Epigraph

vi   *Build in Kamchatka*: Glynn Barratt, *Russia in Pacific Waters, 1715–1825* (Vancouver: University of British Columbia Press, 1981), 14.

Preface

xi   *"We meet here"*: John F. Kennedy remarks to New Mexico State Democratic Convention, John F. Kennedy Presidential Library and Museum, June 4, 1960.

xiii   *"Even though one"*: Author interview with Steve Cowper, June 9, 2015.

xv   *Putin himself laughed:* Shadee Ashtan, "Vladimir Putin Says Alaska Is Too Cold to Annex," *Huffington Post*, April 17, 2014.

Prologue

1   *Outfitted in thick fur:* Dan O'Neill, *The Last Giant of Beringia: The Mystery of the Bering Land Bridge* (Boulder, CO: Westview Press, 2004), 11–14.

1   *Across that new land bridge:* David M. Hopkins, editor, *The Bering Land Bridge* (Stanford: Stanford University Press, 1967), 1–5.

1   *That was the setting:* Stephen Haycox, *Alaska: An American Colony* (Seattle: University of Washington Press, 2002), 53. See also Lydia T. Black, *Russians in Alaska 1732–1867* (Fairbanks: University of Alaska Press, 2004), for details about early Russian exploration of North America.

3   *The surviving crew:* Haycox, *Alaska: An American Colony*, 51–52.

3   *A German doctor*: Owen Matthews, *Glorious Misadventures: Nikolai Rezanov and the Dream of a Russian America* (London: Bloomsbury Publishing, 2014), 214.

4   *Baranov used the time*: Ibid., 227.

4   *The company later launched*: James R. Gibson, *Imperial Russia in Frontier America: The Changing Geography of Supply of Russian America, 1784–1867* (New York: Oxford University Press, 1976), 25.

5   *Even more troubling to Russia*: Haycox, *Alaska: An American Colony*, 136.

5   *The British, their hands*: Matthews, *Glorious Misadventures*, 311.

6   *The United States would buy*: Haycox, *Alaska: An American Colony*, 153.

6   *The editor of the New York Herald*: Claus-M. Naske and Herman E. Slotnick, *Alaska—A History of the 49th State* (Grand Rapids, MI: Wm. B. Eerdmans Publishing Co., 1979), 57.

7   *"The last moments"*: Matthews, *Glorious Misadventures*, 312. See also Haycox and Black for accounts of the transfer ceremony.

7   *Upon the election*: Mike Dunham, "He bought Alaska, but that's just one reason Seward was among the most important men in history," *Alaska Dispatch News*, October 8, 2015.

7   *A provision in the purchase*: Naske, *Alaska—A History of the 49th State*, 58.

7   *Although Army Gen. Jefferson C. Davis*: Truman R. Strobridge and Dennis L. Noble, *Alaska and the U.S. Revenue Cutter Service 1867–1915* (Annapolis: Naval Institute Press, 1999), 12.

8   *Sitka's population topped out*: Haycox, *Alaska: An American Colony*, 176.

8   *Within a decade*: Black, *Russians in Alaska*, 287.

8   *Retired University of Alaska*: Michael Krauss, "Crossroads? A Twentieth-Century History of Contacts across the Bering Strait," *Anthropology of the North Pacific Rim* (Washington, DC: Smithsonian Institution Press, 1994), 366.

8   *Measles, influenza, gonorrhea*: John R. Bockstoce, *Furs and Frontiers in the Far North: The Contest among Native and Foreign Nations for the Bering Strait Fur Trade* (New Haven: Yale University Press, 2009), 319.

9   *In 1938, the Soviet*: Visits to Siberia by American Eskimos, exchange of notes at Washington, DC, February 7, March 26, and April 18, 1938, files of the US Department of State.

Chapter 1

11   *"I believe that"*: US General Billy Mitchell, Alaska Public Lands Information Center, National Park Service website.

12   *As the nation*: A dramatic account of the Maultsby incident comes from Michael Dobbs, *One Minute to Midnight: Kennedy, Khruschchev and Castro on the Brink of Nuclear War* (New York: Alfred A. Knopf, 2008). Other sources include a manuscript edited by Maultsby's wife, Jeanne, in Brig. Gen. (Ret.) Gerald E. McIlmoyle and Linda Rios Bromley, *Remembering the Dragon Lady: Memoirs of the Men Who Experienced the Legend of the U-2 Spy Plane* (West Midlands, England: Helion & Company Ltd., 2011). Another source on the incident is State of Alaska historian Mark Rice in "Alaska's Cuban Missile Crisis," an unpublished narrative.

15   *In 1940, Anthony Dimond*: Associated Press, "Russians Colonize Isle Just Off Alaskan Coast," *New York Times*, June 15, 1940.

15   *The settlers were reported*: Hallett Abend, "Threat to Alaska Seen in Red Force," *New York Times*, August 11, 1940.

15   *Alaska Natives also reported*: Associated Press, "Bering Sea Air Base of Soviet Confirmed," *New York Times*, July 24, 1940.

15   *"Simultaneously a string"*: *New York Times*, August 11, 1940.

16   *Soviet leader Joseph Stalin*: Alexander Dolitsky, "The Alaska-Siberia Lend-Lease Program during World War II," *Aspects of Arctic and Sub-Arctic History: Proceedings of the International Congress on the History of the Arctic and Sub-Arctic Region*, Reykjavik, June 18–21, 1988, 462.

16   *The Soviet airmen were*: Ibid., 468.

17   *A generation after*: Ibid., 473.

17   *A few months after*: Winthrop Griffith, "Detente on the rocks," *New York Times*, August 17, 1975.

17   *On March 22, 1948*: Krauss, "Crossroads? A Twentieth-Century History of Contacts across the Bering Strait," 369.

18   *Alaska's geographic location*: Laurel J. Hummel, "The U.S. Military as Geographical Agent: The Case of Cold War Alaska," *Geographical Review* 95, no. 1 (January 2005): 48–49.

18   *Compared to prewar expenditures*: Naske, *Alaska—A History of the 49th State*, 130.

18   *Dubbed by code names*: Associated Press, "Alaskan fishermen were trained to be spies during Cold War," September 1, 2014.

19   *Some Alaskans considered*: Norman Brown, editorial in the *Anchorage Daily News*, February 21, 1949, quoted in C. A. Salisbury, *Soldiers of the Mists: Minutemen of the Alaska Frontier* (Missoula, MT: Pictorial Histories Publishing Company, 1992), 84.

19   *Making what officials described*: TSgt. William J. Allen, *Hunting the Soviet Bear: A Study of Soviet Aircraft Intercepts near Alaska 1961–1991* (Elmendorf Air Force Base: 11th Air Force Office of History, 1992), 4.

Chapter 2

21   *"Never, perhaps, in the postwar decades"*: Mikhail Gorbachev, "The Soviet 'War Scare' of 1983," George Washington University National Security Archive, 1990.

21   *At four a.m.*: Author interviews with Leo Rasmussen, October 14, 2015, and June 28, 2016.

22   *As a Soviet helicopter*: "Whaling Protesters Say Chase Followed Incursion in Siberia," *New York Times*, July 20, 1983.

22   *"I'm thinking to myself"*: Author interview with Leo Rasmussen.

23   *After tracking the plane*: Thom Patterson, "The downing of Flight 007: Thirty years later, a Cold War tragedy still seems surreal," CNN, August 31, 2013.

23   *President Reagan called*: Ibid.

24   *For example, Willis Walunga's father*: Author interview with Willis Walunga, June 12, 2015.

24   *"The reality was"*: Author interviews with Jim Stimpfle, June 26, 2015, and June 27, 2016, and Stimpfle's oral interview with Project Jukebox, University of Alaska Fairbanks archives, March 7, 2007.

25   *One of the first:* Jeff Berliner, "Siberian port now open to U.S. ships," UPI, September 24, 1987.

26   *As the ship crossed*: Author interview with Sathy Naidu, October 29, 2015.

27   *A dashing Hollywood playboy*: Lael Morgan, *Eskimo Star: From the Tundra to Tinseltown: The Ray Mala Story* (Kenmore, WA: Epicenter Press, 2011).

27   *Around 1980, Mala*: Author interview with Dr. Ted Mala, July 10, 2015. See also George Bryson, "Unlocking the Door to Siberia," *Anchorage Daily News, We Alaskans* magazine, May 31, 1987.

28   *Mala and then-UAA chancellor*: Martha Eliassen, "UAA officials, Soviet school agree on pact for exchange," *Anchorage Daily News*, January 22, 1983.

28   *For one of his early*: "Alaskans, Soviets Agree in Principle to Health Exchange," *Anchorage Daily News*, August 2, 1986.

28   *In 1989, Mala*: John Wolfe, "Institute director calls UAA leaders 'unethical'," *Anchorage Times*, August 30, 1989.

29   *They wintered over*: David Lewis and Mimi George, *Icebound in Antarctica* (New York: W.W. Norton & Company, 1988), 1.

29   *The two first visited*: Ann Chandonnet, "Across the Strait—Separated by 40 Long Years," *Anchorage Times*, September 6, 1990, and author interview with Mimi George, January 25, 2016.

Chapter 3

31   *"Our land and people"*: Chuna McIntyre, "Siberia-Alaska Cultural Exchange" brochure, Cam'ai, 1986.

31   *Peace activist Dixie Belcher*: Author interviews with Dixie Belcher, July 13, 2015, and August 3, 2016.

32   *"Dixie, bless her"*: Jay Hammond, *Anchorage Daily News*, January 4, 1987.

33   *He welcomed Belcher*: *Moscow News*, Weekly No. 5, 1986.

33   *He coined the term*: *Los Angeles Times*, November 29, 1990.

34   *"When she asked me to go"*: Author interview with Bella Hammond, July 28, 2015.

34   *Belcher and other*: *Juneau Empire*, December 27, 1988.

35   *That September, the United States*: H. W. Brands, *Reagan—The Life* (New York: Doubleday, 2015), 564.

35   *The Juneau Empire*: *Juneau Empire*, September 3, 1986.

35   *"One of the terrifying"*: Video documentary about the Soviet concert trip produced by KYUK public television, Bethel, Alaska, 1986.

36   *"When the curtain"*: *Moscow News*, Weekly No. 46, 1986.

37   *In brief remarks*: Ibid.

37   *For gospel singer Shirley Staton*: Author interview with Shirley Staton, July 23, 2015.

37   *After the obligatory toasts*: "Cowper Urges Soviet Consular Office in Alaska," press release, Office of the Governor, April 23, 1988.

38   *Gingerly making his way*: Claire Richardson, "Villagers give visitor warm welcome," *Anchorage Daily News*, April 26, 1988.

38   *A Hollywood B-movie*: *New York Times*, May 30, 1988.

39   *"Taking into account"*: Moscow Summit, *Department of State Bulletin*, August 1988.

Chapter 4

41   *"You have embodied"*: President Ronald Reagan, September 11, 1987, Lynne Cox press kit, 1988.

41   *"He was the one"*: Author interview with Lynne Cox, August 3, 2015.

42   *In her dramatic autobiography*: Lynne Cox, *Swimming to Antarctica: Tales of a Long-Distance Swimmer* (Orlando: A Harvest Book, Harcourt, Inc., 2004).

42   *"There's something poetic"*: Author interview with Cox.

43   *"When the secretary"*: Author interview with Ed Salazar, August 17, 2015.

43   *Dave Karp, manager*: Author interview with Dave Karp, August 20, 2015.

44   *A major concern*: Cox, *Swimming to Antarctica*, 146–159.

45   *Just days before*: Ibid., 269.

46   *KNOM radio reporter*: Author interview with Claire Richardson, July 31, 2016.

46   *Too numb to climb*: Author interview with Cox.

47   *At the White House*: Cox, *Swimming to Antarctica,* 305.

Chapter 5

49   *"Now, with a suddenness"*: Jay Mathews, "From Nome, Trying to Open the Back Door to the Soviet Union," *Washington Post,* December 7, 1987.

49   *Between 1985 and June 1987*: Oliver Scott Goldsmith, "Alaska's Economy: What's Ahead," report by the University of Alaska Anchorage Institute of Social and Economic Research, Vol. XXIV, No. 2, December 1987.

50   *To balance the State's books*: "The Cowper Administration: Transition into the 1990s," Office of the Governor, November 1990.

50   *George Krusz, who*: Author interview with George Krusz, July 10, 2015.

50   *Another participant was*: Author interview with Mead Treadwell, July 24, 2015.

51   *The fourteen-page document*: Siberian Gateway Project summary, author unknown, fall 1987.

51   *But in Washington*: A chronology of letters and press releases by Senator Murkowski are listed in a handout he distributed on the Friendship Flight, "The Nome-Provideniya Friendship Flight: A Real Alaska Success Story," 1988. These were supplemented by an author interview with Murkowski, June 23, 2015.

52   *It met a lukewarm*: Robert J. Serling, *Character & Characters: The Spirit of Alaska Airlines* (Seattle: Documentary Media, LLC, 2008), 290.

52   *A couple of weeks*: Ken Wells, "Gateway to Siberia? Nome, Alaska Feels It Has a Certain Ring." *Wall Street Journal,* September 25, 1987.

53   *The airline also contacted*: Author interview with Bill McKay, January 30, 2015.

53   *The green-light call*: Author interviews with Bob Poe, June 24, 2015, Ginna Brelsford, May 21, 2015, and Jim Stimpfle, March 11 and June 26, 2015.

54   *"We were in Nome"*: Author interview with Jim Rowe, August 16, 2015.

54   *When a state legislator*: Author interview with Bob Poe, June 24, 2015.

55   *"Did Sen. Frank Murkowski"*: *Anchorage Daily News,* June 12, 1988.

56   *Cowper invited former Governor*: Walter J. Hickel, *Who Owns America?* (Englewood, NJ: Prentice-Hall, 1971), 209.

57   *A few months earlier*: *Alascom Spectrum* magazine 9, no. 3 (August 1988).

57   *The King Air flight*: Author interview with Lee Wareham, February 11, 2015.

58   *After becoming separated*: Salisbury, *Soldiers of the Mists,* 124.

Chapter 6

61   *"Now glasnost has come"*: Wilbur E. Garrett, "Air Bridge to Siberia," *National Geographic*, October 1988.

62   *"I have drawings"*: Author interviews with Darlene Orr, May 18, 2015, and May 12, 2016.

63   *Alaska Native Ora Gologergen*: Garrett, *National Geographic*, October 1988, 504–9.

64   *Gambell's Willis Walunga*: Author interview with Willis Walunga, June 12, 2015.

64   *King Island hunter*: Author interview with Francis Alvanna, June 12, 2015.

64   *Wall Street Journal reporter*: Carrie Dolan, "In the Age of Glasnost, Being Sent to Siberia Can Be a Real Trip, First-Wave Visitors to Provideniya Find," *Wall Street Journal*, June 15, 1988.

64   *"Only Senator Frank Murkowski"*: David Postman, "Yes, Even Cynics Warm to the Trip," *Anchorage Daily News*, June 14, 1988.

65   *"Mother? I'm in Provideniya"*: Walter Hickel in *The Alaska-Siberia Connection*, video written and produced by Connections, Ltd. of Anchorage, for Alascom, Inc., 1988.

65   *"Naturally she spoke"*: Author interview with Professor Michael Krauss, June 29, 2015.

65   *After descending the stairs*: Author interviews with Orr.

Chapter 7

69   *"Business, cultural and educational"*: Alaska Governor Steve Cowper, letter to President George H. W. Bush, November 27, 1989.

70   *As a Yale undergrad*: Author interview with Gunnar Knapp, July 20, 2015.

70   *Before most Alaskans*: Gunnar Knapp, *Alaska and the Soviet North: A Brief Comparison of Population Data,* Institute of Social and Economic Research Working Paper 87.4, University of Alaska Anchorage, November 1987.

70   *At the governor's request*: Gunnar Knapp and Elisa Miller, *Alaska-Soviet Far East Trade: Opportunities and Strategies,* Alaska Office of International Trade, April 1988.

70   *"I was the almost-sightless"*: Author interview with Knapp.

71   *Born in Berlin*: Victor Fischer (with Charles Wohlforth), *To Russia with Love: An Alaskan's Journey* (Fairbanks: University of Alaska Press, 2012), and author interviews with Fischer, January 19, 2015, March 6, 2015, June 22, 2015, and May 28, 2016.

72   *A month after*: Ginna Brelsford, "Soviet Far East Trip Report," produced for governor's Office of International Trade, July 26, 1988.

73   *Peska was dubious*: Author interview with Garrey Peska, November 15, 2015.

74   *The trip produced*: Ginna Brelsford, "Alaska Trade and Friendship Mission to the Soviet Far East," produced for governor's Office of International Trade, October 29, 1988.

74   *"The special significance"*: Ibid, 5.

Chapter 8

78   *John Handeland, then Nome's mayor*: Author interview with John Handeland, October 11, 2015.

78   *Charles "Chick" Trainer*: Author interview with Charles Trainer, November 9, 2015.

78   *Mayor Kulinkin took on*: Associated Press, "Soviet visit to Nome ends 40-year break," *Northland News*, October 1988.

80   *Within hours of their arrival*: Hal Bernton, "Soviet traders hit a snag at customs," *Anchorage Daily News*, February 22, 1989.

80   *Dixie Belcher envisioned*: Glasnost Folkfest program, February 24, 1989, and author interviews.

81   *"At age forty-seven"*: Andrew Perala, "The Heat Exchange: Soviet Union's Hottest Rocker Looks to West for Guidance," *Anchorage Daily News*, February 20, 1989.

82   *"It was a love fest"*: Catherine Stadem, "Folkfest: Building bridges through song," *Anchorage Times*, February 26, 1989.

82   *She had counted on*: "The Price of Glasnost," *Anchorage Daily News*, April 3, 1989.

83   *One was Perry Eaton*: Author interview with Perry Eaton, July 28, 2016.

83   *Another was Mead Treadwell*: Email exchange between the author and Treadwell, August 25, 2016.

Chapter 9

85   *Soviet icebreakers sail*: Bruce Bartley, "Soviet icebreakers sail toward whales," *Anchorage Times*, October 24, 1988.

85   *Arctic Alaska was experiencing*: Richard Mauer, "The Real Story Behind 'Big Miracle,'" *Anchorage Daily News*, February 3, 2012.

87   *Two Soviet ships*: UPI reporter Jeff Berliner, "Soviets Begin Ice Assault to Rescue Gray Whales," *Parkersburg (West Virginia) News*, October 26, 1988.

88   *"To the cheers"*: UPI, "Whales head for freedom behind ship," *Ashland (Oregon) Times-Gazette*, October 27, 1988.

88   *"I was impressed"*: Ibid.

88   *The human persistence*: Statement by President Reagan, ibid.

Chapter 10

89   *"The purpose: to forget"*: Author interview with Dmitry Shparo, Soviet co-leader of the Bering Bridge Expedition, via email exchange, April 5, 2016.

Much of the material for this chapter comes from the author's personal recollections and files from the Bering Bridge Expedition as a member of Governor Cowper's staff. Other key sources are expedition co-leader Paul Schurke's compelling book about the adventure, *Bering Bridge: The Soviet-American Expedition from Siberia to Alaska* (Duluth, MN: Pfeifer-Hamilton, 1989); media materials produced by the expedition; and several author interviews with Schurke, September 2, 2015, and January 19, 2016. The author also interviewed other expedition members, including Ginna Brelsford, May 21, 2015, and Alexander Belyaev, May 21, 2015, and received written responses to questions posed to Soviet expedition co-leader Dmitry Shparo, May 4, 2016.

The defection of the two Soviet journalists is dramatically detailed by reporter Doug O'Harra, "Flight to Freedom," *Anchorage Daily News, We Alaskans* magazine, June 4, 1989. The Alaska Army National Guard prepared an after-action memorandum on the defection provided to me by its author: Lt. Col. William D. Wortman, Memorandum for Adjutant General of the Alaska National Guard, "After Action Report on Events on Little Diomede Island, 22 through 26 April 1989," May 3, 1989.

96   *"They show up"*: Bruce Melzer, "The Other Diomede," *Anchorage Daily News, We Alaskans* magazine, October 29, 1989.

97   *"Alaska is on"*: Gov. Steve Cowper, in press release from Office of the Governor, April 13, 1989.

Chapter 11

99   *"Jesus, I mean"*: Randle McMurphy, *One Flew Over the Cuckoo's Nest*, directed by Miloš Forman, 1975.

99   *Capt. Dusty Finley*: Author interview with Rex Finley, December 16, 2015.

99   *Finley's superior was*: Author interview with William Wortman, January 8, 2016.

100 *Anatoly Tkachenko's mother*: Much of the account of the defectors' early lives comes from O'Harra's article, "Flight to Freedom."

104 *"We didn't know"*: Interview with Finley.

106 *The INS soon issued*: Press release, US Immigration and Naturalization Service, April 24, 1989.

106 *"Soviets defect at border rite"*: *Times* staff and Associated Press, *Anchorage Times*, April 25, 1989.

106   *Dr. Ted Mala*: "Mala mourns action," *Nome Nugget*, April 27, 1989.

106   *General Schaeffer, the state's*: Hal Bernton, "Soviet defect—Men leave Diomede celebration," *Anchorage Daily News*, April 25, 1989.

106   *Nome Nugget reporter*: Sandra Medearis, "Two Soviets defect at Little Diomede," *Nome Nugget*, April 27, 1989.

106   *Soviet expedition member*: Author interview with Sasha Belyaev, May 22, 2015.

107   *"Crossing more than"*: President George H. W. Bush, Telegram from the White House, in Schurke, *Bering Bridge*, 207.

108   *Two months later*: Anatoly Tkachenko, "On the First Frontier," *Anchorage Daily News*, June 4, 1989.

108   *The US Army Russian interpreter*: Author interview with William Wortman.

109   *En route to California*: "Gorbachevs Visit Minnesota, Dazzle American Heartland," *New York Times*, June 4, 1990.

109   *After a gift exchange*: Author interview with Paul Schurke, January 18, 2016.

Chapter 12

111   *"Glasnost and geography"*: Dean Fosdick, "Glasnost and Geography Make for New Soviet-Alaska Connections," Associated Press, August 29, 1989.

Much of the material for this chapter comes from the author's journal of the trade mission with Governor Cowper. Other sources are specifically noted.

112   *Provideniya was founded*: John Tichotsky, *An Overview of Provideniya District, U.S.S.R.*, Institute of Social and Economic Research, University of Alaska Anchorage, December 1989.

113   *"It's an attractive place"*: Provideniya Mayor Kulinkin, to UPI reporter Jeff Berliner in the *Chicago Sun-Times*, August 7, 1988.

114   *Left unsaid at the time*: Tichotsky, *An Overview of Provideniya District*, 14.

114   *A 1928 American Museum*: Harold McCracken, leader of an American Museum of Natural History expedition to the Diomede Islands, *New York Times*, December 16, 1928.

115   *"The Big Diomeders"*: Roger Menadelook, Secretary of the Little Diomede City Council, "Minutes of the meeting Nov. 30, 1940."

115   *Just two years*: *Nome Nugget*, January 22, 1987. The Alaska National Guard maintained a comprehensive file of sightings and activity in the Bering Strait near the Diomede Islands, summarized in a memorandum by Col. William Shaw to the Adjutant General, January 10, 1988.

116   *Rows of light*: *Anchorage Daily News*, Oct. 29, 1989.

118 *Chairman Kobets jammed*: Documents about the trade mission include a large binder, "Governor Cowper's Trade and Friendship Mission to the Soviet Far East, Aug. 30–Sept. 10, 1989," and the author's personal journal of the trip.

120 *"Although the Soviets"*: President Gerald R. Ford, *A Time to Heal* (New York: Harper and Row, 1979), from the Ford Presidential Library and Museum website.

121 *Brown called for*: Alaska State Rep. Kay Brown letter to Governor Cowper, August 5, 1989.

122 *To the one thousand*: Address of Alaska Governor Steve Cowper to U.S.-U.S.S.R. Trade and Economic Council, Moscow, May 22, 1990, author's personal files.

123 *Slight, with a bushy*: "Russia plants flag on North Pole seabed," Tom Parfitt, *The Guardian*, August 2, 2007.

Chapter 13

125 *"Many Native people"*: Statement of Intent, signed by Alaska Governor Steve Cowper and Magadan Chairman Vyacheslav Kobets via speaker phone between Little Diomede, Alaska, and Nome, Alaska, April 23 (in the US), 1989.

125 *The two proposed*: Protocol on the meeting between Steve Cowper, governor, State of Alaska, and Vyacheslaw I. Kobets, chairman, Magadan Region Executive Committee, April 23, 1989.

126 *"The Baker-Shevardnadze meeting"*: "Yes on Start, for Now," *New York Times*, September 27, 1989.

126 *Signed on September 23, 1989*: Bering Straits Regional Commission, Agreement between the United States of America and the Union of Soviet Socialist Republics, signed at Jackson Hole, Wyoming, September 23, 1989.

127 *In a 2000 memo*: Bering Straits Regional Commission, "Expanding Visa-Free Travel Across the Bering Strait for Natives of Alaska and Russia," Memorandum by Charles Johnson, Alaska chief commissioner, to Deputy Secretary of State Strobe Talbott, August 17, 2000.

127 *The Aleutian Pribilof Islands Association*: "United States & Russian Aleuts Visa-Free Travel Fact Sheet," Memorandum prepared for Deputy Secretary of State Talbott by the Aleutian Pribilof Islands Association, Inc., August 2000.

128 *Between 1993 and 2015*: U.S. Customs and Border Patrol statistics provided to the author under a Freedom of Information request by the author, April 26, 2016.

128 *Nearly a quarter of a century*: Agreement on Cooperation in the Field of Environmental Protection Between the United States of America and the Union of Soviet Socialist Republics, signed in Moscow by President Richard Nixon and N. V. Podgorny, chairman of the Presidium of the Supreme Soviet of the U.S.S.R, May 23, 1972.

129   *Three years later*: D. P. Galvin and I. G. Ivanov, *Beringian Heritage: A Reconnaissance Study of Sites and Recommendations*, US National Park Service and USSR Gasstroy, October 4, 1989.

129   *In the Alaska State House*: CS for House Joint Resolution No. 15 (RES), by the House Resources Committee, March 31, 1999, House Journal: 633–634.

129   *According to retired*: Author interview with Loretta Bullard, April 4, 2016.

130   *In part, it said*: Resolution 91-62, passed at the 1991 annual Convention of the Alaska Federation of Natives, Inc.

130   *"Everybody thought this"*: Author interview with Bob Gerhard, March 10, 2016.

131   *In 1993, the Chukotka*: Author interview with Russian Beringia Park administrator Vladimir Bychkov, June 30, 2016.

131   *Republican US Sen. Rand Paul*: Hannah Hess, "Rand Paul uncovers grant-funded 'X-Files' project," *E&E*, March 30, 2016.

Chapter 14

133   *"This year, 4,000 nonconformists"*: Alaska Airlines newspaper ad advertising service to the Russian Far East, 1990.

133   *"Lovely stewardesses"*: Alaska Airlines tourism brochure, circa 1970.

133   *Charles F. Willis, Jr.*: Bruce Lambert, obituary of Charles Willis, *New York Times*, March 21, 1993.

134   *In 1957, Willis*: Serling, *Character & Characters*, 50.

134   *To live up to*: Author interview with Jim Johnson, June 5, 2015.

134   *"It was 103 years"*: Stanton Patty, "Airline Begins Service to Siberia," *Seattle Times*, June 11, 1970.

135   *As would occur*: Serling, *Character & Characters*, 102.

135   *Pegge Begich recalled*: Author interview with Pegge Begich, August 1, 2015.

135   *Company public affairs*: Author interview with Jim Johnson, August 29, 2016.

136   *"The Russian trips"*: Archie Satterfield, *The Alaska Airlines Story* (Seattle: Alaska Northwest Publishing Company, 1981) 151.

136   *"With the collapse"*: Author interview with Tom Grady, July 7, 2015.

136   *In its January 1987*: Application of Alaska Airlines, Inc. for a Certificate of Public Convenience and Necessity, by counsel Marshall Sinick, filed before the US Department of Transportation, January 12, 1987.

137   *The company marketed*: Alaska Airlines print advertisement, *Anchorage Daily News*, December 1990.

137   *To safely guide*: Jeff Berliner, UPI, *Shipping Times*, August 7, 1991.

138   *But Mark Dudley*: Author interview with Mark Dudley, March 21, 2016.

139 *After many signed*: Daniel Saddler, *Anchorage Times*, April 4, 1990.

140 *In 1992 and 1993*: US Department of Transportation T100 Segment Data, US-Russia Scheduled Passenger Service for Alaska Airlines.

140 *Peculiar to that*: Alaska Airlines *Alaskaline* employee newsletter, June 18, 1993.

140 *The Alaska jet*: Author interview with Kit Cooper, July 27, 2015.

141 *Despite flying to*: Author interview with Jim Rowe, August 6, 2015.

142 *A decade later*: Ron Zellar, "Glasnost in flight? Soviet airline Aeroflot considering Anchorage connection," *Anchorage Times*, September 10, 1989.

142 *Dick Reeve's earliest*: Author interview with Dick Reeve, October 28, 2015.

143 *"It is a vast"*: Walter J. Hickel, "The Day of the Arctic Has Come," *Reader's Digest*, June 1973.

Chapter 15

145 *"If Boris Yeltsin"*: "Soviets reject Nome's ruble plan," *Anchorage Daily News*, October 25, 1991.

145 *Through his day job*: Author interview with Dave Heatwole, September 2, 2015.

147 *Heatwole was so bullish*: David Heatwole, "Love Story—Arizona Boy Meets Irish Girl in Magadan, Russia," unpublished personal account, December 1994.

147 *By January 1990*: Hal Bernton, "Computer Links Trade Center to the World," *Anchorage Daily News*, January 12, 1990.

147 *"Now it has decided"*: Alaska Ear, *Anchorage Daily News*, May 31, 1992.

147 *Anchorage engineer Kent Lee Woodman*: Hugh Curran, "COSAR envisions Alaska as a Seattle for Far East," *Anchorage Daily News*, December 2, 1992.

148 *Beginning with just eighty-one*: Author interview with Elisa Miller, May 21, 2015.

148 *The center partnered*: Author interview with Carol Vipperman, May 21, 2015.

148 *"I wouldn't have"*: Hal Bernton, "Groups Looking Abroad, Alaskans Search for New Markets," *Anchorage Daily News*, October 26, 1994.

149 *"We're all willing"*: Associated Press reporter Julia Rubin, "Nome entrepreneurs find rubles' only value is goodwill," *Anchorage Daily News*, October 15, 1990.

149 *To dispose of*: Hal Bernton, "Melting the Ice Curtain," *Alaska* magazine, September 1991.

149 *In summer 1991*: Sherri McBride, "Soviet shoppers swap in Nome," *Nome Nugget*, August 15, 1991.

150 *In winter 1987*: Melissa Chapin, "Encounters through a Melting Ice Curtain: The Sister Cities Experience of Yakutsk and Fairbanks Early Year 1987–1991," report

presented to the Alaska Historical Society, September 2009. Chapin was an early participant in Fairbanks-Yakutsk sister-city activities and was still involved in 2016.

150 *Sister-city pioneer*: Molly Lane, "Fairbanks, Yakutsk celebrate 20 years of sister city love," *Fairbanks Daily News-Miner*, October 16, 2011.

151 *In 1993, UAF*: Author interview with Joy Morrison, September 17, 2015.

151 *"We have a"*: Nina Mollett, "Glasnost awakens Yakutsk newspaper," *Pioneer All-Alaska Weekly*, March 15, 1991.

152 *"It reminded me"*: Chapin, "Encounters through a Melting Ice Curtain."

152 *He hoped his*: Author interview with Tom Fink, May 10, 2016.

153 *A year later*: Author interview with Jack Randolph, May 13, 2016.

154 *"While many of them"*: Dermot Cole, "Rotarians gather in Nakhotka," *Fairbanks Daily News-Miner*, May 2, 1996.

155 *Their ominous warnings*: Victoria E. Bonnell, Ann Cooper, and Gregory Freidin, editors, *Russia at the Barricades: Eyewitness Accounts of the August 1991 Coup* (New York: M.E. Sharpe. Inc., 1994), 33.

Chapter 16

157 *"Gorbachev was physically"*: Arkady Ostrovsky, *The Invention of Russia: From Gorbachev's Freedom to Putin's War* (New York: Viking, 2015), 117.

157 *Six decades later*: Victor Fischer, *To Russia with Love: An Alaskan's Journey* (Fairbanks: University of Alaska Press, 2012), 312–317.

158 *Among the coup*: A detailed account of the coup and its aftermath are included in Bonnell et al., *Russia at the Barricades*.

159 *Natalie Novik was*: "Shortwave discoveries—Soviet Coup: Reactions from Chukotka," *Arctic Sounder*, August 30, 1991.

160 *Because of Alaska's*: Author interview with Lee Gorsuch, May 20, 2015.

160 *"The number of"*: News release, Office of the President, University of Alaska, September 25, 1989.

160 *The son of*: Author interview with Jerry Komisar, January 29, 2016.

161 *More than four hundred*: Ted Spencer, curator, Whittier Museum, blog about Sen. Ted Stevens's World War II Service, August 19, 2010.

161 *Stevens estimated that*: Interview with Sen. Ted Stevens, *Russian-American Business* magazine, February 14, 2007.

161 *"Alaska has much"*: Vic Fischer, letter to Senator Stevens, October 29, 1990.

161 *Stevens responded with*: Ted Stevens, letter to Fischer, November 16, 1990.

161 *A longtime member*: Joel Connelly, "Ted Stevens: 'Emperor of Earmarks,'" *Seattle Post-Intelligencer*, August 10, 2010.

162 *"Lack of sufficient"*: Fischer, to Alaska Gov. Steve Cowper, October 25, 1990.

164 *The abortion rate*: Asta Corley, "Alaskan Organizes Russian Women's Conference," *Anchorage Daily News*, July 12, 1993.

164 *Grady initially worked*: Author interview with JoAnn Grady, July 13, 2015.

Chapter 17

167 *Millions in international aid*: Hal Bernton, "Millions in international aid flows though Alaska's Capitalism U," *Anchorage Daily News*, July 23, 1995.

167 *ARC director Charlie Neff*: Charles B. Neff, "Russia's Booming Far-East Frontier," *Anchorage Daily News*, August 27, 1993.

168 *The twenty-seven-year-old Juneau*: Author interview with Tiffany Markey, April 26, 2016.

168 *In spring 1994*: Hal Bernton, "Trying out capitalism, Russians come to Anchorage to learn the basics," *Anchorage Daily News*, April 6, 1994.

169 *A 2000 performance audit*: "Evaluation of USAID Programs to Develop Business Skills in Russia," CARANA Corp., Arlington, VA, July 2000, pp. 28–32.

170 *A 1997 Alaska legislative*: "Report on the University of Alaska's American Russian Center, Alaska Center for International Business, Institute for Social and Economic Research, and Office of Russian Affairs," Alaska State Legislature, Legislative Budget and Audit Committee, September 25, 1997.

170 *A former State Department*: Chip Blacker, Institute for International Studies at Stanford University, Memorandum to Richard Morningstar, special advisor to the president and the secretary of state on assistance to Russia and the new independent states, and Carlos Pascual, director of Russian, Ukrainian, and Eurasian affairs directorate of the National Security Council, April 30, 1998.

170 *"It is by no means"*: Final Report to the US Information Agency, *Cultural and Educational Exchanges between Alaska and the Russian Far East*, grant period July 24, 1995–Aug. 31, 1997, by the American Russian Center, University of Alaska Anchorage.

171 *According to an ARC*: MH Consulting, Inc., "Final Report: Building Oilfield Service Technology and Management Training Capacity in the Russian Far East," August 14, 2004.

171 *ARC detailed its*: Russell B. Howell, letter to Senator Stevens, June 6, 2008.

172 *In 1989, Fischer*: Fischer, *To Russia with Love*, 325.

172 *In 1993, Mitchell*: Memorandum from Cecile Mitchell to Larry Kingry, UAA vice chancellor of student services, October 28, 1993, and author interview with Cecile Mitchell, May 5, 2015.

172   *Between 1991 and 2015*: Author interview with Leslie Tuovinen, UAA education abroad coordinator, April 21, 2015.

Chapter 18

175   *"If ever once"*: David Germain, AP, "Remote Russian island in a hurry for prosperity," *Anchorage Daily News*, May 19, 1997.

176   *"We finally buried"*: David Germain, AP, "Quake survivors await help," *Anchorage Daily News*, July 12, 1995.

177   *"By the year 2000"*: Nancy Pounds, "Alaska Abroad," *Journal of Alaska Business and Commerce*, March 16, 1998.

177   *"There aren't many"*: Patricia Jones, "Great hope, great risk," *Fairbanks Daily News-Miner*, May 18, 1997.

177   *"It was natural"*: Author interview with Tony Knowles, April 27, 2016.

178   *In 2000, the state*: News release, "Federal Grant to Continue Alaska-Russia Relationship," Office of the Governor, July 12, 2000.

178   *As part of that*: Report from David Rose, chairman of Alaska Permanent Capital Management Company, to Jeff Berliner, Russian Far East trade specialist for the State of Alaska, July 12, 2002.

179   *Each time he returned*: Author interview with Fran Rose, September 9, 2015.

179   *A founder of*: Alexey A. Dudarev, Valery S. Chupakhin, and Jon Oyvind Odland, "Health and Society in Chukotka: An Overview," *International Journal of Circumpolar Health* 72 (2013): 3.

179   *In 1993, he emerged*: Hal Bernton, "Hickel the 'godfather' of new Russian state," *Anchorage Daily News*, February 26, 1993.

180   *"We can't allow"*: Alexey Peskov, "Chukotka—How Can We Live Without You?" *Evening Moscow*, date uncertain.

181   *He coupled his*: "Russia's Wretched Farthest East," *The Economist*, November 9, 2000.

181   *Sedwick, a former*: Author interview with Debby Sedwick, May 4, 2016.

182   *Between Abramovich's investments*: Dudarev et al., "Health and Society in Chukotka," 3.

183   *"What is not in doubt"*: Dominic Midgley and Chris Hutchins, *Abramovich: The Billionaire from Nowhere* (London: HarperCollins, 2005), 70.

Chapter 19

185   *Eighty years later*: Author interview with Dave Heatwole, May 5, 2016.

186   *"The crisis of August"*: Andre Shleifer and Daniel Treisman, *Without a Map: Political Tactics and Economic Reform in Russia* (Cambridge, MA: MIT Press, 2000), 177.

186   *Two months after*: Author interview with Dennis Mitchell, December 9, 2015.

188   *"It had the unintended"*: Author interview with Dave Parish, May 4, 2016.

189   *Thousands of reindeer*: Author interview, May 5, 2016. Another key source on the Drum experience is reporting from Hal Bernton, "Showdown in Magadan—Alaska businessman sees Russian deal slip away," *Anchorage Daily News*, January 17, 1993.

190   *After burning the*: Hal Bernton, "People of the Reindeer," *Anchorage Daily News, We Alaskans* magazine, January 17, 1993.

190   *The Washington Post*: Jay Matthews, "For Wealthy Alaska, Soviet Far East, A Cautious Courtship across Cold Sea," *Washington Post*, February 14, 1991.

191   *In spring 2016*: Author interview with Doug Drum, May 11, 2016.

Chapter 20

193   *In Kolyma, winter*: Stephan, *The Russian Far East*, 225.

194   *"All of Russia"*: Christian Caryl, "Russia's deep freeze—In the Far North, the hardest winter in a generation," *U.S. News and World Report*, January 25, 1999.

194   *She was so taken*: Author interview with Gretchen Bersch, May 23, 2016.

194   *In just four days*: "Magadan—Food for the body, hope for the spirit," editorial, *Anchorage Daily News*, April 22, 1999.

195   *After his three days*: Author interview with Rick Mystrom, February 5, 2016.

195   *Even one of Alaska's*: Mike Doogan, "Food drive nears its end with Alaska-Russia benefit concert," *Anchorage Daily News*, April 2, 1999.

196   *"Just as Alaska"*: Strobe Talbott, "Alaska and the World," speech to the World Affairs Council of Anchorage, August 22, 2000.

197   *"Compared to the billions"*: Joseph Henri, "Bering railroad tunnel will bond nations in era of peace," *Anchorage Times*, August 3, 1991.

198   *Passenger traffic was estimated*: B. H. Cooper, Jr., "Bering Strait tunnel and railway project will boost Pacific development," *Executive Intelligence Review*, September 16, 1994.

198   *"If presidents signed"*: Natasha Shanetskaya, "Building Bridges to Billion-Dollar Dreams," *Moscow Times*, January 12, 2001.

198   *The new President Putin*: Anders Aslund, Peterson Institute for International Economics, "An Assessment of Putin's Economic Policy," *CESifo Forum*, July 2008.

198   *The highest-profile act*: A detailed account is contained in Martin Sixsmith, *Putin's Oil: The Yukos Affair and the Struggle for Russia* (New York: Continuum International Publishing Group Inc., 2010).

199   *"Finally somebody was"*: Author interview with Dave Parish, May 4, 2016.

199   *The Duma in 2015*: Aleksandr Gorbachev, "Russian Parliament Creates a 'Patriotic Stop-List'," *Newsweek*, July 8, 2015.

199   *After a four-hour*: Author interview with Russ Howell, April 21, 2016.

199   *Around 2004, he*: Author interview with Andrew Crow, May 18, 2016.

Chapter 21

201   *"The sable was"*: Yvegeny Yevtushenko and Boyd Norton (photographs), *Divided Twins: Alaska and Siberia* (New York: Viking Penguin Inc., 1988), 41.

204   *In 2005, Magnitsky*: Bill Browder, *Red Notice: A True Story of High Finance, Murder and My Fight for Justice in Putin's Russia* (London: Transworld Publishers, 2015), 276–278.

204   *"Your commitment to"*: Boris Nemtsov, letter to US Sen. Mark Begich, January 24, 2011.

205   *Launched in 1960*: James Voorhees, *Dialogue Sustained: The Multilevel Peace Process and the Dartmouth Conference* (Washington, DC: U.S. Institute of Peace Press, 2002).

206   *On the evening of*: Masha Lipman, "A March of Mourning for Boris Nemtsov," *New Yorker*, March 3, 2015.

Chapter 22

209   *"Over the last decade"*: Andrei Soldatov and Irina Borogan, *The New Nobility: The Restoration of Russia's Security State and the Enduring Legacy of the KGB* (New York: PublicAffairs, 2010), 3.

210   *After the Soviet Union*: Andrew Higgins, "Russia Looks to Populate Its Far East. Wimps Need Not Apply," *New York Times*, July 14, 2016.

210   *"But the Native people"*: Ludmilla Ainana, Mikhail Zelensky, and Vladimir Bychkov, *Preservation and Development of the Subsistence Lifestyle and Traditional Use of Natural Resources by the Native People (Eskimo and Chukchi) in Selected Coastal Communities (Inchoun, Uelen, Lorino, Lavrentiya, Novoye Chaplino, Sireniki, Nunligran, Enmelen) of Chukotka in the Russian Far East During 1998* (Submitted to US National Park Service and North Slope Borough, March 2000), 3.

211   *In 1995, five*: "Social Transition in the North: Research team obituaries," *Arctic Anthropology* 33, no. 1 (1996).

213   *Guarded and bureaucratic*: Interview with Provideniya Deputy Administrator Vladimir Paramonov, July 12, 2016.

213   *Despite efforts to*: Interview with Vladimir Bychkov, director of Beringia Park, June 30, 2016.

216   *Of the approximately*: Interview with Lorino Mayor Victor Kalasnikov, July 8, 2016.

217   *The number of Russians*: World Population Review, http://worldpopulation review.com/countries/russia-population/

217   *In the cramped offices*: Interview with Alexey Ottoy, Lorino marine mammal hunters' association director, July 8, 2016.

218   *Our host, Alexey Ryrultet*: Interview with Alexey Ryrultet, July 8, 2016.

220   *"It was so emotional"*: Author interview with Etta Tall, July 12, 2016.

220   *Once home to*: Elizaveta Dobrieva, Evgeniy Golovko, Steven Jacobson, and Michael Krauss, *Naukan Yupik Eskimo Dictionary* (Fairbanks: Alaska Native Language Center, 2004), v.

221   *Wearing sweatpants from*: Interview with Stanislov Nuteventin, July 4, 2016.

221   *In Uelen, Chukchi*: Interview with Tatyana Zhukovskaya, July 4, 2016.

224   *But visits today require*: Interview with Mayor Valentina Kareva, July 5, 2016.

224â   *Just a month after:* Karen Schwartz, "Arctic cruise raises hopes and environmental concerns," *Alaska Dispatch News*, July 11, 2016.

Chapter 23

227   *"I am sure"*: William H. Seward, Speech to citizens of Sitka, August 12, 1869, Alaska State Library and Museum.

228   *There he was received*: Daniel Henry, "Kaalaxch' and the Great Tyee: Moving Heaven and Earth in Klukwan," *Across the Shaman's River: John Muir and the Last Tlingit Stronghold,* unpublished paper, Sharing Our Knowledge: Tlingit Clan Conference, Sitka, Alaska, April 2016.

228   *Tongass chief Ebbit*: June Allen, "William Henry Seward 1801–1872," *Sitnews*, Ketchikan, Alaska, 2005.

218   *Alaska's Lt. Gov.*: Author interview with Byron Mallott, July 27, 2016.

239   *The nation, he wrote*: Haycox, *Alaska*, 171.

230   *The surprise 2016 election*: Neil MacFarquhar, "For Russia and Putin, a Surprise Gift from America," *New York Times*, November 9, 2016.

231   *After the September 11, 2001*: David Remnick, "Trump and Putin: A Love Story," *New Yorker*, August 3, 2016.

231   *He continued the diplomatic*: Yereth Rosen, "Obama, Nordic leaders pledge Arctic unity," *Alaska Dispatch News*, May 14, 2016.

232   *Joint research already*: "Alaska-Russia Collaborations," Memorandum by the International Arctic Research Center at the University of Alaska Fairbanks, prepared for a visit to the UAF campus by Lt. Governor Mallott, December 2015.

232   *Yet that cooperation*: Editorial, "Trapped in a bear hug," *Nature*, November 3, 2016.

233   *The 1988 Friendship Flight*: Author interview with Michael Krauss, June 29, 2015.

233   *His colleague, UAF professor*: Author interview with Lawrence Kaplan, June 21, 2016.

233   *Organized by local activist*: Maisie Thomas, "Russians Visit Savoonga to Celebrate Shared Ancestry," *Nome Nugget*, July 8, 2016.

233   *"That's my passion"*: Author interview with John Waghiya, August 17, 2016.

233   *Despite reforms adopted*: Jennifer Monaghan, "Bilateral Visa Waiver Announced for Indigenous Peoples of Alaska, Russia's Chukotka," *Moscow Times*, July 23, 2015.

234   *President Obama made*: Julie Hirschfeld Davis and Steven Lee Myers, "Obama Makes Urgent Appeal in Alaska for Climate Change Action," *New York Times*, August 31, 2015.

234   *Russia announced plans*: Heather A. Conley and Caroline Rohloff, *The New Ice Curtain: Russia's Strategic Reach to the Arctic* (Washington, DC: Center for Strategic & International Studies, August 2015), ix.

234   *The thoughtful Washington, DC*: Ibid., xv–xvii.

235   *An entirely new*: Heather Conley and Matthew Melino, *An Arctic Redesign: Recommendations to Rejuvenate the Arctic Council* (Washington, DC: Center for Strategic & International Studies, February 2016), 17.

235   *A Brown University institute*: Jeremy McKenzie, Samuel Klarich, Catherine Ardrey, and Kristopher Lagor, *The Bering Strait: Reducing Risk Through International Cooperation and Capability Improvements*, Watson Institute for International and Public Affairs, US Coast Guard Academy Center for Arctic Study and Policy, and World Wildlife Fund Arctic Program, June 2016.

235   *Countries such as Russia*: Andrew Kramer, "Russia Stakes New Claim to Expanse in the Arctic," *New York Times*, August 4, 2015.

236   *"My colleagues and I"*: Author interview via email with retired Magadan Governor Vyacheslav Kobets, July 25, 2016.

236   *"Since the collapse"*: "Russia: High-Profile Killings, Attempted Killings in the Post-Soviet Period," *Radio Free Europe/Radio Liberty*, October 19, 2006.

236   *More recently, the*: Andrew Kramer, "More of Kremlin's Opponents Are Ending Up Dead," *New York Times*, August 20, 2016.

237 *A sizable contingent*: Yereth Rosen, "After hiatus, Alaska returns to Northern Forum," *Alaska Dispatch News*, July 28, 2016.

237 *Janna Lelchuk was born*: Author interview with Janna Lelchuk, August 4, 2015.

238 *"I love living"*: "Educator Spotlight: Janna Lelchuk," *Juneau Empire*, December 21, 2014.

238 *As a ten-year-old*: Author interview with Larry Rockhill, May 15, 2016.

239 *Elena Farkas grew up*: Author interview with Elena Farkas, June 3, 2015.

239 *Susan Kalina, a former*: Author interview with Susan Kalina, August 30, 2016.

239 *Father Michael Shields*: Author interview with Father Michael Shields, August 27, 2016.

240 *This sharing of memories*: Michael Shields, John Newtown, and Terry Murphy, *Martyrs of Magadan: Memories of the Gulag* (Surrey, UK: Aid to the Church in Need, 2007).

240 *The Church estimates*: Ed West, "Prayer is absolutely essential—or you die," *Catholic Herald*, March 10, 2011.

Epilogue

243 *More than seven thousand*: Andreas Parsch, "Douglas M31/M50/MGR-1 Honest John," Directory of U.S. Military Rockets and Missiles, http://www.designation-systems.net/dusrm/r-1.html.

244 *The US Air Force captain*: Dobbs, *One Minute to Midnight*, 341.

244 *Between 1961 and 1991*: Allen, *Hunting the Soviet Bear*, 8.

244 *Today, those intercepts*: Email exchange of July 20, 2016, between the author and US Air Force Capt. Anastasia D. Wasem, director of public affairs, Alaskan NORAD Region/Alaskan Command/11th Air Force.

246 *Neither the museum*: Email exchange between author and Angela J. Linn, senior collections manager, ethnology and history, at the University of Alaska Museum of the North, August 2015.

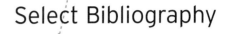

Select Bibliography

Archival Sources

Alaska Airlines archived files, Seattle, Washington

Library of Congress, Washington, DC

National Archives, Washington, DC

Ronald Reagan Library, Simi Valley, California

State of Alaska archives, Juneau, Alaska—Administrations of Governors Steve Cowper and Tony Knowles

University of Alaska Anchorage—Archives of Victor Fischer, Gunnar Knapp, and US Sen. Mark Begich

University of Alaska Fairbanks—Archives of US Sen. Frank Murkowski

Books

Applebaum, Anne. *Gulag: A History*. London: Doubleday, 2003.

Black, Lydia T. *Russians in Alaska 1732–1867*. Fairbanks: University of Alaska Press, 2004.

Bockstoce, John R. *Furs and Frontiers in the Far North: The Contest among Native and Foreign Nations for the Bering Strait Fur Trade*. New Haven: Yale University Press, 2009.

Bonnell, Victoria E., Ann Cooper, and Gregory Freidin, editors. *Russia at the Barricades: Eyewitness Accounts of the August 1991 Coup*. New York: M.E. Sharpe. Inc., 1994.

Bradshaw, Michael J. *The Russian Far East and Pacific Asia: Unfulfilled Potential*. Richmond, UK: Curzon Press, 2001.

Browder, Bill. *Red Notice: A True Story of High Finance, Murder and My Fight for Justice in Putin's Russia.* London: Transworld Publishers, 2015.

Cox, Lynne. *Swimming to Antarctica: Tales of a Long-Distance Swimmer.* Orlando: Harcourt Books, 2004.

Dobrieva, Elizaveta, Evgeniy Golovko, Steven Jacobson, and Michael Krauss. *Naukan Yupik Eskimo Dictionary.* Fairbanks: Alaska Native Language Center, 2004.

Dolitsky, Alexander B., editor. *Pipeline to Russia: The Alaska-Siberia Air Route in World War II.* Anchorage: National Park Service, 2016.

Durell, Ann, editor. *The Big Book for Peace.* New York: Dutton Children's Books, 1990.

Fairhall, David. *Cold Front: Conflict Ahead in Arctic Waters.* United Kingdom: I.B. Tauris & Co. Ltd., 2010.

Figes, Orlando. *Natasha's Dance: A Cultural History of Russia.* New York: Metropolitan Books, 2002.

Fischer, Victor (with Charles Wohlforth). *To Russia with Love: An Alaskan's Journey.* Fairbanks: University of Alaska Press, 2012.

Garrels, Anne. *Putin Country: A Journey into the Real Russia.* New York: Farrar, Straus and Giroux, 2016.

Gibson, James R. *California through Russian Eyes 1806–1848.* Norman, OK: The Arthur H. Clark Company, 2013.

———. *Imperial Russia in Frontier America: The Changing Geography of Supply of Russian America, 1784–1867.* New York: Oxford University Press, 1976.

Goodwin, Doris Kearns. *Team of Rivals: The Political Genius of Abraham Lincoln.* New York: Simon & Schuster, 2005.

Haycox, Stephen. *Alaska: An American Colony.* Seattle: University of Washington Press, 2002.

Hickel, Walter J. *Crisis in the Commons: The Alaska Solution.* Oakland, CA: Institute for Contemporary Studies, 200.

Hickel, Walter J. *Who Owns America?* Englewood, NJ: Prentice-Hall, 1971.

Hoffman, David E. *The Oligarchs: Wealth and Power in the New Russia.* New York: Perseus Books Group, 2002.

Hopkins, David M., editor. *The Bering Land Bridge.* Stanford: Stanford University Press, 1967.

Legvold, Robert. *Return to the Cold War.* Malden, MA: Polity Press, 2016.

Lewis, David, and Mimi George. *Icebound in Antarctica.* New York: W.W. Norton & Company, 1987.

Jensen, Ronald J. *The Alaska Purchase and Russian-American Relations.* Seattle: University of Washington Press, 1975.

Kaiser, Robert G. *Why Gorbachev Happened: His Triumphs and His Failure.* New York: Simon & Schuster, 1991.

Kennan, George. *Tent Life in Siberia.* New York: Skyhorse Publishing, 2016.

Kerttula, Anna M. *Antler on the Sea: The Yup'ik and Chukchi of the Russian Far East.* Ithaca: Cornell University Press, 2000.

Marston, "Muktuk." *Men of the Tundra: Alaska Eskimos at War.* New York: October House Inc., 1969.

Matthews, Owen. *Glorious Misadventures: Nikolai Rezanov and the Dream of a Russian America.* London: Bloomsbury Publishing, 2014.

———. *Stalin's Children: Three Generations of Love, War, and Survival.* New York: Walker Publishing Company, 2008.

Mezrich, Ben. *Once Upon a Time in Russia.* New York: Atria Books, 2015.

Midgley, Dominic, and Chris Hutchins. *Abramovich: The Billionaire from Nowhere.* London: HarperCollins, 2005.

Miller, Elisa, editor. *The Russian Far East: A Business Reference Guide.* Seattle: Russian Far East Update, 1995.

Murphy, Claire Rudolf, and Charles Mason (photographer). *Friendship Across Arctic Waters: Alaskan Cub Scouts Visit Their Soviet Neighbors.* New York: Lodestar Books, 1991.

Naske, Claus-M., and Herman E. Slotnick. *Alaska—A History of the 49th State.* Grand Rapids, MI: Wm. B. Eerdmans Publishing Co., 1979.

O'Neill, Dan. *The Last Giant of Beringia: The Mystery of the Bering Land Bridge.* Boulder, CO: Westview Press, 2004.

Ostrovsky, Arkady. *The Invention of Russia: From Gorbachev's Freedom to Putin's War.* New York: Viking, 2015.

Rytkheu, Yuri. *A Dream in Polar Fog.* Trans. Hona Yazhbin Chavasse. Brooklyn: Archipelago Books, 2005.

Salisbury, C. A. *Soldiers of the Mists: Minutemen of the Alaska Frontier.* Missoula, MT: Pictorial Histories Publishing Company, 1992.

Satterfield, Archie. *The Alaska Airlines Story.* Seattle: Alaska Northwest Publishing Co., 1981.

Saunt, Claudio. *West of the Revolution: An Uncommon History of 1776.* New York: W.W. Norton and Company, 2014.

Schurke, Paul. *Bering Bridge: The Soviet-American Expedition from Siberia to Alaska.* Duluth, MN: Pfeifer-Hamilton Publisher, 1989.

Shields, Michael, John Newtown, and Terry Murphy. *Martyrs of Magadan: Memories of the Gulag.* Surrey, UK: Aid to the Church in Need, 2007.

Shleifer, Andre, and Daniel Treisman. *Without a Map: Political Tactics and Economic Reform in Russia.* Cambridge, MA: MIT Press, 2000.

Sixsmith, Martin. *Putin's Oil: The Yukos Affair and the Struggle for Russia.* New York: Continuum International Publishing Group Inc., 2010.

Smith, Barbara Sweetland, and Redmond J. Barnett, editors. *Russian America: The Forgotten Frontier.* Tacoma: Washington State Historical Society, 1990.

Soldatov, Andrei, and Irina Borogan. *The New Nobility: The Restoration of Russia's Security State and the Enduring Legacy of the KGB.* New York: PublicAffairs, 2010.

Steller, Georg Wilhelm. *Journal of a Voyage with Bering 1741–1742.* Ed. O. W. Frost. Stanford: Stanford University Press, 1988.

Sterling, Robert J. *Character & Characters: The Spirit of Alaska Airlines.* Seattle: Documentary Media LLC, 2008.

Strobridge, Truman R., and Dennis L. Noble. *Alaska and the U.S. Revenue Cutter Service 1867–1915.* Annapolis, MD: Naval Institute Press, 1999.

Tichotsky, John. *Russia's Diamond Colony: The Republic of Sakha.* Amsterdam: Harwood Academic Publishers, 2000.

Vitebsky, Piers. *The Reindeer People: Living with Animals and Spirits in Siberia.* New York: HarperCollins, 2005.

Voorhees, James. *Dialogue Sustained: The Multilevel Peace Process and the Dartmouth Conference.* Washington, DC: US Institute of Peace Press, 2002.

Wohlforth, Charles. *The Fate of Nature: Rediscovering Our Ability to Rescue the Earth.* New York: Thomas Dunne Books, 2010.

Yevtushenko, Yvegeny, and Boyd Norton (photographs). *Divided Twins: Alaska and Siberia.* New York: Viking Penguin Inc., 1988.

Newspapers and Magazines

Alaska Dispatch News
Alaska Magazine
Anchorage Daily News
Anchorage Times
Arctic Sounder
Ashland (Oregon) Times-Gazette
Economist
Fairbanks Daily News-Miner
Huffington Post
Journal of Alaska Business and Commerce
Juneau Empire
Los Angeles Times
Moscow News
National Geographic
New York Times
Nome Nugget
Parkersburg (West Virginia) News
Seattle Post-Intelligencer

Seattle Times
Shipping Times
New Yorker
U.S. News and World Report
Wall Street Journal
Washington Post

Government Publications

Ainana, Ludmilla, Mikhail Zelensky, and Vladimir Bychkov. *Preservation and Development of the Subsistence Lifestyle and Traditional Use of Natural Resources by the Native People (Eskimo and Chukchi) in Selected Coastal Communities (Inchoun, Uelen, Lorino, Lavrentiya, Novoye Chaplino, Sireniki, Nunligran, Enmelen) of Chukotka in the Russian Far East During 1998.* Submitted to US National Park Service and North Slope Borough, March 2000.

Alaska State Legislature, Legislative Budget and Audit Committee. *Report on the University of Alaska's American Russian Center, Alaska Center for International Business, Institute for Social and Economic Research, and Office of Russian Affairs,* September 25, 1997.

Allen, TSgt. William J. *Hunting the Soviet Bear: A Study of Soviet Aircraft Intercepts Near Alaska 1961–1991.* Elmendorf Air Force Base: 11th Air Force Office of History, 1992.

Brelsford, Ginna. *Soviet Far East Trip Report.* Produced for the governor's Office of International Trade, Juneau, July 26, 1988.

———. *Alaska Trade and Friendship Mission to the Soviet Far East.* Produced for the governor's Office of International Trade, Juneau, October 29, 1988.

Cowper, Steve. *The Cowper Administration: Transition into the 1990s.* Juneau: Office of the Governor, 1990.

Goldsmith, Scott Oliver. *Alaska's Economy: What's Ahead.* Report by the University of Alaska Anchorage Institute of Social and Economic Research, Vol. XXIV, no. 2, December 1987.

Knapp, Gunnar. *Alaska and the Soviet North: A Brief Comparison of Population Data.* Institute of Social and Economic Research Working Paper 87.4, University of Alaska Anchorage, November 1987.

Knapp, Gunnar, and Elisa Miller. *Alaska-Soviet Far East Trade: Opportunities and Strategies.* Produced for the governor's Office of International Trade, April 1988.

Knapp, Gunnar, Diddy Hitchins, Lee Gorsuch, John Tichotsky, and Ron Miller. *Alaska-Soviet Far East Trade and Research Cooperation.* Preliminary Trip Report, University of Alaska Anchorage, Alaska Office of International Trade, Alaska International Airport System, June 1–July 22, 1989.

Knapp, Gunnar, and John Tichotsky. *Alaska-Soviet Far East Air Routes: Opportunities and Strategies*. Prepared for Alaska International Airport System, Institute of Social and Economic Research, August 1989.

Ramseur, David. *Index of Protocols/Agreements between Alaska and Foreign Countries*. Alaska State House Special Committee on International Trade and Tourism, 1991.

Tichotsky, John. *An Overview of Provideniya District, U.S.S.R.* Institute of Social and Economic Research, University of Alaska Anchorage, December 1989.

Wortman, Lt. Col. William D. *Memorandum for Adjutant General of the Alaska National Guard: After Action Report on Events on Little Diomede Island, 22 through 26 April 1989*. May 3, 1989.

Nongovernmental Reports

Conley, Heather A., and Matthew Melino. *An Arctic Redesign: Recommendations to Rejuvenate the Arctic Council*. Washington, DC: Center for Strategic & International Studies, February 2016.

Conley, Heather A., and Caroline Rohloff. *The New Ice Curtain: Russia's Strategic Reach to the Arctic*. Washington, DC: Center for Strategic & International Studies and Rowman & Littlefield, August 2015.

Dolitsy, Alexander. "The Alaska-Siberia Lend-Lease Program during World War II." *Aspects of Arctic and Sub-Arctic History: Proceedings of the International Congress on the History of the Arctic and Sub-Arctic Region*. Reykjavik, June 18–21, 1988.

McKenzie, Jeremy, Samuel Klarich, Catherine Ardrey, and Kristopher Lagor. *The Bering Strait: Reducing Risk Through International Cooperation and Capability Improvements*. Watson Institute for International and Public Affairs, US Coast Guard Academy Center for Arctic Study and Policy and World Wildlife Fund Arctic Program, June 2016.

Journals

"The Alaska-Siberia Connection." *Alascom Spectrum*. Anchorage: Public Affairs Department, Alascom Inc., August 1988.

Dudarev, Alexey A., Valery S. Chupakhin, and Jon Oyvind Odland. "Health and Society in Chukotka: An Overview." *International Journal of Circumpolar Health* 72 (2013).

Hummel, Laurel J. "The U.S. Military as Geographical Agent: The Case of Cold War Alaska." *Geographical Review* 95, no. 1 (January 2005).

Krauss, Michael. "Crossroads? A Twentieth-Century History of Contacts across the Bering Strait." *Anthropology of the North Pacific Rim*. Washington, DC: Smithsonian Institution Press, 1994.

Electronic Media

Circumpolar Expedition video and KTUU-Channel 2 stories supplied by Tandy Wallack.

Documentaries of Bering Bridge Expedition, videotape supplied by Bering Bridge Expedition member Sasha Belyaev.

Leo B. Rasmussen collection, seventeen videotape recordings covering events in Nome, St. Lawrence Island and Provideniya, USSR, between 1987 and 1989. Alaska Film Archives, Elmer E. Rasmuson Library, University of Alaska Fairbanks.

The Alaska-Siberia Connection. Video about the Friendship Flight written and produced by Connections, Ltd. of Anchorage, for Alascom, Inc., 1988.

Interviews

Francis Alvanna, Native elder, Nome

Nils Andreassen, Institute of the North

Donna Anger, UAF international programs director

Pegge Begich, widow of the late Alaska US Rep. Nick Begich

Mark Begich, former Alaska US senator

Dixie Belcher, Juneau peace activist

Sasha Belyaev, Russian arctic explorer

Richard Beneville, Nome mayor

Jeff Berliner, former state of Alaska international affairs Russian specialist

Gretchen Bersch, UAA education professor emeritus

Bruce Botelho, former Alaska attorney general, Juneau mayor

Ginna Brelsford, former State of Alaska international affairs Soviet specialist

Loretta Bullard, former Kawerak, Inc. CEO

Vladimir Bychkov, Beringia Park director, Provideniya

Mimi Chapin, Fairbanks-Yakutsk Sister Cities

James Collins, former US ambassador to Russia

Don Conrad, Alaska Airlines archivist

Kit Cooper, retired Alaska Airlines operations

Steve Cowper, former Alaska governor

Lynne Cox, cold-water endurance swimmer

Andrew Crow, UAA Business Enterprise Institute, longtime Russian interpreter

Doug Drum, Indian Valley Meats

Mark Dudley, AirRussia, Seattle

Paul Dunscomb, UAA history professor

Perry Eaton, former Alaska-Russian businessman

Patricia Eckert, retired State of Alaska Office of International Trade

Elena Farkus, Anchorage School District Russian immersion teacher

Tom Fink, former Anchorage mayor

Rex "Dusty" Finley, former Alaska National Guard captain

Victor Fischer, former director of UAA Russian Relations, author of *To Russia with Love*

Marianne "Mimi" George, anthropologist

Bob Gerhard, retired National Park Service Beringia Program

Lee Gorsuch, former UAA chancellor

JoAnn Grady, former director, Foundation for Social Innovations

Bella Hammond, former Alaska first lady

John Handeland, former Nome mayor

Stephen Haycox, retired UAA history professor

Dave Heatwole, former ARCO executive and Alaska-Russia entrepreneur

Diddy Hitchins, former UAA political science professor

Russell Howell, former director, UAA American Russian Center

Jim Johnson, former Alaska Airlines senior vice president of public affairs

Andrei Kaininan, Beringia Park ranger, New Chaplino, Russia

Victor Kalasnikov, mayor of Lorino, Russia

Susan Kalena, former UAA Russian professor

Lawrence Kaplan, UAF linguistics professor

Valentina Kareva, mayor of Uelen, Russia

Dave Karp, former Alaska Village Tours manager, Nome

Brian Kassof, UAF Russian history professor

Vaycheslav Kobets, former Magadan governor

Leonid Kokaurov, former staff at UAA American Russian Center, Russian interpreter

Jerry Komisar, former UA president

Leslye Korvola, Fairbanks Sister-Cities and International Rotary

Gunnar Knapp, retired director of UAA Institute of Social and Economic Research, Russian scholar

Tony Knowles, former Alaska governor

Janis Kozlowski, retired National Park Service Beringia Program

Michael Krauss, retired UAF linguist

George Krusz, former director Alaska State Chamber of Commerce

Mark Langland, Northrim Bank

Janna Lelchuk, Juneau Russian public school teacher

Bill McKay, former Alaska Airlines regional vice president

Dr. Ted Mala, former director, Alaska-Soviet Medical Exchange

Byron Mallott, Alaska lieutenant governor

Tiffany Markey, former American Russian Center staffer

Nancy Mendenhall, Nome Chukotka advocate

Vera Metcalf, visa-free commissioner, Nome

Kevin Meyer, former head of Russia relations, ConocoPhillips

Elisa Miller, former University of Washington Russian scholar, consultant

Cecile Mitchell, late UAA international student coordinator

Dennis Mitchell, Lynden Transport

Joy Morrison, former UAF journalism professor

Tom Moyer, former Fairbanks state legislator

Frank Murkowski, former Alaska governor and US senator

Rich Mystrom, former Anchorage mayor

Sathy Naidu, former UAF fisheries professor

Charles Neff, former director UAA American Russian Center

Steve Nelson, former Foundation for Social Innovations

Derek Norberg, Council for US-Russia Relations

Natalie Norvick, NANA Russian specialist

Donald O'Dowd, former UA president

Tom O'Grady, retired Alaska Airlines attorney

Darlene Pungowiyi Orr, National Science Foundation, Sitka

Dave Parish, former Alaska-Russian businessman

Kyle Parker, US House Foreign Relations Committee staff

Eric Pedersen, UAA associate vice chancellor, Enrollment Services

Garrey Peska, former chief of staff, Alaska Governor Cowper

Bob Poe, former State of Alaska international trade director

Joe Ralston, retired Air Force general

Jack Randolph, former Alaska Rotary regional officer

Leo Rasmussen, former Nome mayor

Glenn Reed, Pacific Seafood Processors Association

Richard Reeve, former Reeve Aleutian Airlines CEO

Claire Richardson, former KNOM radio reporter

Malcolm Roberts, former aide to Governor Wally Hickel

Larry Khlinovski Rockhill, former Kenai teacher

Brian Rogers, former UAF chancellor

Matt Rojansky, director of Kennan Institute at the Woodrow Wilson Institute, Washington, DC

Fran Rose, widow of the late Alaska Permanent Fund executive director Dave Rose

Jim Rowe, Bering Air CEO, Nome

Ed Salazar, former US State Department Soviet desk officer

Paul Schurke, arctic explorer and author

Debby Sedwick, former Alaska commerce commissioner
Ron Sheardown, Alaska-Russia mining business executive
Mike Sfraga, former UAF vice chancellor and arctic expert
Father Michael Shields, Magadan priest
Susan Soule, Alaska Department of Health and Social Services
Shirley Staton, Anchorage gospel singer
Sue Steinacher, Nome Russian affairs advocate
Jim Stimpfle, Nome realtor
Bernadette Alanna Stimpfle, Nome Native language teacher
Etta Myrna Tall, former Little Diomede Native
Francine Taylor, Anchorage film preservationist
Terri Tibbett, Juneau-Vladivostok sister cities
John Tichotsky, Alaska governor's office, Russian interpreter
Charles "Chick" Trainer, former Nome customs inspector
Mead Treadwell, former Alaska lieutenant governor
Leslie Tuovinen, UAA Education Abroad Coordinator
Fran Ulmer, chair, US Arctic Research Commission
Carol Vipperman, Senator Henry Jackson Foundation, Seattle
John Waghiyi, Native of St. Lawrence Island, advocate of Alaska-Russian exchanges
Bob Wagstaff, former director, Alaska Bar Association
Tandy Wallack, Circumpolar Expeditions
Willis Walunga, Native elder, St. Lawrence Island
Lee Wareham, former Alascom telecommunications
Margaret Williams, World Wildlife Fund Bering Sea Ecoregion Program
William Wortman, former Alaska National Guard colonel
Oksana Yashchenko, Beringia Park deputy director, Provideniya
Tatyana Zhukovskaya, Chukchi language teacher, Uelen, Russia

Acknowledgments

MY PACK-RAT TENDENCIES finally paid off. For better than three decades, a growing number of boxes stuffed with Russian newspaper clippings, reports, and trinkets collected dust in my Anchorage garage. I always thought some library or historian could make use of them to shed light on Alaska-Russia interactions in the 1980s and beyond. Nobody ever came knocking.

So when my political career came to a premature end in 2015, I decided to crack them open. Before memories faded entirely and more of the pioneers passed from the scene, I determined that the story of melting the Ice Curtain needed to be told. Fortunately, scores of others had also squirreled away their Russian memorabilia. Many of the nearly 130 people I interviewed for this book shared their files and remembrances, which formed the basis of my research.

My closest rival for sheer volume was Jeff Berliner, who oversaw the State of Alaska's Russian desk for years and graciously shared his extensive collection. Alaska-Russia groundbreaker Vic Fischer provided access to his archived papers at the University of Alaska Anchorage and was incredibly gracious with his time and guidance throughout my book-writing efforts and, for that matter, my career.

Gunnar Knapp, director of the university's Institute of Social and Economic Research, opened his well-organized files and impeccable memory. Russ Howell and Charlie Neff, former directors of UAA's American Russian Center, shared a wealth of knowledge about ARC's operations. Andrew Crow, who helped open

ARC's business centers in the Russian Far East and interpreted many of the developments since 1989, was helpful with boxes of memories. Staff at several archives, including the State of Alaska, Reagan Library, and National Archives were helpful.

My work for three of Alaska's finest statesmen led me to the Soviet Union, and then to Russia after it disintegrated. I'm grateful to Governors Steve Cowper and Tony Knowles and Anchorage Mayor and US Senator Mark Begich for the opportunities they provided me and our state in improving relations across the Bering Strait.

I'm indebted to UAA library director Stephen Rollins for providing me access to the extensive collections and to reference librarian Ralph Courtney for showing me how to use them. Many other University of Alaska faculty and staff provided insights and assistance. At UA Anchorage, they included Lee Gorsuch, Gretchen Bersch, Steve Haycox, Marcia Trudgen, Diddy Hitchins, John Tichotsky, Lexi Hill, Ted Mala, and the late Cecile Mitchell. At UA Fairbanks, they included Brian Rogers, Michael Krauss, Joy Morrison, Suzan Hahn, and Suzanne Bishop. Thanks to two former UA presidents for their early recollections: Jerry Komisar and Donald O'Dowd.

Several Alaska Airlines current and former staff were especially helpful in reconstructing the early history of service to the Russian Far East, including Jim Johnson, Bill MacKay, Paula Marchitto, Don Conrad, Kit Cooper, Mark Dudley, and Ginny Carruthers. My neighbor and former Reeve Aleutian CEO Dick Reeve helped me understand the early days of Alaska-Russia aviation.

Four members of the Bering Bridge Expedition were especially gracious with their time about their harrowing adventure: Paul Schurke, Ginna Brelsford, Sasha Belyaev, and Dmitry Shparo. For the drama on Diomede, I'm grateful to Capt. Rex "Dusty" Finley and Lt. Col. William Wortman, who provided me invaluable government reports, photos, and remembrances.

Many people can claim pioneer status when it comes to melting the Ice Curtain but two deserve special recognition for their persistence to the cause and assistance to me: Dixie Belcher of Juneau and Jim Stimpfle of Nome. Darlene Pungowiyi Orr was invaluable in helping me understand the significance of this era to Alaska and Russian Native peoples. Sue Steinacher rescued an invaluable collection of newspaper clippings and oral interviews in Nome and shared them.

Thanks to US Sen. Frank Murkowski for his thoughts and willingness to open his archived papers at UAF. Unfortunately, the family of US Sen. Ted Stevens declined my request—and that of other researchers—for access to his papers. Former Lt. Gov. Mead Treadwell also opened his personal files and detailed memory to me.

Hundreds of Alaskans and others traveled to Russia to improve relations across the Bering Strait and were invaluable with their insights and assistance, including JoAnn Grady, Steve Nelson, Garrey Peska, Dave Heatwole, Dennis Mitchell, Bruce Botelho, Margaret Williams, Mimi Chapin, Carol Vipperman, Tandy Wallack, Dermot Cole, and Claire Richardson. Thanks, too, to many of the aforementioned and others for sharing photographs.

Many Russians provided their perspective on this era, including former Magadan governor Vyacheslav Kobets, Alexander Pelyasov of the Center for the Arctic and Northern Economies, and Oksana Yashchenko and Vladimir Bychkov from the Beringia Park in Provideniya.

Three Washington, DC, colleagues helped with invaluable contacts and wisdom: Kyle Parker of the US House Foreign Relations Committee; Matt Rojansky, director of the Kennan Institute; and Russian opposition leader Vladimir Kara-Murza.

I'm grateful to several colleagues and friends for reading early chapters and attempting to steer me toward literary clarity: Patty Ginsburg, Kathleen Tarr, Charles Wohlforth, Tom Kizzia, Parry Grover, Jo Antonson, and members of the Turnagain Writers Group. Thanks to Ric Wilson and Keith Labay at the Anchorage US Geological Survey for producing the maps.

Thanks to Bob Harper for helping me understand something of the book publishing business. Jenny Evans showed great patience with my limited computer skills as she provided invaluable technological assistance. My former Russian teacher, Leonid Kokaurov, was my Russian translation go-to guy. Katie Dougherty transcribed endless hours of interviews about people and places she could barely pronounce. My former editor at the *Fairbanks Daily News-Miner*, Kent Sturgis, helped edit a mass of memories into what I hope is a readable history.

For the scores more who dug deep into their memories and aging files and whom I failed to mention here, thank you.

Thanks to the Rasmuson Foundation for generous support to help get this book published. Thanks, too, to former University of Alaska Press manager Amy Simpson for taking a chance on a first-time book author and for walking me through the publishing process.

Finally, thanks to my partner of thirty-five years, Susan Wibker, for her steady encouragement, common-sense insights, and more than three decades of wild and crazy adventure in Alaska.

Index

Page numbers with an *f* refer to a figure. *Insert* refers to the 16-page color insert.

About the Author

D AVID RAMSEUR MOVED to Alaska in 1979, where he reported on politics and government in the state and national capitals for the *Fairbanks Daily News-Miner* and *Anchorage Times*. Starting in 1986, he served for nearly thirty years as press secretary, communications director, chief of staff, and foreign policy advisor to Alaska Governors Steve Cowper and Tony Knowles and to Anchorage Mayor and US Senator Mark Begich.

Ramseur has published numerous articles about Russia in Alaska newspapers, the *Foreign Trade and Investment Review*, and with the Kennan Institute, a leading Washington, DC, Russian think tank. He holds a bachelor's in political science from the University of North Carolina–Asheville and a master's in journalism from the University of Missouri. Ramseur is a visiting scholar in public policy at the University of Alaska Anchorage's Institute of Social and Economic Research and board member of the Alaska World Affairs Council. He lives in Anchorage with his spouse, attorney Susan Wibker.